Twilight
on the
Line

Twilight
on the
Line

Underworlds and
Politics at the U.S.-Mexico
Border

SEBASTIAN ROTELLA

W. W. NORTON & COMPANY

New York • London

For information about permission to reproduce selections from this book,
write to Permissions, W. W. Norton & Company, Inc., 500 Fifth Avenue,
New York, NY 10110.

The text of this book is composed in Adobe Times with the display
set in Bureau Agency.
Desktop composition by JoAnn Schambier.
Manufacturing by The Courier Companies, Inc.
Book design by Charlotte Staub.

Library of Congress Cataloging-in-Publication Data

Rotella, Sebastian.
    Twilight on the line: underworlds and politics at the U.S.-Mexico border /
Sebastian Rotella.
        p.   cm.
    Includes index.

    1. Drug traffic—Mexican-American Border Region. 2. Gangs—Mexican-
American Border Region. 3. Crime—Mexican-American Border Region.
4. Illegal aliens—Mexican-American Border Region.
I. Title.
HV5831.M46R67 1997
363.45'0972'1—dc21   97-11890
                                                                       CIP

W. W. Norton & Company, Inc., 500 Fifth Avenue, New York, N.Y. 10110
http://www.wwnorton.com

W. W. Norton & Company Ltd., 10 Coptic Street, London WC1A 1PU

1 2 3 4 5 6 7 8 9 0
ISBN: 978-0-393-33759-4

For

Carmen and Valeria
with love

Contents

My thanks to:

The many editors and reporters at the *Los Angeles Times*—a wonderful place to work—who have shared with me their kindness and wisdom every step of the way, especially Alan Acosta, Simon Li and Dale Fetherling: three good and kind bosses. And Patrick McDonnell, Mark Fineman, Don Bartletti, and Juanita Darling, admired colleagues and friends with whom I had the pleasure of working. And my friends and colleagues in the San Diego office.

My friends in the press corps in Tijuana and elsewhere in Mexico. I am indebted to them for their hospitality, solidarity, courage and sense of humor, especially Miguel Cervantes, Dora Elena Cortés, Manuel Cordero, Sergio Haro and Ignacio Rodríguez Reyna.

A list of dedicated and helpful people including Alan Bersin, Víctor Clark Alfaro, Gustavo De La Viña, Miguel Escobar, Antonio García Sánchez, Marcela Merino, Adolfo Gonzalez, Roberto Martinez, Rudy Murillo, José Luis Pérez Canchola, Gabriel Rosas, Gov. Ernesto Ruffo, Claudia Smith, Javier Valenzuela, Manuel Valenzuela and colleagues at the College of the Northern Border, and Vicente Villalvazo.

Jorge Alberto Duarte for his help and hospitality and a lesson in courage and sacrifice.

Numerous and necessarily anonymous men and women in law enforcement and government in the United States and Mexico who helped me see a hazy world more clearly, sometimes at considerable risk. They were invaluable and they have my thanks and admiration.

The migrants and working people on both sides of the line who took time out of their journeys to talk to a stranger.

Bonnie Nadell, an agent from heaven, and Alane Mason, a talented and dogged editor.

Bruce Springsteen, for the inspiration and for the border songs.

Jim Shepard and George Garrett with respect and gratitude.

My brothers, Carlo and Sal, for trenchant comments and musketeer-like solidarity.

My parents for everything, especially for teaching me that work is good for you.

My parents-in-law for eleventh-hour assistance, the relatives on both sides of the ocean, and the memory of those departed.

The fellas, Chicago and Michigan chapters.

The good folks at Seventh near B and Big Boy.

Last but most important: Carmen for her love and patience; as always, she helped me understand what I had seen and what I had not; without her there would be no border stories. And Valeria, the best border story of all.

Twilight
on the
Line

CHAPTER ONE

The View from Big Boy

In the movie *Casablanca,* everybody went to Rick's Café Américain.

In Tijuana, the Mexican border city that has taken on a cinematic air of intrigue, everybody goes to Bob's Big Boy (El Big).

Cops, journalists, spies, lawyers, gangsters, entrepreneurs, political bosses, human rights activists, former, current and future government officials—they all haunt the diner with the statue of the short fat guy in front. El Big serves around-the-clock coffee, burgers, enchiladas, the classic trans-border menu. But the hottest item is the conversation about news and politics, crime and conspiracy: a web of whispers as labyrinthine and melodramatic as the reality of the border itself.

Big Boy occupies a prime location on Agua Caliente Boulevard, Tijuana's main drag. Agua Caliente Boulevard starts near the border in the old downtown, the fabled Avenida Revolución tourist district, and extends across this city of about 1.5 million, the biggest Mexican metropolis on the international line. The boulevard runs past the bullring, past the Agua Caliente racetrack owned by Jorge Hank Rhon, a flamboyant tycoon from one of Mexico's wealthiest political clans. His racetrack security guards assassinated

Héctor (Gato) Félix, columnist and co-editor of the crusading magazine *Zeta,* in 1988. Although journalists accused Jorge Hank of ordering the murder, he denied guilt and was never charged. On a side street near his racetrack are the offices of *Zeta,* whose editor, Jesús Blancornelas, still prints an accusatory page every week, white block letters on a funereal black background, in which the slain columnist demands justice from the grave: "Hank: Why Did Your Bodyguards Kill Me?"

Agua Caliente Boulevard curls southeast below the hills topped by the mansions of the Tijuana elite, mansions built with border money of the clean, dirty and ambiguous variety: construction, manufacturing, tourism, gambling, exports, imports, smuggling, drugs, political thievery. Periodically, federal police hunting for the Arellano Félix brothers, the elusive barons of Tijuana's narco-underworld, raid the hilltop palaces. The police blow open doors with explosives, roust families and confiscate empty safes, luxury cars and sophisticated eavesdropping equipment. But the Arellanos are always one step ahead. At a busy intersection farther down the boulevard, the walls of a corner market are scarred by bullet holes from an epic gun battle in which the Arellanos' corrupt state police bodyguards fought off federal police so that the gangsters could escape.

Changing names, the boulevard becomes Díaz Ordaz. It slants through the fast-food joints and mini-malls of the middle-class flatlands. It empties finally into the industrial belt of low-wage, multinational factories and junkyards surrounded by dusty, sprawling shacktowns where the factory workers live. The workers keep arriving from the south. The city keeps expanding, squatter colonies sprouting in the parched foothills. The migrants build their shacks and save their money, many of them hoping to go north across the border one day.

Big Boy is in the center of town, just across Agua Caliente Boulevard from the bullring and a few blocks from the police stations and the courthouse. The all-night diner with the low red roof has been an institution for twenty years. Its gravel parking lot is invariably filled with Tijuana's most characteristic forms of transport: shiny Jeep Cherokees, Chevrolet Suburbans, aging battleship Caprices and Impalas from Detroit's glory days, relics of a time before auto industry jobs started migrating south of the border. Tijuana's movers and shakers hang out at Big Boy, and Denny's, and VIPS, the roomy, brightly lit, U.S.-style coffee shops that are preferred meeting places in urban Mexico. The crowd at Big Boy thins out around lunchtime, suggesting that the appeal is more social than culinary. Otherwise, the diner is thick with talk about sinister topics: after the latest scandal, shootout or gangland murder, reporters hit Big Boy to work their sources, sift through versions, swap theories. If someone draws on a napkin, it usually involves homicide scenes, angles of gunfire or the kind of diagram used to chart mob hierarchies. Often the regulars knew the victim: a prosecutor, a police commander. Sometimes it is just another story to chase; sometimes it hurts. Poor bastard, they mutter. He was in here just the other night. I interviewed him a couple of days ago and he told me to get back to him, he might have a tip for me.

The grim and speculative litany begins. Drug trafficking is usually to blame, but there might be other motives: political feuds, corruption debts, smuggling of immigrants or guns or contraband, a deadly cocktail of the above. Did they kill him because he took the money or because he didn't? Is it riskier to do business with the bad guys or to stand up to them? These are years of living dangerously in Tijuana. To the chagrin of the hardworking citizenry, who point out that the average pedestrian is safer on the streets of Tijuana than

in Los Angeles or Washington, Tijuana has become synonymous with bloodshed and corruption.

Nonetheless, in a juxtaposition typical of Tijuana, Big
Boy is also homey and wholesome. Parents bring their children; it is not unusual to see a family slurping milk shakes
at one table and agents of National Security, the federal espionage service, looking vaguely furtive in sunglasses at the
next table. A group of *ganaderos,* grizzled and dignified
men who make their living in the livestock trade, use the
diner as an unofficial office: in the morning they slide
behind the tables by the front windows, unholster cellular
phones, snap open briefcases. They do business casually,
deliberately, paced by coffee and conversation. Big Boy's
green-uniformed waitresses are pleasant and efficient. The
simple facade, circular booths and laminated tables invite
you to linger. Big Boy evokes the feeling of shelter that
Ernest Hemingway described in "A Clean, Well-Lighted
Place," the story about an old man who sits at night in a café
in Madrid because he is alone and in despair.

Especially at night, Big Boy exudes a whiff of the milieu
where politics, police, and the press intertwine. Mexican and
U.S. reporters spend hours here in a haze of nicotine, caf-
feine, rumors, body counts, conspiracy theories. Dora Elena
Cortés and Manuel Cordero, the Tijuana correspondents for
the national newspaper *El Universal,* are day-and-night
denizens. They occupy a strategically located booth by the
front entrance—she sips coffee, he stirs a cup of tea.
Cordero is the consummate Tijuana police reporter. He has
prematurely white hair, a rasping laugh and a hard-boiled
habit of referring to newsmakers as "monkeys," as in: "That
monkey is going to give a press conference at one o'clock."
Cordero is a martial-arts expert who moves easily through
the swamps of Tijuana law enforcement. He once taught
self-defense at the police academy, so the police respect

him: some know from experience that he can beat them up.

Cortés, *El Universal*'s chief correspondent, is relentlessly cheerful and cheerfully relentless. She talks at the speed of an assault rifle. She has billowing curls and a vivacious, down-to-earth charm. Her legion of sources includes relatives, high school chums, political insiders and a large percentage of the regulars at El Big. "Instead of chasing around town after the news, you go to Big Boy," Cortés says. "And the news comes to you."

Neither Cortés nor Cordero has a university degree, but they won Mexico's National Journalism Prize for their coverage in 1994 of the assassination of presidential candidate Luis Donaldo Colosio. In their forties, with a combined four decades of experience, they are quintessential representatives of the Tijuana press corps: a band of fast and fearless warriors whose swagger and stark working conditions recall the 1930s Chicago style that has faded away north of the border. Journalism in Mexico has become increasingly independent; publications such as *Proceso, Reforma* and *Zeta* have led the fight for democracy. Computers and cellular phones are tools of the trade. But it is still a world of danger and drudgery where survival depends on instincts, contacts and hustle, where you assume that the phones are tapped by the security forces and the mafias, where you do business face-to-face in a public place. Like Big Boy.

"It is a refuge of police and politicians," says Manuel Valenzuela Arce, a sociologist who studies the popular culture of the border. "Probably some of the best and worst things that have happened to us in Tijuana were planned there."

Some of the best and worst things that ever happened to Tijuana happened during the 1990s. The stories at the border got bigger and crazier. Mexico came to resemble a detective novel; Tijuana was the heart of the mystery.

The action never stops at the border. There is no other place like it on the globe. The international boundary stretches for almost two thousand miles, from the Pacific Ocean through the mountains, the deserts, the valleys of the Rio Grande to the Gulf of Mexico. The region is a vast world unto itself. And the westernmost, fourteen-mile strip between San Diego and Tijuana, the border's biggest and richest cities, is the most intense microcosm of that world. The U.S. Border Patrol records half a million yearly arrests of illegal immigrants here, accounting for almost half of all its arrests. This is the corridor for billions of dollars worth of cocaine, heroin, methamphetamine and marijuana smuggled by the international drug cartels that have converted Mexico into the supply route to the United States, the world's hungriest consumer of narcotics. And Tijuana has historically served as a hub for gambling and money laundering, as well as southbound guns, stolen vehicles and trunkloads of drug profits.

Simultaneously, this is the busiest international border crossing in the world, the commercial crossroads of the United States, Latin America and the Pacific Rim, a hotbed of investment and industry. The region is the border's biggest media market and the portal between California, a state with the economy and personality of a nation, and Baja California, one of Mexico's most prosperous and politically modern states. Baja's recent history of simultaneous democratization and violence represents the progress and the calamities that are remaking Mexico. The best and the worst of the two societies collide and blend here: the border is the future in the making.

"At the border," says Javier Valenzuela, the psychologist-turned-cop who founded Grupo Beta, an elite Tijuana police unit designed to protect migrants, "you always have the sensation that *something* is about to happen."

The last decade of the century has been an extraordinary time in this extraordinary place. Profound political, economic and cultural forces converged at the international line. After the fall of the Iron Curtain, old borders blurred and new ones materialized around the world. Political revolutions combined with revolutions in communications and transportation to spur migration to developed nations from Latin America, Asia, Africa. These revolutions put most places on the map within a twenty-four-hour, $1,000-journey from First World capitals. Electronic media created an equality of aspiration, bombarding the populations of developing countries with images of the United States, Europe, Japan. Philip Martin, a professor at the University of California at Davis, told an economic conference in San Diego in 1995: "During the last thirty to forty-five years, nations have removed many of the barriers to trade and capital flows. There has been a drastic reduction of prices and interest rates. But the labor wage gap has increased. . . . This simultaneous narrowing and broadening spurs migration."

While the global surge in migration was a recent phenomenon, immigration from Mexico to the United States had flourished along routes that dated back to midcentury and earlier. The migrants were pushed by poverty and aspiration and pulled by the evolving labor demands of the global economy, which in the 1990s produced a historic free-trade agreement between the United States and Mexico. Crime also became increasingly globalized: international mafias expanded, confronting and infiltrating governments. As a result, corruption and organized crime posed one of the most urgent threats of the post–Cold War period to fragile and established democracies alike: Russia, Colombia, Italy, Mexico. In some nations, the disintegration of authoritarian dynasties raised hopes for democracy. But often the immediate price was a suddenly chaotic landscape littered with the wreckage of political systems that, as in the case of Mexico, had preserved stability for decades.

All those fuses ignited a series of crises in Mexico in 1994. The Mexican writer Carlos Monsiváis called it "the year in which it was impossible to be bored in Mexico." There was political and drug violence, kidnappings of tycoons, a guerrilla uprising, monumental scandals and the economic collapse of December, which sent aftershocks as far as Tierra del Fuego and raised fears in the United States of ever more desperate immigration. Continuing a tradition of alternately ignoring or misunderstanding Mexico, the Bush and Clinton administrations had accepted the image promoted by the administration of President Carlos Salinas de Gortari. It was a mirage of a modernizing, stable democracy whose neoliberal economic renaissance would be crowned by the ultimate continental partnership: the North American Free Trade Agreement (NAFTA). The collapse of the mirage caught policymakers, journalists and other observers off guard.

Much of the violence was concentrated in Tijuana; Big Boy was buzzing. From the vantage point of the border, particularly street-level outposts such as El Big, Mexico's crisis was less surprising. It was the logical outcome of the economic and political injustice that had spawned illegal immigration, drug smuggling and political corruption. It was a consequence of the power of the border mafias that had corroded the economy and politics. And it was the self-destruction of an authoritarian system that, as the rest of the society opened up, had tried to stay closed, leading to internal feuds and external attack. The contradictions that reached the breaking point in Mexico—between modernization and corruption, reformers and gangsters, urban north and rural south, international commerce and migratory misery—were especially evident at the border.

At the border, enormous legal and illegal flows of goods, people, cultures and ideas overlap, generating energy that is constructive, destructive and overwhelming. It happens out in the open at the San Ysidro port of entry, the world's busiest border crossing. On a busy summer day in the concrete arena of the U.S. inspection station, a thousand engines grumble in the heat. The lines of cars bound for San Diego stretch like steel serpents in the northbound lanes, inching under ramps and over bridges toward the concrete hulk of the port of entry. Wisps of sound drift from car radios—rock music, classical, ranchera, news reports describing how bad the border traffic is. Their faces glazed behind sun-spattered windshields, the drivers yawn, read newspapers, gulp cold drinks. They snarl and honk at an obnoxious Buick Regal, 1970s funk blasting from the sunroof, that tries to cut into line. And they wait. The caravan crawls through a motley bazaar boiling with motion and free enterprise. Wading on foot through the herky-jerk traffic are travelers, commuters, tourists (Tijuana calls itself "the most visited city in the world"), taxi drivers, vendors, shawled indigenous women selling crucifix necklaces knit from black thread, haunting indigenous children who chew on the paper cups with which they beg for coins. The stalls lining the traffic islands sell a global village of iconography: plastic figurines of Bart Simpson, Jesus Christ, the Power Rangers, St. Francis of Assisi, Michelangelo's *David,* the Virgin of Guadalupe, Mickey Mouse.

The San Ysidro port of entry records more than 40 million legal crossings a year, mostly by law-abiding, middle-class Mexicans like the families that go to Big Boy. While hundreds of thousands of Mexicans risk their lives sneaking across the line, hundreds of thousands of others cross legally and casually. They either meet the modest financial criteria required for a border-crossing card, which permits trips in the immediate area, or they have U.S. resident status because they were born or have lived north of the line. They go to San Diego to work, shop, see a movie (the proximity of San Diego multiplexes has all but wiped out movie theaters in Tijuana), visit Sea World, meet friends and relatives. On weekends, in suburban shopping centers and diners north of the line, journalists from Tijuana run into the Mexican government officials and human rights advocates they cover during the week. Mexicans spend an estimated $2.6 billion a year in San Diego. Mexican executives and politicos own condominums in the genteel coastal resorts of La Jolla and Coronado. So do gangsters: in 1993, shortly after the Catholic cardinal of Guadalajara died in a mysterious shoot-out involving the Arellanos of Tijuana, the wife of one of the fugitive drug lords was spotted in a department store in San Diego's Fashion Valley mall. Designer boutiques and discount stores depend on business from south of the border. But for years, the long lines at the San Ysidro port of entry have symbolized the lack of trust between the United States and Mexico.

Politicians may talk about free trade and economic partnership, but things are different out here on the concrete, says Lalo, a veteran border vendor leaning on a cart full of newspapers for sale. Lalo is a sawed-off street pundit with a solid gut in a blue sweatshirt, a baseball cap, sunglasses; he has the chunky look of a panda bear. He says: "On weekends, when you get all the tourists coming back and the people who went drinking, whoof"—Lalo gestures skyward with a stubby arm—"it's disorder. Pure disorder."

As is often the case at the international line, though, it is more orderly than it looks. The border vendors are required to carry municipal permits and membership cards in a labor union controlled by the ubiquitous Institutional Revolutionary Party. And the area around the port of entry is a headquarters of the smuggling underworld, which has boomed as the buildup of U.S. defenses makes crossing over open land more difficult. The smuggling artists can be slick and secretive, but at the port of entry they perform in public: U.S. inspectors have a videotape of a uniformed Tijuana municipal police officer—who was assigned to direct the legal traffic—selling fake documents to vehicle passengers on the U.S. turf that begins a few hundred yards south of the inspection booths. Smuggling recruiters in the crowd hawk fraudulent documents to families, who prefer using fake papers to hiking through the dark and forbidding canyons. Arrests of women outnumber those of men at the port of entry, while accounting for only about 20 percent of the arrests by the U.S. Border Patrol on open land. Smuggling "packages" at the port cost as much as $1,000: you can rent a fake or stolen "green card" (residency permit) or buy a contorted ride in the hollowed-out stereo speaker of a van.

Sometimes the brash smugglers merely give their clients a quick lesson in how to bluff a harried inspector who screens 120 entrants an hour; then they lead the way through the indoor pedestrian lanes. Veteran border-crossers float back and forth with ease—like the homeless street kids and boy prostitutes who frequent Balboa Park in San Diego and who became the tragic stars of news reports and a song by Bruce Springsteen. Some of the boys pride themselves on being able to fake their way into the United States without papers. Carlitos, an angelic-looking, husky-voiced fourteen-year-old with bangs over his forehead swaggers up to the inspector and proclaims "U.S. citizen" with a dead-on California accent and emphatic eye contact. U.S. citizens rarely have to produce documents at the port; most of the time the inspectors just wave Carlitos on. If they are suspicious, he has a rapid-fire answer for every question.

"Usually they just send me through to shut me up," Carlitos says.

The inspectors are on guard for smugglers trying to blend in with commerce, but corruption and disarray weaken the defenses. Smuggling spotters use cellular phones and binoculars to direct vehicles loaded with drugs and people to U.S. border inspectors selected because they are lax or on the take. One gang deployed youths on bicycles to spot three notoriously unenthusiastic inspectors on whom they bestowed nicknames: Spock, an inspector resembling the *Star Trek* character; Tequila, who unfailingly inquired if tourists were bringing back tequila from Tijuana; and Nails, who did her nails in the booth. The smugglers sent carloads of clients with fraudulent documents past the three inspectors, six at a time.

Until 1996, when U.S. border authorities made a concerted effort to add inspectors and reduce waiting times, the intersection of the visible and invisible crossing flows was too much for the inspection station to handle. The wait for legal crossers sometimes lasted two hours: a nerve-wrenching, brake-grinding, carbon-monoxide-sucking, fistfight-provoking nightmare. Gustavo Guzmán, thirty-one, a genial father of three, commmuted across the line every day to a maintenance job in a San Diego office tower. He entered the slow steel river of traffic at dawn, part of a trans-border workforce of about forty thousand. He passed the time with prayer and *cumbia* music. "I pray the Rosary and then I turn on the radio," he said. "The closer you get, the more aggravated you get, because you can see how slow they are going."

The loudest voices at the border don't talk much about economic interdependence because they are the most polarized. Border politics produces mainly antagonistic rhetoric or polite generalities. The border remains mysterious for many Southern Californians, let alone the leaders and bureaucrats in Washington and Mexico City. San Diego and Tijuana seem dissimilar neighbors. Elsewhere—in Calexico and Mexicali, or in the twin towns named Nogales on the Arizona line—the U.S. and Mexican communities flow together almost without interruption; the population on the U.S. side is heavily Mexican-American, connected by kinship ties to the southern side. Alone among U.S. border cities, San Diego remains resolutely Anglo. San Diego has sleek skyscrapers, a water wonderland of bays and beaches, a conservative suburban landscape and mentality. For many years, the city did its best to ignore the proximity of Latin America; the colors, sounds, and crowds of the Latino neighborhoods of Los Angeles resemble Tijuana more than San Diego does. And Tijuana retains the stereotypical image of the garish, lawless border town: the front door to the Third World.

But headlong growth has transformed Tijuana—and the rest of Baja California—into an industrial powerhouse. Assembly plants, known as *maquiladoras,* make televisions, toys, trucks, garments and plastic goods for export. The U.S. and Asian manufacturing corporations often house their executives and administrative offices in San Diego. Together the cities market a logical partnership—white-collar and high-tech in the north, blue-collar and labor-intensive in the south. Tijuana's levels of income, education, car ownership and employment are among the highest in Mexico. The migrant shantytowns are squalid; the enclaves above the Agua Caliente racetrack are typically ostentatious. But the real story of Tijuana is all the people in between—professionals, managers, entrepreneurs. Tijuana is a bastion of the middle class that has taken root in northern and urban Mexico and fostered political change.

Historically, leaders in Mexico City have regarded the

border cities as Americanized beachheads vulnerable to
their northern neighbor's penchant for invasions. After a
two-year war ending in 1848, the United States wrested
away the northern half of Mexico: the Treaty of Guadalupe
Hidalgo created the border and seared another painful memory of conquest into the Mexican consciousness. In the following decades, wealthy Southern Californians joined in
periodic armed conspiracies with U.S. and Mexican adven-
turers and political activists trying to colonize Baja
California. Tijuana was viewed with particular suspicion by
Mexico City because Baja's deserts and mountains cut
Tijuana off from the rest of Mexico. The only way to reach
the city was to cross into the United States and approach
from the north. In this century, Tijuana's economy depend-
ed on its northern neighbors' appetites for vice: gambling,
prostitution, liquor during Prohibition. U.S. dollars were the
dominant currency until the 1970s and are still ubiquitous.
The Mexican government has tried to defend Mexican identity with cultural programs that have fed border states a diet
of mariachi music, *charros* (cowboys) and other icons of the
interior. This seems to have been a waste of time. Tijuana's
population is a mix of migrants from all over Mexico.
Although they might regard natives of Mexico City, or *chi-
langos,* as imperious, Tijuanans are just as patriotic as other
Mexicans. Perhaps more so, scholars have suggested,
because the border defines their sense of national identity
more sharply. They are culturally agile, moving between the
two sides and making the most of each.

So Tijuana and San Diego are closer than they appear;
they share an economic horizon. And the very walls tell a
story about an evolving hybrid culture. The teenage graffiti
artists of Tijuana took the border by storm in the early
1990s, splattering bilingual graffiti across the port of entry,
the shopping centers on Agua Caliente Boulevard, the trol-

ley that runs from San Ysidro to downtown San Diego.
Contradicting the complaints in California that social ills
ooze north from Mexico, "los taggers" were mostly English-
speaking, middle-class youths who commuted to schools in
San Diego or former immigrants who brought back the hip-
hop/graffiti craze with them. An enterprising Tijuana youth
from a wealthy family that owned a garment factory in Los
Angeles tapped a curious and lucrative market. He opened a
corner store on Agua Caliente Boulevard called Madness. It
was a paint-drenched clubhouse for taggers which sold the
tools and regalia of the trade: baseball caps, baggy jeans, ski
masks, backpacks for toting spray-paint cans on clandestine
"bombing" runs in which the youths taunted police by
adorning their scrawled monikers with the number 1036, the
police code for "fleeing suspect." When the officers of the
elite Special Tactical Group caught the taggers, they administered street justice by spraying them head to foot with their
own confiscated paint cans.

"All of the fashions of the United States arrive sooner or
later," said Federico Benítez, the bespectacled, reformist
police chief who in early 1994 organized an antigraffiti campaign by police and social workers. "The movement of people back and forth is large. It brings these influences."

The graffiti craze burst the confines of working-class
neighborhoods in Tijuana, catching on with children of
Mexican millionaires and with nonconformists in their thirties—"what in other times would have been called hippies,"
Chief Benítez said. In fact, the taggers were the latest in a
procession of defiant trans-border subcultures: the zoot-suit-
ed *pachucos* of the 1940s, the hippies of the 1960s, and the
cholo gang members of today. A more destructive form of
this cultural ferment swallowed up a group of Mexican-
American gang members from the Logan Heights barrio of
San Diego in 1993. Recruited as traveling gunmen by the

Arellano drug lords, the young men of the Thirtieth Street gang ended up in the middle of the murder of the cardinal of Guadalajara; they were hunted down while their bosses disappeared and the mysteries of drugs and politics went unsolved.

In comparison to the young narco-soldiers, the graffiti "crews" were mere nuisances. But they caused a lot of indignation and discussion in Tijuana about insidious foreign influences on local youth. The crews were hundreds strong and had names like Fool Krew, Homeless Altamira Punks and HEM, the Spanish acronym for Made in Mexico. "I like the name HEM because it's 100 percent Mexican," declared Bens, seventeen, a rebellious rich kid sitting cross-legged on the counter of the Madness store. His tag adorned a giant HEM insignia on a white wall across the boulevard from Madness dated 1993, the year of the tagger invasion. Bens (as in Mercedes) had lived for two years in Southern California with cousins who were avid taggers. He did not work or go to school, and he spent nights at a time without seeing his family, whom he described sourly as *"muy* stuck-up." Bens and his crew spoke a rollicking Spanglish patois full of terms like lonche (lunch), raite (ride), underground, wannabes, get-a-life.

"What do I have to do with Mexico City or Sinaloa, if I spent my life shopping here in San Ysidro at Ralph's and Safeway?" growled another graffiti artist, eighteen-year-old Fran Ilich, slurping a Coke at a Jack-in-the-Box a quick walk north of the San Ysidro port of entry. Ilich was edgy and skinny with short disheveled hair, an appropriately bohemian-looking leader of Tijuana's guerrilla counterculture. He was also an aspiring novelist, journalist and filmmaker. "Before being Mexican, I am from Tijuana. Taggers, raves, techno—those are words you can't translate. I have to like this transculturation, this hybrid language: that's what I am."

The beauty of Tijuana lies in this cheerfully eclectic vitality, which U.S. visitors do not always see. The Cultural Center of Tijuana, whose globe-shaped edifice dominates the downtown landscape, offers Picasso exhibits, Tito Puente concerts, a classical orchestra made up of Russian expatriate musicians and paintings inspired both by Baja California indigenous folk drawings and the murals of East Los Angeles barrios. Young writers frequent the cantinas of the red-light district, scribbling ideas on paper napkins, soaking up material. One playwright wrote a drama entitled *The Journey of the Minstrels,* based on the true story of eighteen illegal immigrants who suffocated to death in a railroad boxcar. "The stereotype of the city does not necessarily bother us; if fact, we take it as a point of thematic departure," says Leonardo Saravia, a magazine editor who oversaw the translation of a Dashiell Hammett story set in 1920s Tijuana. And Miguel Escobar, a novelist from the northern state of Sonora and consular press attaché in Southern California, says: "The border has its own very healthy culture based precisely on the clash, the disparity of the two cultures, which in a way end up complementing each other. It is a cultural phenomenon that has a certain appeal."

In the United States, the border appeals mainly to political instincts for exploiting the fear and anger of the voters. The border is an irresistible stage for political theater, as more and more politicians have discovered. Although it seemed marginally significant at the time, the visit by Patrick Buchanan to San Diego during the 1992 presidential campaign turned out to be prophetic. Buchanan, who was running a maverick protest campaign against President George Bush, held a press conference on a plateau above Smugglers Canyon. The canyon, a popular entry point for illegal immigrants, overlooked a panorama of boulders, brush, farmland, the ocean shimmering on the west. At a gap in the border

fence, vendors manning a makeshift tabletop stand sold soft
drinks and sandwiches to migrants on the Mexican side waiting to sneak across. Buchanan's bodyguards chatted with the
migrants; the press turned out in modest numbers; no one
was holding space on the front page.

His shoes and suit dusty, Buchanan grinned pugnaciously
and tore into President Bush on the immigration issue.
Buchanan demanded that the line be reinforced with ditch-
es, fences, checkpoints, agents and troops. He proposed
charging a fee to legal border-crossers to pay for the
buildup. He thundered about what he called "a national dis-
grace: the failure of the national government of the United
States to protect the borders of the United States from an
illegal invasion that involves at least a million aliens a year.
As a result, we have social problems and economic problems. And drug problems."

Behind the candidate, the migrants on the Mexican side
of the line tried to make sense of the pin-striped invasion of
Smugglers Canyon. They had heard only vaguely of
Buchanan.

"He's a presidential candidate?" asked a man named
Guillermo, squinting behind thick tinted glasses. "Does he
speak Spanish? Ask him if he can pull the Migra out of here
for twenty-four hours, then he can do whatever he wants.
Ask him if he can give me a ride to Los Angeles."

Next to Guillermo, Filoberto was not impressed with
Buchanan's tough talk. The seventeen-year-old Filoberto
had a greyhound's build and wore a single black racing
glove. He leaned slightly forward, loose-limbed, like a
sprinter about to crouch into the blocks.

"They have all kinds of technology," said Filoberto. "But
we are smarter. People are smarter than machines. We are
still going to cross. In fact, as soon as all you people get out
of here, we are going to go for it."

Filoberto and Buchanan's aides reacted with displeasure to a raucous handful of extremists who showed up on the U.S. side to yell insults about immigrants, Republicans and Democrats. One protestor wore a hard hat that depicted running immigrants crossed out by the international "No" slash. He spoke with a thick East European accent and distributed leaflets advertising a video telling the "truth" about illegal immigrants: "They are coming by the millions, and they are all pregnant!"

Buchanan's candidacy fizzled. But during the next few years, the illegal immigration story got very hot. And just about every proposal Buchanan made in the seeming political isolation of Smugglers Canyon was espoused by leaders across the ideological spectrum, from Governor Pete Wilson to Senator Dianne Feinstein to Attorney General Janet Reno: imposing border-crossing fees, doubling the Border Patrol, calling in the National Guard, erecting fences and high-tech fortifications. Liberals and conservatives elbowed each other aside to glare across Smugglers Canyon and declare war on illegal immigration. Rhetoric about an immigration crisis crescendoed during the successful campaigns by Governor Wilson and the proponents of Proposition 187, the California ballot measure denying social services to immigrants, leading up to the 1994 elections in California. The border press corps covered stories that dramatized the urgency of the problem: In the summer of 1993, an onslaught of smuggling ships from China displayed the global might of the mafias that trade in humans and sent the regulars at Big Boy chasing Chinese illegal immigrants back and forth across Baja and the border.

California was key to winning the presidency; and the immigration issue was perceived as the key to winning California. During the 1996 presidential campaign, a chorus of Republicans—Buchanan gleefully leading the way

again—denounced the hydra of illegal immigration, drugs
and corruption, bashed Mexico and accused President
Clinton of failing to defend the border. The Clinton administration responded with an industrious public relations
campaign about how it had fortified the line with unprecedented expenditure. Visits to the San Diego border by the
attorney general and the immigration commissioner—infre-
quent safaris in the past—became routine media events
drumming home a message that was part hype, but also part
fact: It was getting more difficult for illegal immigrants to
cross the line.

This was an ironic aspect of the rise of anti-immigrant
politics. Illegal immigration had been downplayed for a long
time because of a lack of interest in Washington and because
of the strength of California's economy, which faded along
with the defense and aerospace industries in the early 1990s.
But the political and journalistic "discovery" of the issue did
not mean that illegal immigration was much worse than
before. Measuring the number of illegal entrants was tricky.
Solid statistics are elusive at the border. The best barometer
of illegal crossing was Border Patrol arrests, an imperfect
tool subject to diverging interpretations and manipulation
through deployment. Even with the best of intentions, how
do you go about counting those who get away, who are
caught repeatedly or who are discouraged from crossing?
During the early 1990s, the overworked, underfunded
Border Patrol was accused of inflating the arrest numbers to
gain resources. After Washington responded with more
funds, the Patrol was promptly accused of deflating the
statistics in order to look successful.

It was undeniable, however, that the San Diego–Tijuana
line became a safer, more controlled place. Mexico took an
increasingly conscientious and cooperative approach to border policing by creating the Grupo Beta police unit, which

reduced anarchy, corruption and crime against illegal immigrants. By 1997, U.S. federal agencies could say they had imposed a measure of order at the immediate border and that they were slowing—not stopping—the advance of immigrants. Yet there was a harsh consequence: the buildup pushed more immigrants into the hands of smuggling mafias, which, like other border businesses, grew increasingly sophisticated and global in scope. The smuggling of humans is a growth industry, parallel and sometimes linked to the smuggling of drugs.

Illegal immigration has a dramatic impact south of the line, pouring billions of remittance dollars into the Mexican economy. Migration feeds Tijuana's population boom and industrial workforce and chokes the city's streets, sewers, water supply and social services. Many migrants from central and southern Mexico stop and settle in Tijuana or return there after sojourns in the United States. Tijuana has grown in reckless lunges across a hazardous landscape of hills and canyons where floods wreak destruction. Not long after the city dug out from deadly floods in 1993, civil defense workers conducted a helicopter tour and discovered entire squatter communities, founded in flood zones by recent migrants, that had not existed months earlier.

Tijuana has an ambivalent attitude toward migrants, whether they stay in Tijuana or keep going north. The Mexican government praises the bravery and determination of illegal immigrants and loudly defends them against human rights violations in the United States—alleged, spurious or genuine. Most Mexicans feel sympathy for countrymen who go north. But Baja tends to be conservative. "Natives" of Tijuana sound surprisingly like Californians when they blame new arrivals from the states of Sinaloa and Oaxaca for poverty and crime; a hint of backlash occasionally creeps into the city's animated radio talk shows. Crusty crime reporters deliver breathless renditions of the day's police blotter, punctuated with routine references to cowboy holdup men of "Sinaloan appearance" and indignant editorial comments: "Imagine that, ladies and gentlemen, robbed of $300 by two good-for-nothings of Sinaloan appearance—and they stick a shotgun in your nose for good measure. Where are the police when you need them?"

If the natives looked back a generation or two, however, they would probably find that their own families had come from somewhere else as well. So, like U.S. citizens of immigrant stock, they celebrate the migrant spirit. "Migration has made us very rich in that there are people here from so many parts of Mexico," says Ernesto Ruffo Appel, who served as governor from 1989 to 1995. "Because they make this difficult decision of leaving their land, they are very hardworking people, with many necessities. And that's why they push so hard. Maybe that's why I'm here. Maybe that's why this is the first state in Mexico with a different government."

Ruffo was thirty-seven when he was elected the first opposition-party governor in modern Mexican history. Ruffo led Baja's peaceful political revolution. The governor was a short man with a slight lisp that accentuated his unflappable good cheer. His somewhat woolly hair grayed at the temples during his six-year tenure and receded over a high forehead. His face was open, round, not quite chubby. He was direct and disarming. He spoke the folksy, unadorned language of Baja's independent-minded middle class and mixed easily with dockworkers and executives alike. In the informal border style, he avoided suits and ties in favor of leather jackets and open-collared shirts. Ruffo had little in common with the florid, old-school bosses of the ruling party, bloated by self-importance and decadence. Nor could he be mistaken for one of the slick, severe, foreign-educated technocrats of the Salinas generation. Ruffo was a self-admitted rookie. His success was based on instincts, luck, good timing and a sense of innovation.

"I never studied for this or thought it was going to be my career or anything," Ruffo said in 1994. He drifted into politics while working as an executive at a seafood company in Ensenada, the port city south of Tijuana. The catalyst was the greed he encountered in the seafood industry among federal regulatory officials shaking down businesspeople for bribes. This corruption, to Ruffo's mind, was symptomatic of the rot in the ruling Institutional Revolutionary Party, or PRI. The party formed in the late 1920s after the Mexican Revolution and evolved into one of the world's most formidable political machines, once described by the Peruvian author Mario Vargas Llosa as "the perfect dictatorship." The party was the government and the government was the party, a tightly disciplined structure commanded by an almost monarchical presidency. Mexico favored populist rhetoric at home and expressions of leftist Third-World solidarity in foreign affairs. But the oligarchy enriched itself. The economy stayed closed and statist. The political apparatus used muscle, charm and systemic, systematic corruption to control assorted social forces: labor unions and journalists, peasants and urban squatters, magnates and generals. The PRI always held elections and almost always won. Since 1939, the main opposition was the National Action Party, or PAN, an amalgalm of conservatives, Catholics, businesspeople and the middle class in big cities and northern states. The PAN won a few municipal elections in the north; it contested races in Baja so closely that the security forces had to disperse crowds enraged at the PRI's electoral larceny. In the 1990s, the other major opposition force nationwide became the Party of the Democratic Revolution (PRD), a breakaway faction created by former leaders of the PRI and longtime leftists whose denunciations of injustice and human rights violations brought an often violent response from those in power.

Ruffo joined the PAN and ran for mayor of Ensenada in 1986. "I figured I didn't have a chance, but I'll give them a real battle here so we can win somewhere else." But he won. Three years later, he ran for governor at a propitious moment. Carlos Salinas had just been elected president in a very close national election in 1988. Salinas beat the popular Cuauhtémoc Cárdenas, who led a left-of-center coalition that was the forerunner of the PRD. The victory was tainted by a suspicious crash of the vote-counting computer system and widespread accusations of fraud. President Salinas had big plans to remake the economy with a massive program of privatization, deregulation and opening to foreign investment. To overcome the public relations debacle of his questionable election, he struck a reformist pose, locking up a few drug lords and a corrupt union boss. He seized on the elections in Baja to reinforce his image as a democrat. President Salinas ousted Baja's governor, Xicotencatl Leyva, a PRI "dinosaur" whose administration had floundered in scandal and disarray. This set up a competitive race in Baja. Ruffo, the PAN challenger, campaigned in a climate of festivity and anticipation dubbed "Ruffomania." Crowds lined the streets when Ruffo passed, sensing that they were witnesses to history. In the August elections, the PRI quickly conceded. Ruffo was "allowed" to take office. President Salinas attended the inauguration, his presence blessing the PAN's breakthrough (and sending a positive message to observers across the border).

Today the PAN controls major states and cities and poses a serious challenge for the presidential elections of 2000. But in 1989, Ruffo was on his own and feeling a bit of trepidation. Baja was under intense scrutiny. The state was a laboratory of democracy that could make Ruffo a hero or blow

up in his face. The political sages and street operatives who
kibitzed in Big Boy and other figuratively smoke-filled
rooms did not give him great odds. "In the beginning, when
I took office, there were people who even placed bets that I
would not finish," Ruffo said. "Some said I would last six
months, others a couple of years. And there were so many
comments that I said, 'Gee, am I going to make it?' But I
have never been pessimistic about the future."

   Ruffo's first move was a pioneering reform of the election
system which became a model for Mexico. The state of Baja
California pressured the federal government into relinquish-
ing control of voter rolls and electoral councils, the tools
with which the PRI had multiplied its voters and caused
opposition votes to vanish. The electoral registry was
cleaned up and computerized. The governor unveiled the
ultimate weapon for slaying the electoral "alchemists" of the
ruling party's back rooms: a piece of plastic. Baja introduced a photo identification card for voters, designed by
Polaroid, with a laser-printed security seal and other state-
of-the-art protections. It was copied by the federal government, one of the few in the world that uses a photo
identification document for elections.

   Electoral corruption disappeared with remarkable speed.
Elections in Baja, which routinely draw a turnout above 70
percent, were soon regarded as the cleanest in Mexico. This
was impressive because disputes over allegedly stolen elections continued in other states as late as 1996. After years in
which the citizenry "saw democratic elections as exceptions
or concessions," Baja's identification card was a badge of
political maturity, said Tonatiuh Guillén López, a political
scientist at the College of the Northern Border in Tijuana.

   There were other advances: a public works boom, a land
reform campaign that broke the thuggish bosses of squatter
communities. Ruffo became the first governor in Mexico to

create an independent ombudsman to defend human rights. The ombudsman was José Luis Pérez Canchola. Pérez had operated a center for the study of migration issues with another activist, Víctor Clark Alfaro, who then founded the independent Binational Center of Human Rights. Pérez and Clark became two of the most important voices in Baja California, denouncing official abuse and corruption at considerable personal risk. Pérez was an eloquent, weathered-looking bulldog of a man who was active in the Party of the Democratic Revolution. Clark was a diminutive anthropologist with a neat black beard, owlish glasses and an air of intent intellectual curiousity. In their very separate ways, Pérez affiliated with the government and Clark on the outside, they acted as the consciences of the state during harrowing times. When frightened migrants, whistle-blowing cops and accused political assassins needed help, they called Víctor Clark or José Luis Pérez. This crusading duo and the aggresive press corps reaffirmed Baja's place in the vanguard of free speech in Mexico.

In other areas, such as the battle against law enforcement corruption, the Ruffo administration stumbled over its inexperience and self-interest. Progress was not a matter of the comparative virtues of political parties. Baja grew more democratic because, after decades of uniform one-party control, different parties ran the state and federal governments. "It's pure checks and balances," Guillén said. "One ambition against another ambition. And the result is good."

Just as the immigration issue heated up in the United States at a time when authorities imposed a measure of control at the line, the strife in Baja was partly the result of positive change. Political competition forced conflict and corruption into the open. Baja was a complicated place; geography made the state a magnet for industry, jobs and hardworking, politically sophisticated migrants who laid the seeds for progress. But the state's proximity to drug-hungry California also made it an ideal base for international organized crime. As a U.S. crackdown in the Caribbean pushed drug smuggling to the Mexican land route in the late 1980s and early 1990s, Tijuana became a world capital of the narcotics trade.

The casualties of the border traffickers had piled up for years: anonymous gunmen, small-time dealers, dirty cops. Nobody paid much attention. To the outside world, the drug wars were frenzied and murky. For the participants, the violence had very specific codes and objectives, a logic all its own. The gangsters perfected the art of using murders to send messages. The choice of the victim, the method and the location were often calculated to make a statement. They might make a point of shooting a former chief prosecutor in daylight in a busy place to show the current chief prosecutor how vulnerable he was. A beefy veteran detective of the Baja state police—thick gold chains around a thick neck, a gold bracelet, a steady stare—described the semiotics of murder to a cross-border visitor as he drank beer and ate lamb in the wood-paneled booth of a spacious restaurant. "You shoot someone in the back, it means they betrayed someone. You shoot them in the face, it means they talked. It all has meaning. It is like a language."

The messages grew loud and ominous during the final years of Governor Ruffo's term. Violence and scandal engulfed Ruffo's administration and left the governor in fear for his life. Nationwide conflicts in the underworlds of drugs and politics converged with explosive results: Tijuana was ground zero. The journalists, cops and politicos who hung out at Big Boy found themselves on the front lines. It got scary even for old gladiators like David Rubí, the chief of the Special Tactical Group of the municipal police. Part SWAT team and part flying squad of yore, the Tactical

Group consisted of about sixty young men and women who rolled around town in black jumpsuits, hanging off the sides of blue pickup trucks, children cheering and running along-side. The officers were chosen for their athleticism, skill with firearms and reverence for their swashbuckling chief, who during late 1993 and early 1994 led an offensive against the drug mafias that had frightened, bought or killed off just about everybody else.

Rubí dressed in black and called his AK-47 assault rifle "my baby." He was a sly, granite-faced, bristle-mustached warrior; not particularly big, but a master of the lethal arts. Rubí was a celebrity gunslinger and he knew it. He held court at Big Boy, a thin cigar smoldering between his fingers, an earphone wired to his radio keeping him abreast of potential mayhem. As the night wore on, his war stories got more hair-raising. His eyes danced with bluster and merriment. His cigar stabbed and parried. "Give me twice as many officers," Rubí once exclaimed, "and Tijuana would tremble!"

Tijuana trembled in 1994, and so did the rest of Mexico. The casualties were suddenly figures of power—"excellent cadavers," in the parlance of the Sicilian mafia wars, another bloody struggle with comparable political implications. The first illustrious corpse was Juan Jesús Posadas Ocampo, the Catholic cardinal who fell in Guadalajara in 1993. It was the battle for Tijuana that killed him. Then came March 1994: the federal police and Baja state police engaged in a shoot-out with each other on Boulevard Diaz Ordaz which left five combatants dead, including a reputed Lebanese gangster and associate of the Arellanos who was a frequent customer at El Big. The revelation that the police were fighting on the wrong side in the drug war seemed like a big scandal until three weeks later, when a gunman assassinated Luis Donaldo Colosio, the man on the verge of becoming the president of Mexico, in the shacktown of Lomas Taurinas. The repercussions of the first top-level political assassination in a half century threatened to tear the system apart. In the paranoid, convoluted aftermath, the less-than-savory, PRI-connected ex-cops who had served as Colosio's volunteer security guards huddled at Big Boy during the days when they were being hauled in as suspected conspirators. When Colosio's death was followed by the assassination of city police chief Federico Benítez, who had unleashed the Tactical Group against the drug lords, Baja's deadly spring of 1994 had grown into a national crisis.

If the rebellion in the state of Chiapas posed an unexpected threat of Central American–style guerrilla conflict on Mexico's southern border, Baja California came to represent another Latin American danger in the north: the challenge of the drug mafias. The Colombian and Mexican cartels consolidated Mexico's position as the smuggling gateway into the United States even as the free-market overhaul of the economy created two dozen Mexican billionaires and enriched foreign industrialists and speculators. Hailing Mexico's "miracle" of economic liberalization, U.S. leaders downplayed the dark side: the new moneymaking was tainted by the old graft and cronyism. At the level of U.S. domestic politics and policy, the drug mafias got little attention—far less than illegal immigration—until the violence spiraled out of control. This was partly because immigration was a more visible, visceral issue. Everyone worried about drug use in the United States, but there was little understanding of the shadowy forces by which the drugs reached the streets from foreign lands. In addition, before 1994 it was neither polite nor politically correct in mainstream government circles to talk about the power of the Mexican traffickers and thereby question the thesis that Mexico was a safe partner for the twenty-first century. The

Bush and Clinton administrations systematically ignored "drug trafficking in Mexico during NAFTA consideration," said Peter Smith, director of the Center for Iberian and Latin American Studies at the University of California at San Diego. "President Salinas was consummating a reconfiguration of the power structure in Mexico, and one element of the power structure was international billionaires. People who qualify for membership in that group include the leaders of the drug cartels."

The flood of drug money emboldened the gangsters and enabled them to infiltrate business and industry as well as the government. "There are honestly earned fortunes in Mexico," said Pérez, the Baja ombudsman. "But during the Salinas administration, multimillionaires appeared under rocks, like mushrooms, people for whom it was impossible to make so much money so fast by legal means."

Baja became a battlefield obscured by a fog of fear, subterfuge and political rivalry. Friends blurred into foes, victims into villains, police into thieves. Soon the fog spread to Mexico City, bringing new violence and extraordinary accusations about gangsterism at the top. It seemed that despite their Ivy League degrees, refined tastes and impeccable English, a sector of the Mexican elite spoke the same murderous language as the border drug lords. It was sometimes unclear where the political mafias ended and the criminal mafias began. "It is getting hard to tell which area you are in, drugs or politics," said Governor Ruffo in 1995. "Things are heading in a dangerous direction."

Mafias, drugs, immigration, globalization, democratization: the tectonic shifts of the 1990s reshaped the border, Mexico and the relationship between Mexico and the United States. The repercussions at the San Diego–Tijuana line were palpable. The secret and very organized structures beneath the apparent anarchy became fleetingly visible. The stories of the border were more urgent and spectacular than ever because they showed raw history at work. The border told stories about individuals swept up and transformed by vast forces, caught in a singular place and moment. The stories were bleak, heroic, crazy, tragic. Some of the protagonists were Mexican immigrants. Others were street children, Chinese refugees, human rights advocates, gang members, police officers, upstart politicians. Many were outsiders or neophytes to the border. They shared a common experience: in one form or another, voluntarily or not, they made the figurative leap into the underworlds of the border. They tried to survive, to make sense of the mysteries; some risked their lives to make a difference.

The border was magical and deadly and ambiguous. The allure of the border drew the reporters back to the diner across the boulevard from the bullring in Tijuana every night. The reporters joked, whispered, talked fast, always on edge, always on the prowl for a tip, a source, a story. They stayed at Big Boy long into the night. They found it hard to leave, hard to stop. They were the storytellers of the border. And there was no better story in the world.

CHAPTER TWO

El Brinco (The Leap)

The border begins at the bus station.

A ponderous steel herd of buses rumbles day and night over a bleak urban mesa in east Tijuana. The buses nose into the dock behind the terminal about two miles south of the international line, fuselages rippling through fumes and dust. One hundred and seventy-five buses and five thousand passengers a day, 70 percent of the travelers bound for the United States. Known as the Central Camionera, the bus station is a migratory hub, a smuggler's gold mine and the gateway to a frontier of dreams and nightmares.

The buses disgorge migrants from the classic "sending states"—Oaxaca, Michoacán, Guanajuato, Sinaloa—where immigration is embedded in the economy and culture. The cavernous terminal receives them with its harsh loudspeakers, circling flies and barefoot children, its crowds dazed by travel, aspiration and fear. Babies have been born in the Central Camionera. Families camp on the floor among their plastic bags and bundles tied with twine. Street urchins come and go, paying their way to other stations by running errands and washing windows for bus drivers. Once, a migrant afflicted with AIDS came here to die: after wandering from Los Angeles to the Mexican interior to Tijuana, he spent his final agonized days on one of the blue plastic benches.

The magical reality of the border transforms the terminal

into a refuge. Maria de los Angeles Delgado keeps vigil at a counter by the exit. Stacked in front of her are pamphlets offering shelter and meals at La Casa del Migrante, a Tijuana hostel run by the Scalabrinians, Italian priests who minister to migrants all over the world. Perched on her stool, Delgado, a breathless twenty-five-year-old volunteer for the shelter, watches the advance of humanity bound primarily for Southern California, but also for Chicago, Denver, New York, Minneapolis, Florida and the other destinations configuring the Mexican diaspora.

"I see so much," Delgado says. "A woman with six children who can't afford a smuggler. Men who have been here for three months and send for their families from the south. They thought it would be better with their families here. Then it doesn't work and they spend weeks living in the station. All of them intending to cross one day."

Delgado tells them to be careful. Migrants are preferred crime victims in Tijuana. She hands out cards inscribed with "The Prayer of the Traveler," which reads in part: "You, Lord, are always with the poor and You became a traveling companion for we undocumented immigrants, refugees, migrants or simply those on the path toward You." Tijuana is a mecca for an epic modern-day pilgrimage. And the bus station is a kind of temple, filled with the collective energy of where these people come from and where they are going, who they were and who they are in the act of becoming.

The migrants pass through the glass doors. Marked as prey by their backpacks and soft rural cadences, they emerge blinking into the pale sunlight of their future. Into the pack of men who prowl the sidewalk in sunglasses, cowboy boots and gaudy shirts. The men have elevated loitering to a predatory art form, a languid matador's dance. They are *talones*. (The word suggests both "ticket" and "claw.") In the hierarchy of the multimillion-dollar industry that smuggles immigrants into the United States, the *talones* are recruiters. Swooping past the halfhearted parries of security guards with truncheons, they gesture, jostle and mutter a gruff incantation: *"Los Angeles."*

The sidewalk scene appears frenzied. But it is a deceptively well-organized business ritual supervised by the border underworlds. The *talones* generally turn the client over to a taxi driver, who drives to a safe house. The migrant gets a meal, maybe a phone call to relatives in California to arrange payment; the longtime fare of $300 has crept up hundreds of dollars since a U.S. border crackdown in 1994. Acrobatic *coyotes* lead the actual crossing, aided by scouts, or *checadores,* who run interference against the Border Patrol. The smugglers are an athletic, reckless and scruffy army who assault the ramparts with shovels, ladders, blowtorches, human pyramids. When it rains, the smugglers use ropes and makeshift rafts to cross flooded streams and marshes. They are fence-jumpers, hill-climbers, trail-hikers, marathon runners. Once across, the migrants are turned over, or sold, to daredevil drivers-for-hire, *raiteros,* who take them north. In Los Angeles, enforcers at safe houses collect payment. Sometimes the smugglers jack up the price upon arrival, rape the women, punish clients who don't pay by shaving off their hair and eyebrows. There is a thin line between smuggling and kidnapping.

Not all smugglers are vicious and not all of them work for organized crime. Kinship networks between Mexican villages and U.S. big cities have spawned a legion of "weekend" or occasional smugglers, often young men with legal status. Freelancing and subcontracting abound. But small-timers don't work the lucrative sidewalk turf at the bus station unless they have a connection. The smuggling mafias pay officers of the federal police and Mexican immigration service for operating rights: $200 per shift per smuggler, as much as $40,000 a month for nearby safe houses. "Perhaps in all of Mexico, the bus station is the most important point for the movement of illegal immigrants," says Javier Valenzuela, chief of Grupo Beta, the elite border police unit in Tijuana. "It has been a cave, a hotbed of corruption. Any police action there is delicate because of the interests involved."

The kingpins have a lower profile than the swaggering barons of the drug trade, but their wealth and influence is prodigious. Organized along family lines, they also traffic in Asians, Central Americans, East Europeans—the lucrative specialty known by the U.S. Border Patrol as OTMs (Other Than Mexicans). The roster of picturesquely named smuggling kingpins includes Manuel (the Prophet) García Rodríguez, two hard-as-nails women racketeers named La Brenda and Doña María, and a gang called the Wasps. They are based in border areas such as the Zona Norte red-light district, with its foot-stomping dance halls and gloomy brothels, and Colonia Libertad, the hillside neighborhood east of the San Ysidro port of entry which offers a view of Border Patrol helicopters at work.

A typical example of the volume of the smuggling business: In 1995, U.S. investigators estimated that the Peralta clan of Tijuana were moving a thousand clients and earning a million dollars a month. The three Peralta brothers commanded an organization extending from Guatemala to Southern California. They used trucks, buses and a ranch in the central Mexican state of Guanajuato, where hundreds of non-Mexican immigrants were housed in barracks as they waited to move north. The Peralta clan knew the best routes, such as the rugged mountain trails east of San Diego. They built a pipeline of corrupt law enforcement allies in both nations. One of the Peraltas' routes was an inspection lane at the San Ysidro port of entry, the workplace of one of their most effective henchmen: U.S. Customs Inspector Guy Henry Kmett. He was arrested in October 1994, after fellow inspectors on roving foot patrol at dawn discovered three Chevrolet vans packed with a total of seventy illegal immigrants—crushed together like sardines, no pretense of concealment—waiting in line at Kmett's booth. The same vans, minus immigrants, had been followed to Kmett's house days earlier by Border Patrol investigators conducting surveillance in a separate case. The passengers were Salvadorans, Dominicans, Guatemalans and an Egyptian—all recruited in Guatemala and charged $5,000 each to be smuggled as far as Virginia and Boston. The drivers of the vans, one of them Kmett's girlfriend, each received $1,000 for the day's work.

Kmett, thirty-six, pleaded guilty. The eight-year veteran had been fired once for allegedly sneaking a Mexican woman across the border, prosecutors said. But he had been reinstated on appeal. His cellular phone records showed repeated calls to a Peralta house. He had spent $100,000 in cash in the course of less than a year on televisions, computers, a swimming pool—more than double his yearly salary. Investigators could only guess how many vehicles full of human contraband he had waved north, a crime entailing a few seconds of risk.

"When you've got an inspector," said Jeff Casey, the deputy special agent in charge of Customs Enforcement in San Diego, "you've got the keys to the kingdom."

Many illegal immigrants are Mexicans who cannot afford such first-class smuggling services. Some fend off the *talones* at the bus station, hoping to cross on their own or with a low-priced solo guide. They take a bus or share a taxi to the border. Dense Tijuana housing and industry give way abruptly to U.S. industrial parks, farmland, sudden open space; pigs from Tijuana *colonias* root in the grass on the north side. The border fence is both symbol and reality: stark, rusty, ten feet tall, fourteen miles long, fashioned from iron landing mats used by the U.S. military for runways in temporary air bases. The Border Patrol acquired the material on the cheap—used Pentagon goods for a secondhand peacetime conflict. Extending from the Pacific Ocean to Otay Mountain, the fence assumes multiple personalities, juxtaposed against children playing soccer, shacks, satellite dishes, mansions, jets descending into the Tijuana airport. People decorate the fence with murals and political graffiti. The fence generates indignation in Mexico: fences are not neighborly. Meanwhile, U.S. politicians extol the virtues of the fence and curse wimpy bureaucrats for not building more of them. Despite the huffing and puffing, the barrier is not exactly the Iron Curtain. It has not stopped border-crossing, but did anyone really think it would? The fence has reduced violent confrontations and incursions by smuggling vehicles. The fence creates a demarcation, a semblance of order.

Government policies have human consequences. Emergency room doctors in the San Diego area have identified recurring injuries—shattered feet, ankles and legs—suffered by migrants dropping over the fence. Perhaps the most spectacular casualty was an immigrant whose hand got caught as he scrambled back into Mexico ahead of pursuing Border Patrol agents. He lost his balance and toppled. The sharp metal edge sliced off his finger. The migrant fell on the north side, his hand spewing blood. His finger fell on the south side. Yelling and scrabbling around in the dirt, migrants and Border Patrol agents recovered the amputated finger, but the doctors could not reattach it.

The crossing routes evolve in response to the U.S. defenses, the flow shifting among the landmarks: Goat Canyon, the canyon known as the Soccer Field, the riverbank near the Tijuana headquarters of the Institutional Revolutionary

Party. The PRI's green, boxlike building has a modernistic facade adorned with the Mexican eagle and the motto "Liberty and Social Justice." These are the last words that many Mexicans see before they leave.

The immigrants use a poetic phrase to describe the act of illegal crossing. They call it El Brinco: "The Leap." It is a word full of meanings. Crossing in either direction, legally or illegally, is a leap between worlds. The border region has leapt forward politically, culturally, economically. Life for illegal immigrants, smugglers and other denizens of the border is a continuous and harrowing series of leaps back and forth. They inhabit a shadow world that defies notions of law and order, culture and nationhood. The fantastic becomes routine, but the life rarely gets easier.

Early on a November morning at the crossing point known as Stewart's Bridge, not far from the headquarters of the PRI, migrants huddle in a drainage culvert beneath Calle Internacional, the Tijuana highway that parallels the international line. Traffic thunders overhead. The dank, low-ceilinged chamber smells of ashes and exhaust fumes. Gathered at two campfires in the predawn chill, wrapped in blankets and hoods, the voyagers peer like primeval subterranean creatures through a twenty-foot-wide gap beneath the fence; floodwaters have opened a doorway to El Norte. The view consists of a small bridge, a stream bed full of garbage and an idling Border Patrol Blazer, the squat silhouette taking shape as sunrise approaches.

The conversation in the tunnel beneath the highway comes in murmurs, monosyllables, soft laughter. Hands in pockets, Mario reclines against a sooty cement wall. The graffiti around his head resembles cave drawings in the firelight. Mario has been dozing fitfully, one eye on the Border Patrol vehicle, ready to slip through a gap in the metal grillwork covering the culvert.

"It's getting tougher," says Mario. "I used to cross almost every weekend, go to Tijuana to go shopping. It was real easy to get back in those days."

Mario hunches his shoulders against the cold; he wears a frayed crimson sweatshirt and jeans. His face was handsome once, but it has acquired a stubbled layer of jowl. The twenty-four-year-old has slept for several nights in the tunnel after being caught twice and returned by the Border Patrol. "Now they have more agents, and lights, and fences. And the agents who sneak up on you in plainclothes. They're real despotic, too. I tell them, 'Treat us like human beings.' And they get mad. They don't like that, if you know your rights. I've got a brother-in-law who's a [Border Patrol agent]. He never says he's Mexican. He just says, 'I'm an American citizen.' I don't like him much."

Sliding back and forth between Spanish and English, Mario explains that he left Guadalajara and crossed the border for the first time at sixteen. Alone. He lived in Los Angeles for eight years, surviving gang and drug trouble to settle down and marry a Chicana. He worked at a Japanese restaurant in Hollywood. The owners did not care about your immigration status as long as you worked like a beast. "They're cheapskates," he chuckles, savoring the English slang. "But you know what? I like their food. Different. Raw fish, all that. I learned how to make it. Sometimes I worked in the kitchen, sometimes busboy."

Mario does not have a special crossing route planned out. "Just imagination, man." Once he makes it across, he plans to hop a train at the Amtrak station in downtown San Diego and fake his way past the Border Patrol agents making spot checks. "They stop me a lot of times, ask me where I'm from. I say, 'L.A., man.' I'm not scared anymore. I can go anywhere. I don't really feel illegal anymore."

As the sun rises, the traffic picks up on the road over the

drainage tunnel. Tijuana awakes, its back turned to the border. Schoolchildren and commuters line bus stops, facing south in front of roadside vending stands that cater to migrants. Joggers in designer warm-up suits chug past migrants crouching on junked refrigerators to look over the fence. In the culvert below, the migrants stamp out the campfires, smoke twisting into the sunlight. Mario and the rest of the temporary community hunker down for the day. They are still waiting fifteen hours later when the cold and dark return, when the campfires start up again, flames dancing behind the grillwork.

Three days underground have left Mario looking haggard. He puts it in perspective by recalling a television documentary he once saw about the Berlin Wall. In comparison, he says, the U.S.-Mexico border is a "piece of cake. They killed people in Berlin. They were real tough. The show had this guy talking, a German. And he said this border, the Mexican one, is the best in the world. Because they don't punish. And it's true."

There are no mines or sharpshooters here, but immigrants run a gauntlet of dangers. In the late 1980s and early 1990s, the southernmost I-5 freeway became a slaughtering ground for illegal immigrants, the embodiment of border anarchy. It was perhaps the only highway in the developed world to be perennially crowded with pedestrians. Debilitated by their journeys, the immigrants forded eight lanes of traffic hurtling at speeds some had never seen before. Dozens of silhouettes trudged north on the median after dark, swept by headlights. Forlorn families held hands, replicating the image on the yellow warning signs installed by the state of California: a running man, woman and little girl with pigtails flying out behind her. Transvestites clopped along on wobbly heels, heading for the seamy fringes of downtown San Diego. Strolling shirtless toughs drank beer in the sun.

On rainy nights, a mist steamed up off the black pavement, swirling with the ghosts of dozens of victims.

Speed made the traffic deaths spectacular even by the macabre standards of California Highway Patrol old-timers: people sent flying out of their shoes, people mangled by multiple impacts. A smuggler named El Turi once saw a car tear a little girl out of her mother's grip. The smuggler turns his head and grimaces at the memory. "The car wiped her out. I said, Please, for the love of God. I'm not even going to look at this. Let's go."

El Turi bears part of the blame for the carnage because it was smugglers like him who methodically converted the freeway into a pedestrian thoroughfare. El Turi trolls for clients at the entrance from Tijuana to the U.S. immigration facility at the San Ysidro port of entry. If you enter the covered walkway, turn around and walk back south, El Turi detaches himself from a wall, where he has been murmuring with a stocky young woman in a baseball warm-up jacket who has high corners painted onto her eyes and a mane of strawberry-tinted hair. El Turi eases alongside you: he is a raffish, skull-faced twenty-seven-year-old with grim eyes and a short leather coat. He thinks you are one of the dejected would-be pedestrian crossers whom the U.S. inspectors reject because of unconvincing claims to legality.

"What happened?" he rasps, his scraggly curls bobbing. "They wouldn't let you through? Don't worry, we'll take care of you. We are international guides. We have served dentists and musical groups. We have served Cubans, Chinese, Indians, Albanians. We had a Russian last week. We take care of our clients."

This feral gatekeeper has been in the business for thirteen years. His strategy relies on straight-ahead machismo. "This is my little piece of the line. We take you right up the middle. We screw the *Migra*." El Turi assembles small groups of clients near the vehicle inspection booths. He waits until afternoon, when southbound traffic bunches and slows on the Interstate-5 freeway with returning Mexican shoppers and workers. El Turi tells his clients to take off their shirts, so U.S. agents can't identify them by the color. Then he leads the charge: sprinting through traffic past the inspectors into the southbound freeway lanes. The bare-chested port-runners scurry among cars, horns honking, drivers gawking, to the center divider. El Turi's objective is the San Diego trolley east of the freeway, the light-rail system that runs north to downtown San Diego. He knows that the Border Patrol has strict orders not to chase people on the freeway.

"I am responsible," El Turi says. "We try to cross the people during daylight. Look, the canyons are dangerous too. It's tricky terrain. There are swamps. There's a lot of muggers. It's very dangerous everywhere. These are poor people. And we are poor people. We are leading them to a better life. We are doing them a service. The risk is necessary."

The issue of freeway anarchy erupted publicly in 1992 when Gustavo De La Viña, the chief of the Border Patrol in San Diego, quietly deployed an extraordinary number of agents on the front lines. He knew that illegal immigration has well-defined rhythms. Border-crossing declines from the fall to the Christmas holidays, when many immigrants go home laden with purchases and tales from the new world. The crossing activity surges in January, when they return north, and climbs into the summer. De La Viña wanted to test the defenses against the early-year increase. Sure enough, the returning crossers ran up against the Border Patrol reinforcements. The smugglers grew frustrated. The pressure bulged toward the San Ysidro port of entry and burst: El Turi and his smuggler cohorts organized charges of fifty migrants at a time through the southbound Mexican

Customs lanes onto the freeway. The Border Patrol dubbed
the incursions "Banzai Runs." The smugglers called them
"Viva-Villas," in honor of the Mexican revolutionary Pancho
Villa.

The footage of men, women and children stampeding into
traffic was televised around the world. It was a public scene
from the usually private duel between the Patrol and the
smugglers. There was a specific logic and timing behind the
seemingly abrupt confrontation. The Patrol chiefs were
making a stand. If the result was publicity about illegal border-crossing which brought action in both nations, it was
apparently worth the confrontation. And the smuggler field
marshals, who were often callous about putting clients at
risk, were not going to back down easily.

The Border Patrol demanded that Mexican police stop the
runners and threatened to station twenty-five agents on foot
on the freeway, slowing Tijuana-bound traffic to a crawl.
Mexican diplomats responded that their Constitution (and
virulent public opinion) prevented them from interfering
with immigrants leaving Mexican soil. Advocates of immigrants accused the Border Patrol of intentionally provoking
the charges and exploiting the images to get more funding.
But Mexico relented. Officers of the plainclothes Grupo
Beta unit broke up groups near the freeway crossing and
locked up smugglers. On the California side, state and federal agencies built a wire-mesh fence along the center
divider to prevent people from crossing through traffic and
hurdling the median. The California Highway Patrol dispatched a special team to coax immigrants off the freeways.
The deaths and freeway-running declined.

The Banzai Runs of 1992 remained emblazoned in the
minds of politicians and the public in the United States: a
defining moment. Governor Pete Wilson won reelection two
years later with a campaign propelled largely by a get-tough

stand against illegal immigration. A Wilson campaign ad showed the immigrants streaming onto the freeway beneath the "Mexico" sign on the customs station. A narrator intoned an ominous message: "They keep coming." The choice of imagery was ironic. If the freeway-runners epitomized anything, it was the bravery and vulnerability of illegal immigrants. Their confrontation with onrushing death was a challenge to two nations. Neither the United States nor Mexico wanted these people, but both profited from their toil. Hounded by poverty and politicians, smugglers and police, the immigrants kept coming; they kept running.

The clash between growing despair in the south and growing hostility in the north has its ultimate expression in places like the Robin Hood Homes and cases like the story of Humberto Reyes. He and Javier Rodríguez grew up together in Teloyucan on the outskirts of Mexico City. Reyes was four years older; they were neighbors, went to school together, played basketball. "Best friends, like cousins, like brothers," Rodríguez later said. Rodríguez completed high school, no small achievement for his work-ing-class generation. After graduating, he continued to describe himself on official documents as a student. His friend Reyes made three trips to California and returned full of enthusiasm, telling Rodríguez that the future was in the north.

In early 1992, the two left for Los Angeles, planning to find jobs and study English. Reyes was twenty-three and Rodriguez was nineteen. The first stop was Tijuana, where they joined the perennial floating population of migrants. They worked at a taco stand and a lumber supply business to raise money. Six weeks later, Reyes found a smuggler. They set a price of $350 and a rendezvous for Sunday, April 19, at El Bordo. El Bordo is border Spanish for "the Edge"; it refers to a section of the concrete levee of the Tijuana River that runs northwest through Tijuana and cuts into U.S. territory about half a mile west of the San Ysidro port of entry. It was after midnight when Reyes and Rodríguez clambered onto the riverbank among migrants, smugglers and vendors selling burritos and plastic bags to guard the feet against the shallow river's foul brew of industrial toxins and sewage. They saw the enticing lights of San Diego beyond the dark Tijuana River Valley.

Rodríguez, a slender youth with a smudge of a mustache, felt more exhilaration than fear. "We knew that many people had been run over on the freeway. But you never think that's going to happen to you. It didn't seem dangerous. We were mainly nervous about being caught by immigration."

The guide led them across at dawn, taking advantage of the Border Patrol shift change. Sunrise illuminated a mile-long trek through marshes that brought them to the Robin Hood Homes. It was one of those housing tracts that fulfill California's promise to the working middle class: relatively affordable, generic-looking. The small lots belonged largely to federal employees, many of them Filipinos. The placid air was deceiving. The first neighborhood past the marshes constituted a second border, a bastion on the edge of a no-man's-land. Frenzied guard dogs barked all night at the hundreds of border-crossers hurrying through streets, yards and driveways, racing the Border Patrol to the freeway.

The smuggler led the way over a wall that was scuffed and blackened with footmarks from previous climbers. The group crept through backyards, a shortcut to the I-5 freeway that angles northwest beyond the subdivision. The houses bristled with bars and barbed wire. Fences sagged. A few homeowners had simply left their gates open, giving in to the trespassers whose dashes were as much a part of neighborhood rhythms as cars pulling out of driveways and children walking home from school. In a backyard on Wardlow Street, a barking dog charged the migrants and a voice in the house yelled, "Get 'em!" The group stumbled frantically over fences to the street. Rodríguez noticed a two-door sedan go by, the driver looking back as they ran a final block down Valentino Avenue into a cul-de-sac, approaching the last wall before the freeway. The men helped the woman over the wall first. As Rodríguez alighted, he heard the shriek of brakes behind the wall, where Humberto Reyes was preparing to climb. And then the unmistakable crack of gunshots.

"I thought it was the Border Patrol," Rodríguez said. "But why would they be shooting? I didn't know. I thought, I'm going to give myself up, because I'm with him. And then I saw it was a young kid shooting."

The dark sedan Rodríguez had seen earlier had skidded to a stop in the circular arena of the cul-de-sac. The youthful black-haired gunman, dressed incongruously in a T-shirt, shorts and thongs, crouched next to the open driver's door.

Two days later, Rodríguez described the moment during a conversation in San Diego's federal Metropolitan Correctional Center, where he was being held as a material witness. His eyes wet and shining, teeth bared, Rodríguez locked his arms in front of him to demonstrate the two-hand-ed, police-style shooting stance. "He didn't say anything. He just fired, and then he drove away. Humberto just said, 'Oh, he got me.' "

Reyes collapsed. Rodríguez jumped back over the wall. "I lifted his shirt to see, because there wasn't any blood. And that was when I saw the bullet wound. He got up and he climbed over the wall with me, he still had strength. And then he said, 'Stop a car, an ambulance or something, because I feel bad, I'm getting dizzy.' And then he said, 'Javier, hurry, quick.' And then he fell like this, as if he had fainted. And then he didn't say anything else."

The smuggler and the couple ran on. Illegal immigrants

lined the shoulder of the freeway, the morning rush north, but none stopped. Cars droned past. Rodríguez hurried to a freeway call box that did not work. Finally, a Border Patrol vehicle arrived.

After an ambulance left with the body, the cul-de-sac on Valentino Avenue filled with yellow tape, officers with clipboards, detectives crouched over expended cartridges. Rodríguez sat on the cement and cried. A woman neighbor gave him a soda.

The San Diego Police moved fast. Detectives developed a list of cars registered in the area that resembled the descriptions given by Rodríguez and a neighbor. Officers pulled over Harold Ray Bassham in a Datsun sedan and found a .25-caliber semiautomatic pistol. The unemployed Bassham, nineteen, had a juvenile record for burglary and weapons possession and lived two blocks from the murder scene. He confessed. He said he thought Reyes was a smuggler who had run through Bassham's yard in the past and had hit the family dog with a brick. Bassham's mother, Pilnan Beard, was a Korean immigrant married to an Anglo. She said that her son had complained about all the trespassers. "They run through all the time, they never bother anybody, " she said tearfully, standing in her doorway. Of her son, she said: "I was pushing him to go to school or get a job. I didn't want him getting in trouble."

Not all the neighbors were surprised by the killing. The daily siege had ratcheted up tensions: they complained about noise, trampled lawns, stolen cars, vandalism. And insolent young rogues who knocked on their doors and asked to use the phone. "I knew it was going to happen one of these days," said Roberto Juan, whose house had been burglarized. "Maybe not this violent, but I thought somebody might chase some immigrants or throw rocks at them or something. People are mad."

Jerome Hinman's property was continuously overrun because it was on a cul-de-sac facing the marshes. But he took a tolerant view. "If there's any crime element, it's on this side of the border," said the retired air force colonel, a tall, stooped and serene man with a receding white crown of hair. "The philosophy of [the immigrants] is to get the hell out of here, get up north and make a few bucks."

Puttering in his socks by a motorboat in his driveway, Hinman barely looked up when three young men hoisted themselves over the subdivision wall fifty feet away. Two wore sweaters and sweatpants; the third was outfitted more for a disco than a chase—pleated pants, pointed loafers, long hair tumbling down the back of a shiny white windbreaker. The trio clattered down the street. It went on all day like that, Hinman said. He had become a student of the border. He counted the immigrants. He videotaped them. He monitored Border Patrol transmissions on a scanner and watched agents herd prisoners into vans. "We get between 80 to 120 people coming through a day, seven days a week. The holidays and weekends they are busy with little children. You'll see little guys less than a year old. It's a tormenting thing to see."

The slaying resembled two previous cases in San Diego County in which angry working-class young people had shot Mexican immigrants. But sympathies in the Robin Hood Homes leaned toward the victim. The community, literally on the front lines of the immigration debate, could not be dismissed as racist or reactionary. Many neighbors, themselves immigrants, made a distinction between honest crossers and thugs.

During the trial, Bassham's lawyer argued that Reyes was really a smuggler, that he had injured Bassham's dog and that Bassham fired because Reyes had threatened him with a rock. The jury deadlocked 9 to 3 in favor of conviction.

Just before his second trial, Bassham pleaded guilty to
manslaughter and was sentenced to ten years in prison. After
testifying, Javier Rodríguez went back to Mexico.

"If for the simple act of crossing the border this can happen," he said, "I think Los Angeles must be worse. I don't
want to go. What for?"

Rodríguez endured the most extreme—and rarest—form of
retaliation against immigrants. The rhetoric of the immigration debate became increasingly polarized: immigrants were
a benefit or a cost, a scourge or a godsend, victims or preda-
tors. But even Border Patrol agents fed up with saintly depic-
tions of immigrants agreed that most people they caught were
peaceable and hardworking. The immigrants said this: The
day they kick out the Mexicans is the day that the United
States falls apart. Because they are not going to find anyone
to work cheap. We don't beg. The blacks don't want to do
what we do. The whites don't want to do what we do.

"They call us bandits, many things," says a veteran border-crosser named Ramón. "I don't deny there may be some
Mexicans who have done bad things. But the migrant does
not hurt anyone. On the contrary, others take advantage of
you. Since you don't have papers, you are scared of many
things. I made $10 a day when I first came to the United
States. My boss gave me three sandwiches a day. And he let
me sleep in his car. And he charged contractors $50 for me.
He has continued doing the same with many other people
since then."

Ramón is a model citizen who fears he will never become
a citizen. He tells his story in the San Diego office of his
lawyer, his baseball cap on the table next to him. He is a
bantam and somber construction worker in his early fifties
who looks like he would be more comfortable outdoors.
Although undocumented, Ramón has led a meticulously
documented life. The file on the table bulges with receipts,

pay stubs and letters from employers, a priest and the police attesting to twenty years of discipline and self-sacrifice. Ramón lives in a tough barrio of San Diego, but he shrugs off the risks. "Since I don't bother anyone, nobody bothers me."

He was born in rural Michoacán, the eldest of twelve children. He never went to school. In 1974 he left to work in "los fields" of Northern California. Discouraged by frequent Border Patrol raids, in 1979 he tried San Diego on a friend's advice. He ended up joining the small immigrant communi-ty that has chosen not to continue on to Los Angeles, which draws most immigrants because of the wealth of service and industrial jobs. His first boss was the fast-talking subcon-tractor who let him sleep in his car. Ramón's liberation came when his boss loaned him to a construction contractor, an Anglo. The Anglo was infuriated when Ramón told him he earned $10 a day; he hired him on the spot for $40 a day.The new job lasted longer. "Seven years and eight months," says Ramón, who recalls dates with precision. His new boss taught him the trade. Ramón's brown hands trace tools in the air and he switches to English for technical terms. "He taught me everything. From digging the foundation to fin-ishing the house. Inside and outside. Plumbing, sewage lines, tap water, everything."

Following the pattern of many migrant families, some of Ramón's children moved to Tijuana and Mexicali to be clos-er to him. Ramón visited them on weekends. The Border Patrol occasionally caught him sneaking back. "The Border Patrol have a bad reputation. But I have seen many times that, unfortunately, my countrymen provoke them."

At the urging of his boss, Ramón set out to become legal. He made the mistake of going to an "immigration consultant," another of the legion of parasites who feed off immigrants. The swindler promised Ramón permanent residence—fast. He charged $2,300. Ramón received an impressive-looking document stating that his green card was forthcoming. "I thought everything was fine. I realized that nothing was resolved when I was stopped by an agent who told me, "This is worthless." And I argued with him. I told him I had a right to be here. More than one hundred agents had stopped me with this paper and let me go. He looked on his computer and he said, 'There's nothing here with your name.' He laughed at me."

The consultant ended up in jail; the money disappeared; Ramón's lawyer won him a temporary work permit while fighting an uphill battle against his deportation. The fact that Ramón's family stayed in Mexico made him a classic case study for those who argue that immigrants contribute more than they cost. But his chances of being deported were greater because he could not use the standard argument that his family was too established in the United States to leave without suffering great hardship.

Two decades after leaving Michoacán, Ramón's life remains spartan. His most valuable piece of property is a pickup truck. His workweek routinely includes Saturdays and Sundays. He rents a room for $150 in an apartment he shares with a family. Out of about $1,000 in monthly wages, he sends $400 to his family in Mexico. His diversions consist of smoking cigarettes, going to Mass, doing volunteer work at his parish and talking to his family on the phone. Most of his children have returned to Michoacán. He does not mind. He has come to terms with his solitude. "They like the countryside. They should study as much as they can there. The way I suffered, I don't want them to suffer. If when they get older they want to suffer, that's up to them."

Surgery for a back injury forced Ramón out of construction and back to gardening, which pays less. He moves stiffly, racked with pain. But in a society that often glorifies victimization and rewards whining, he has few complaints.

He just wants permission to stay and work. Ramón knows that jobs and tolerance are scarcer for the new generations without papers. But no matter what laws the politicians write, no matter what walls they build, the Mexicans will keep coming. Ramón says this with the certainty of a farmer talking about the seasons, the elements, birth and death. "They are not going to stop it. Because in Mexico we need a great deal. Because in Mexico we don't have work. They can put an agent every meter, but they won't stop it."

Ramón has become a productive member of U.S. society: a modest success. The antithesis of Ramón's story plays out only a few blocks from his lawyer's office, in Balboa Park. The park stretches like a lush front lawn below the sun-glazed high-rises of downtown. It houses the San Diego Zoo, museums, concerts, nature trails and athletic fields. It is beautiful in the sunlight. The boys of Balboa Park live in the shadows; their existence is one of the grimmest possible consequences of the leap into the limbo of the border.

The February afternoon gets off to a typical start: with a Border Patrol raid. Carlitos is near the public rest room when he sees the unmarked Border Patrol van cruise around the circular lane and veer abruptly into an angled parking space. Carlitos fades back against the wall. Two plainclothes officers emerge from the van, a weary Anglo supervisor in sunglasses and a gung-ho Latino rookie, jaws hammering gum, sprinting in a warm-up jacket with rolled-up sleeves.

The boys, who have been reclining on a low grass ridge, scatter. The young agent nabs a couple of them who look too high to react. A second van appears to collect the prisoners. Carlitos hangs back, making faces at the captured boys. El Camarena, an older boy who acts as pimp and bodyguard for the others, saunters up to the agents, surrenders and climbs into the van. He wants to keep the little guys company, he says, and he could use a ride to Tijuana.

When the Border Patrol departs, Carlitos strides into the open, clutching a Coke can. He whistles piercingly.

"They're gone!" Carlitos shouts in Spanish. He pauses to inhale a blast of Octane Booster, a gasoline additive that serves as a makeshift drug, from the can. "I chased them off. Nothing to worry about."

A dozen youths emerge slowly from the trees. Their clothes look like hip teenage wear but are ragged and soiled on closer inspection: army jackets, baggy jeans, wool caps, high-top basketball shoes. Like Carlitos, the youths all carry cans full of Octane Booster (they call it "toncho"). They refuel periodically on the fumes, inhaling deeply and holding their breath as the high floods through them. Addicted, abused, malnourished, homeless, undocumented, they look like the street children who survive on prostitution, petty crime and chemical fumes throughout the Third World. But Carlitos and his friends are from Mexico and Central America. And they live in the heart of a resolutely First World city, subsisting in the corner of the park known as Marston Point, where the cars circle day and night, where the drivers in business suits and BMWs prey on youths for paid sex.

Unfazed by the Border Patrol raid, Carlitos leads the way down into a wooded ravine. He is describing the marvels of the suburban house where a recent client took him. Carlitos is fourteen, still fresh-faced, a shock of black hair tumbling over big eyes, a husky voice that goes from caustic to child-like and back again.

"He has Super Nintendo, a video, a big television, a pool. Like the movies. He took me and Lucas to a place with some go-carts. He gives you food, a place to sleep. And he didn't make us do anything. He just gave us a couple of dollars and dropped us off."

The boys reach a path by the freeway interchange, where

Interstate-5 bisects the park about fifteen miles north of the border. A boy known as the Squirrel totters into the path from the bushes, sleepwalking in a toncho fog, talking to himself. The fourteen-year-old looks frail and undersized in a leather jacket over a hooded sweatshirt; the word is that he was recently diagnosed as HIV-positive. The Squirrel trails behind as they plunge into the traffic, cursing and whistling. They clamber through a multilevel network of bridges, ramps and traffic islands thick with vegetation. Trooping up a final embankment, the crew ducks beneath a bridge. There is a row of blankets in the dirt, backpacks, a stuffed Cookie Monster, schoolbooks, clothes, condoms and, everywhere, discarded white plastic containers of Octane Booster. Graffiti on the wall declares *"No Rifamos, Pero Controlamos"* (roughly: We are not a street gang, but we run things anyway). The spot beneath the bridge is a hiding place, a clubhouse, a refuge where the freeway grumble soothes the boys to sleep at night. The boys call it "the Four Winds Hotel."

"We're from Tijuana, Sinaloa, Mexico City, Guadalajara, Honduras," Carlitos says. "This is our new house."

Carlitos and his friends are the children of the border. As young as nine, they wander an international circuit of streets, parks, jails, homeless shelters, cheap hotels, juvenile halls and immigration lockups. They drift back and forth between Tijuana and Southern California with ease. "For them, the international line is not a dividing line," says Oscar Escalada, director of a YMCA shelter for migrant youths in Tijuana. "It is like a street that has to be crossed to seek better opportunities. With certain dangers, certain obstacles, but nothing more than a street. There is no concept of a dividing line. They are a classic example of the border community: trans-border street children."

The boys, about fifty in all, are too wild for the YMCA

shelter. They beat up, rip off and corrupt other runaways. They manipulate the system, flagging down police cars once they cross the border to get a ride to the county juvenile center. "They have been treated like garbage," says Francisco Velasco, a Mexican doctor at a San Diego health clinic who has made the boys his personal mission. "They have suffered everything you can imagine. They tell me, 'I go with a client, he pays me $20, $40. You come by and bring me food. If I get sick, there are doctors who take care of me. In my country, I don't have anything.'"

Like other immigrants, the boys can make more money north of the border. Monstrous as it seems, they are supply for San Diego's demand: adults solicit their services in broad daylight, even take them on trips. The boys scorn their clients, calling them "chenchos"—fools. Prostitution allows the boys to treat friends at Burger King, play video games and fund other pastimes that unite kids across lines of nationality. A few boys sporadically attend a special high school for the homeless. They stroll across Balboa Park to visit the zoo. They give themselves monikers: Little Dracula, Karate Kid, the Russian. Weaving together profanities, lies, word games, they keep outsiders at bay.

Sitting cross-legged on his blanket, Carlitos explains that he recently spent time in juvenile hall for shoplifting at a department store. "I go and do something at Mervyn's," he chuckles. "Like my jeans? Pure Levi's 501." His English is flawless, so he does not jump the fence from Tijuana: he talks his way past the inspectors if they stop him. He was kicked out of Storefront, a youth shelter, for sniffing toncho. He dismisses the topic of his father with a single word: "Asshole." He says he gives part of his earnings to his mother in Tijuana on the rare days he sees her. Asked if he worries about AIDS, he looks down, the bluster fading for a moment. "Of course. But the money comes first."

A binational coalition of social workers, police and diplomats formed in 1993 to help the boys. The border had produced the problem and frustrated a solution. For every hard-core kid, there were hundreds of young migrants on the verge of entering the same labyrinth of homelessness, crime, drugs and survival sex.

On weekday mornings, the endangered ones filed through the dreary offices of the Mexican immigration service at the Otay Mesa port of entry. The U.S. Border Patrol caught them and sent them back through the turnstile. A sad parade: barefoot youths who lost their shoes running in mud, shivering youths in T-shirts, sawed-off drug runners and protohustlers in leather jackets and gold. Their first stop on the Mexican side was the desk of Rosa Isela Orozco, a social worker who was deceptively sharp beneath her plump good cheer. Wrapped in a sweater against the cinder-block chill of the office, Orozco jousted with them, prodding at their shield of hard-eyed boredom.

"I think you are telling me pure lies," she said to Omar, a sleepy thirteen-year-old with a cough and a bruised nose. Omar's attention jumped to a television in the corner blaring a cartoon about a gunslinging intergalactic space warrior. Omar was a drug mule who swallowed packets of rock cocaine and took it north to Twelfth Street, a wasteland of dealers, gaunt crack whores and the homeless. He said his friends went to Balboa Park, but he did not. He claimed not to remember his family's address in Tijuana. "Send me back to San Diego, to Storefront," Omar insisted in a rare talkative burst. "I like it better there."

Rosa sent him to be questioned by the Grupo Beta police unit, which was gathering files on the youths in the hope of breaking the cycle. The border breeds street kids, their families wrenched apart by migration and poverty. In the early 1990s, social workers noticed an influx of youthful immigrants whom they dubbed "nomads." They differed from the traditional young crossers bent on reuniting with their families in the United States. The nomads journeyed from troubled homes to uncertain destinations, driven by rebelliousness, adventure, pain.

"They can't go back," said Escalada of the YMCA. "There are problems in the home of abuse, behavior. And the boy says: 'I have a cousin who visited us once from Los Angeles with a van. His name is Pedro. He lives on Arlington Street. I'm going to go there too.' These nomads are in great danger of becoming children of the street."

Beneath the bridge in Balboa Park, the boys break out more Octane Booster, pour it carefully into the soft-drink cans and pass the cans around, inhaling deeply. The liquid is a gasoline additive that improves the performance of vehicle engines. In humans, the fumes corrode the brain, heart, lungs and kidneys. The sensation of inhaling it resembles breathing deeply from the gas tank of a car. The drug surging behind their eyes, the boys cackle, whoop, tussle in the dirt. A school notebook goes flying, white pages fluttering out. Peering from beneath his Chicago Bulls cap, Martín squats on his haunches. He announces that his birthday is coming up and he wants a case of toncho as a gift.

"You can get it anywhere," he says in slurred slow motion. "Pep Boys, 7-Eleven. Only $3.99 a bottle and it lasts six guys all day. And gets them good and crazy. Real active. How do you think we got away from the Border Patrol?"

Martín is fifteen. His ears stick out under the cap. He is only a year older than baby-faced Carlitos, but he looks sullen and tormented and has a long-armed boxer's physique. When challenged, he likes to pull his shirt off and fight bare-chested. Martín was born in Michoacán and grew up in Tijuana near the Zona Norte. He claims the scars on his arms were inflicted by his stepfather. His Mexican police file says he was kicked out of the house for trying to rape his sister. A friend enlisted him as a small-time smuggler of immigrants. Their forays took them north to the Twelfth Street corridor, where they worked as errand boys and look-outs for the crack dealers. Then Martín heard that you could make real money a few blocks away in Balboa Park.

Martín is asked if he would be interested in living in a shelter for the boys which social workers have talked about building in Tijuana. "Maybe," he says absently. He drops down to do push-ups, corded muscles straining. "If they let my mother live there too. If they have weights for exercise. And Super Nintendo. And toncho!"

As the afternoon fades, the boys go back to work. They retrace their steps across the freeway, up the ravine through the trees, and plop down on the grass at Marston Point. They watch the cars cruise by. Martín is soaring on toncho, his face a bleary, twisted mask beneath the cap. Thinking that he sees a regular client known as Tío, he stumbles out into the lane bawling "Tío, Tío."

Carlitos lunges after Martín and grabs his arm, all business. He snaps: "*Cabrón*. The cops are going to catch you. Boy, is he tonchoed out."

The boys cheer when Velasco, the doctor from the public clinic, drives up with two bagfuls of groceries. An impromptu picnic ensues, interrupted for a moment by a false sighting of the Border Patrol which sends them fleeing for the trees. Laughing, the boys return to the feast of doughnuts, juice and peanut butter and jelly sandwiches.

"Come back later, *chenchos,*" Carlitos chirps, dismissing a potential client with a regal wave. "We're busy."

As concern spread among police and social workers in early 1993, San Diego discovered the boys of Balboa Park. The press reports were a harsh revelation. The story was another demonstration that the border was not a barrier. It was an especially reprehensible case of exploitation—interdependence as nightmare. And this time the brazen villains were not shadowy foreign smugglers but prosperous-looking Americans. So the city council expressed dismay. The police stepped up operations in the park. Irate citizens videotaped the cars to scare away business. Two boys were murdered, one dumped on the freeway interchange with his throat slashed. The cops and cameras drove some boys elsewhere. Mexican diplomats persuaded a few to go to a Catholic youth home in Guadalajara. After reading a newspaper story about the boys, the rock musician Bruce Springsteen made them famous with a haunting song entitled "Balboa Park."

But they have not all left. You can still see them nodding to the rhythms of the circling cars, hiking on the freeway ramps, curled up under the bridge in the momentary glow of headlights.

Beyond the lurid details, the phenomenon of the boys of Balboa Park was disturbing and fascinating because it reproduced a Third World subculture in such an unlikely setting. The boys didn't live in Lima, Manila or Rio de Janeiro; they lived in the city that called itself "America's Finest." Their case was another indication that the anti-immigration backlash in San Diego, in the rest of California and other states seemed to be about more than immigrants. The loss of control of the border symbolizes a larger, more abstract loss of control: of the economy, neighborhoods, schools, the culture. The obsession with immigration has become a fundamental global issue of the 1990s. Developed nations confront a dilemma: the need for cheap foreign labor on the one hand and the resulting social disruptions on the other. Most of the Balboa Park boys had probably gone north with the same aspirations as the North Africans who brave the

Strait of Gibraltar to reach Spain in rafts; the Cubans and Haitians who wash up, dead and alive, on the beaches of Florida; the Romanians hiding in car trunks to elude West German border guards; the thousands of illegal entrants in South Africa. Or the illegal Chinese immigrants for whom the Baja California–California corridor became a crossroads connecting the mountain villages of China with the urban immigrant villages of New York City.

The number of Chinese and other non-Mexicans caught crossing the U.S.-Mexico border accounts for less than 10 percent of arrests. But one reason fewer Chinese border-crossers are caught is because the smuggling fees—as much as $30,000 each—buy better odds. Estimates of the number of illegal Chinese immigrants entering the United States are in the tens of thousands. Some fly in with fake documents or are simply instructed to ask for political asylum upon reaching the terminal. Until recent legal reforms, the grounds for asylum were broad, loopholes abounded and asylum cases dragged on for as long as seven years. For all practical purposes, once the immigrants touched U.S. soil they had succeeded. The lack of detention space forced the INS to release them on bond with orders to return for an asylum hearing. And they disappeared.

Most Chinese immigrants come from Fujian, a coastal province with a tradition of migration, seafaring and contraband. There are many hotspots for the smuggling of Chinese: Puerto Rico, Hawaii, South America. In 1995, the Italian army stationed one thousand soldiers around Bari, on the heel of the boot, to stop boatloads of illegal Albanians, North Africans and Chinese. The global routes lead to the Chinatowns of New York and, to a lesser extent, San Francisco and Los Angeles—strongholds of Asian racketeers. Immigrants work off the smuggling fees with years of indentured servitude. The conditions harken back to the immigrant experience of past centuries. They toil in sweat-shops, kitchens and factories; they sleep in shifts on crowd-ed tenement bunks.

"Basically, alien smuggling is modern-day slavery," said San Diego federal prosecutor Michael Wheat, an expert on smuggling rings. "The whole idea behind slavery was to move humans to perform labor. The way the aliens are moved, the way they are treated, this is just a sophisticated form of slavery."

In January 1993, Chinese immigrants began showing up on foot among the thousands of Mexicans captured by the Border Patrol in San Diego every week. Mexican federal police and immigration officers were sometimes visible at the line when Chinese crossed; U.S. and Mexican investiga-tors suspected that the officers were protecting the opera-tion. The Mexican smugglers were well trained: they barked orders at their clients in rudimentary Chinese. By April, the Patrol had arrested hundreds of Chinese, compared to thirty-four during the entire previous year. Intelligence reports warned of ships sailing toward the sparsely populated, thou-sand-mile coast of Baja, whose lonely coves and fishing vil-lages are ideal for illicit landings. From there, the objective of the smugglers was to bring the Chinese across the border by land.

On April 26, Mexican police responded to a report of strange activity at a ranch house on the outskirts of Ensenada, the port city an hour south of Tijuana. They dis-covered 306 Chinese migrants, 14 of them women, stuffed into the house and an adjacent trailer: hungry, dehydrated, sick. A Taiwanese ship had brought them via Panama to a rendezvous off the Baja coast with small boats near an inlet named Punta China (Chinese Point). Police arrested four smugglers linked to a well-known local ring run by a clan named Kennedy Valdez. The next day, the Ensenada city jail had crammed more than a hundred immigrants into cells that usually hold a few weekend drunks and petty criminals. The immigrants milled around in the sun, the ordeal still etched on their faces, staring at doctors, camera crews and unarmed police cadets in blue sweat suits serving as extra guards. At a basketball hoop, migrants and police cadets took jump shots and reached tentatively across the cultural and linguistic gulf.

"You like music? Madonna?" said cadet Eduardo Gutiérrez, twenty-four, in English.

"I understand," responded Huang Su Chi, a languid nineteen-year-old in bell-bottoms and a leather jacket. He said he was from Beijing; he acted more self-assured than the rural Fujianese who dominated the group. Huang draped his arm around the shoulders of another young migrant, regarding Gutiérrez with an edgy grin, as the cadet tried dutifully to be hospitable.

"Michael Jordan?" Gutiérrez said hopefully, watching a journalist launch a jump shot from the corner.

"Michael Jackson," Huang said. "Michael Jackson!"

Encouraged by the repartee, a migrant patted the ample belly of a husky cadet, who took the gesture in good humor. The group chortled. Gutiérrez led them in a chorus of "*Gordo!*" (Fatso!).

The Chinese posed an uncomfortable challenge to Mexico. Sentiment on the street was with "*los chinos.*" The people of Ensenada donated blankets, food, medicine, clothes. But Mexico's socioeconomic problems swallowed up resources and permitted little generosity to foreigners. Mexican policy on immigration resembles that of most other nations, granting few rights to illegal immigrants and erecting barriers to political asylum. On the other hand, Mexican foreign policy stresses respect for the rights of Mexican immigrants in the United States, lauding their bravery and determination. Mexican officials often play to nationalistic sentiments by bashing the U.S. Border Patrol. Sometimes the Mexican government appears more concerned about the rights of the citizens who leave than of the ones who stay.

Against this backdrop, the warehousing of the Chinese in Ensenada did not look good. Mexico had to act delicately. While discussions about their fate continued, the prisoners were transferred to Mexicali, the Baja state capital. Mexicali offered an auditorium with more civilized conditions and had one of the largest populations of Chinese descent in Mexico. The city was founded at the turn of the century by contract farm laborers from China. Enduring the blast-furnace heat of the desert, the Chinese pioneers built a town that had fifteen thousand Chinese and two thousand Mexicans by 1919. Chinese-Mexicans became a small but prominent merchant and professional class in Mexicali, which today has more than one hundred Chinese restaurants. The cultural connection spurs Asian investment. A more unsavory connection: U.S. and Mexican investigators suspected that Chinese-Mexicans in Baja were acting as liaisons between Chinese and Mexican smugglers.

The Chinese-Mexican community turned out to welcome the captured immigrants in Mexicali. For two weeks, the auditorium became a combined refugee shelter, recreation center and prison camp. Restaurants donated meals. A brigade of beauticians cut hair and did nails. Volunteers brought Bibles, movies, board games, a volleyball net; plaintive Chinese pop music echoed across the expanse of cots and clotheslines up to the bleachers, where police riflemen paced. Politicians, Chinese diplomats and immigration officials from Mexico City bustled in and out of the gym past the sweaty, exasperated press corps, keeping silent about their plans.

A letter slipped to a visitor expressed the restive mood in

the auditorium. The two-page appeal was signed by two schoolteachers, Hong Jun Chen and Xing Yun Chen. It read in part: "We two are teachers. And teachers belong to the knowledgemen class. We two have special identities (political) in our country, and we will be killed by our government. The others will only be put in prison for a short time. So we want to search for the political protections of the USA government officals [*sic*] in Mexico. If the Mexico government refuse to protecte [*sic*] us—help us."

The letter ended with a threat of suicide: "We two have only one way. That is to die here—kill us by ourselves!!!"

The official response came days later: the immigrants were going to be deported. Federal and city police hustled the prisoners onto the buses and then onto a DC-10 at the airport. But the plane did not move. The United States refused to let the flight stop to refuel on U.S. soil, fearing the passengers would demand asylum. While Mexican officials mapped out a new route, the passengers disembarked and were taken to a hangar used as the airport fire station. During the next twenty-four hours in the hangar, neither the captives nor their police guards slept much. The smothering blanket of heat did not ease after dark. There were fights, more suicide threats. Finally, at about 9 p.m. on May 14, about two hundred immigrants rose up and charged the police. The wall of uniforms gave way; the escapees fled into the desert. The border was only a few miles north. U.S. Border Patrol agents spent the night rounding up exultant fugitives in the farmland around the U.S. city of Calexico. Several dozen escaped altogether. For those arrested in California, there would be no flight home until their case reached a U.S. judge, if then.

The incredible last-minute escape raised immediate suspicions that the whole thing was an elaborate charade in which money had changed hands. Privately, a high-ranking

Mexican Interior Ministry official asserted that the escape was the product of a deal. Several escapees told their lawyer in Los Angeles that the Mexican guards had let them get away in exchange for a bribe. One escapee reportedly carried a map that was slipped to him in the auditorium. But it was never determined whether the escape was genuine or staged.

Because of the distance and the cost, illegal immigration from China is a desperate odyssey through a nightmarish succession of jails and jailers. In their police-state homeland, the smugglers, known as snakeheads, pack immigrants into boats that are little more than floating dungeons. Even immigrants who elude capture remain manacled by the enormous debts owed to the gangsters. Little wonder that at the slightest opportunity, captured migrants try to get away. "They are restless," said senior special agent Wayne McKenna of the INS. "They have been on the boat for thirty to sixty days. They are desperate. They have mortgaged their future. If you give them a chance, they are going to run."

The arrival of the immigrants by sea was highly organized. It grew out of a natural partnership between international conglomerates: Asian and Mexican smugglers. The Chinese mafias were as formidable as the cartels behind the drug trade, and trafficked in heroin as well. "There are millions being pumped into these criminal organizations," said Bill Kerins, the INS director of antismuggling investigations. "The Chinese organizations dwarf the Italian mafia. They are the groups of the future."

The Mexican smugglers had experience and an infrastructure for bringing people and drugs north and stolen vehicles, cash and arms south. The typical boat from China carried a human cargo worth $6 million. That kind of money spread high and wide through the Mexican immigration service and federal police, according to investigators in Mexico and the United States. In early 1993, as the Salinas administration began its slide into disarray, President Salinas ousted Interior Minister Fernando Gutiérrez Barrios, a powerful and feared official who had maintained a firm hand at Mexico's borders. He was replaced by Patrocinio González, the former governor of the troubled state of Chiapas. Human rights advocates denounced what Mexican and U.S. officials were complaining about quietly: new bosses in the immigration service allegedly opened "the valves of corruption" at the border. "The complicity reaches to Mexico City," declared José Luis Pérez Canchola, the Baja human rights ombudsman. "The people who are now in the Interior Ministry are there to take advantage of the position. We have no other recourse but to suspect that the federal authorities are involved. It is not possible to accept the idea that hundreds of Chinese can enter the state without the authorities knowing it. There must be a connection between the smuggling network and the authorities."

In Tijuana, a Mexican immigration inspector earned the nickname "the Orient Express," according to an investigation by human rights advocate Víctor Clark Alfaro. The inspector traveled regularly to Cancún to pick up groups of illegal U.S.-bound Chinese, then flew back to Tijuana and escorted them past the airport checkpoint, dispensing bribes all around. His industrious coworkers at the airport, according to a Mexican officer who conducted an internal investigation, were busy putting a perverse spin on the title of the immigration service. Given cellular phones by the smugglers, the officers made their rounds waiting for calls with instructions about arriving groups of Ecuadorans, Romanians, Indians. The agents met the illegal immigrants at the gate and turned them over to smugglers outside.

An incident on the other end of the continent finally

pushed the smugglers into the sights of political leaders in Washington. On June 7, a freighter crowded with Chinese immigrants ran aground on a beach in Queens, New York, the literal backyard of the television networks. At least seven passengers drowned. The Clinton administration promptly announced a campaign against illegal immigration from China, pledging to improve antismuggling laws and toughen the asylum system against fraud. President Clinton said: "With this plan, the United States signals its abhorrence of the trafficking in human beings for profit and its determination to combat this illegal activity."

Despite the rhetoric, the reality was that the INS was being forced to release boatloads of immigrants after intercepting them. It was embarrassing. Congressional representatives and immigration-control groups were making noise. A new U.S. task force against seagoing smuggling needed to dispel the image of helplessness. They got their chance on the Fourth of July when a U.S. Coast Guard plane on holiday weekend patrol spotted a suspicious-looking 160-foot trawler. A Coast Guard cutter made contact with the Taiwanese-flagged vessel in international waters about 150 miles south of San Diego and 75 miles west of Baja. The trawler carrried 236 Chinese immigrants. Two more boats were intercepted nearby carrying 169 and 254 passengers. Coast Guard boarding parties armed with shotguns and wearing rubber gloves deployed on the vessels. They set up an improvised aquatic penitentiary, separating the crews and smuggling enforcers from the immigrants, distributing food and medicine, and settling down to wait. U.S. officials had no intention of bringing another regiment of asylum applicants ashore. Mexico, equally determined to ward off the problem, dispatched Navy ships to watch for another four smuggling boats detected farther west. An incredulous INS official said: "It's practically an armada coming over here."

Typically, smugglers do little to modify the vessels for passengers, simply assembling them in holds lined with defunct refrigeration units. Food and water tend to run low. The passengers pass the time playing cards, smoking cigarettes, dozing. The three boats fit the profile. The trawler *Long Sen* looked ancient, a dinosaur-boat steaming out of another era. During the voyage, the hot and stuffy hold filled with the sounds of coughing and vomiting. Garbage accumulated. The hold had only one air vent; the stench gathered force, an oppressive, tangible presence. "It had been a place to store fish," a schoolteacher named Liu Jiang recalled afterward. "The passengers were arranged like fish, one by one. . . . The air was bad. When people threw up, it stayed on the floor. It was incredibly dirty."

The voyage leading up to the standoff was particularly brutal. The mafia enforcers kept order with beatings and threats. Liu, a lanky twenty-two-year-old with longish black hair and an earnest, slightly distracted manner, said he was singled out for abuse after the others found out that he was a devout Christian. "They beat me and they also withheld my food. They had prejudice against Christians. I had brought my Bible and crucifix. They threw them into the sea."

Although the Coast Guard put an end to the mistreatment, the mood was ugly. The passengers had cheered and changed into their best clothes when the Coast Guard first appeared, assuming that they would soon land in America and be released. As days passed, the conditions grew abysmal. The Coast Guard sailors quelled a hunger strike and a threat by several women to jump into the ocean. The immigrants pressed onto the decks for fresh air, some smiling, others sick and shell-shocked. They held up hand-painted signs for the U.S. newspaper photographers and camera crews who were brought alongside in a Coast Guard boat.

The signs said: "We Must Go to American," "Longing to Go American," "Bread We Want, Freedom We Want."

The United States, Mexico and China convened talks, each nation arguing that the others should take responsibility. U.S. diplomats urged their Mexican counterparts to take custody of the migrants and deport them, which would prevent them from requesting asylum in the United States. After initial and largely symbolic refusals, Mexico agreed. Mexican authorities described the decision as purely humanitarian. They made it clear that they would not get involved in evaluating refugee claims. The immigrants would spend as little time as possible on Mexican soil. The unmentioned context of the accord was the proposed North American Free Trade Agreement, which would be approved by the U.S. Congress later in the year. By accepting the boats, Mexico helped the Clinton administration look tough on immigration in a case that did not involve Mexicans. The United States hurriedly dispatched immigration officers to the ships, mindful of criticism that it was using Mexico to dodge its obligation to shelter would-be refugees. Speaking with reporters in Washington, Vice President Al Gore argued that the Chinese were economic refugees. "Those with legitimate requests for asylum will be granted asylum," he said. "But those who do not have legitimate requests, and historically that has been the vast majority in these cases, will be returned directly to China."

Human rights advocates responded that the rushed solution violated international human rights norms barring the forcible return of refugees to potential persecution. Previous cases suggested that the deportees would be fined, jailed and otherwise mistreated back in China. As the boats chugged toward a rendezvous with the Mexican navy, the U.S. immigration officers deposited into the heart-wrenching tableau tried to determine whether any passengers had valid cases for political asylum. The ordeal had pushed the immigrants into a collective delirious rage on the other side of exhaustion and fear. The bleary-eyed Coast Guard teams put down mutinies with warning shots, a makeshift water cannon, pepper spray and mass handcuffings. On the vessel *Sing Li,* plunged into darkness by a power failure, dozens of passengers refused to fill out questionnaires, though the INS officials told them they were dooming their chances. Some immigrants tore up the papers and tossed the pieces into the water.

Surrounded by the sounds and smells of despair, Liu, the youthful Christian teacher, felt like Jonah in the belly of the whale. He prayed hard when the immigration examiners selected him to be among fifty-eight cases for closer review. A uniformed officer and a woman interpreter brought him up to the relative calm of a separate deck for a second interview. Liu poured everything he had into the chance to talk his way to freedom. When he told the story later, his face looked the way it must have looked at that moment on the *Long Sen:* wide-eyed with concentration, naïveté and longing, an expression that was part genuine, part calculated.

"My hopes were lifting up," he recalled. "They asked me a lot of questions. I think my replies were good."

Liu told his questioners he came from Lian Jang, a mountain village where cars were a rare sight. His father was a farmer, his grandmother an ethnic Siberian who instilled her Christian faith in him at an early age. He taught classics and Chinese to third graders, but his real passion was a prayer group of about fifty Christians which he organized. He sought converts with priestlike dedication. Grinning sheepishly, he said: "I still haven't had a girlfriend. Being a Christian over there, it is hard to find a girlfriend." The religious group was singled out for harassment. The dreaded cultural unit of the municipal government grilled Liu about the overseas contacts of the church and threatened to lock him up. After a year of unpleasant run-ins, a friend arranged a spot for him on the *Long Sen* at a cost of $10,000. Liu decided to leave while he could. Telling the uniformed Americans about the abuse he had endured during the voyage, Liu implored them not to send him back.

Liu became the fortunate pilgrim. Out of more than 650 potential refugees, the officers decided that he, and he alone, met the criteria to apply for political refugee status. On the morning of Friday, July 16, scant hours before the Coast Guard turned the vessels over to the Mexican navy, the interpreter shook Liu's hand and told him he was going to San Diego. Liu was taken off the ship to a U.S. cutter. Sailors helped him aboard a helicopter. Then he was airborne, ascending out of what he had come to regard as hell—the three captive vessels looking suddenly and ridiculously small against the glittering sheet of blue.

There was only one explanation for his epiphany, Liu said. "Maybe God has secretly protected me. Because in the ship, I was the only one who was a Christian."

While this drama transpired at sea, the scene in Ensenada verged on the bizarre. The peaceful streets near the port came to resemble the base of a paramilitary operation. Hotels and government offices filled with bureaucrats, immigration agents, intelligence officers and hundreds of police, soldiers and sailors. A throng of harried Mexican, U.S. and Asian journalists arrived at the port Friday night and were blocked by soldiers in battle gear. Federal officials also refused entry to a representative of the Baja human rights office who wanted to interview the Chinese about their asylum claims. The standoff on land pitted the old, stolid, secretive ways of doing things in Mexico against the modern realities of an aggressive press and other watchdogs.

The operation inside the port proceeded in the glare of

banks of spotlights. The first vessel docked at about 3:15 a.m. Police and soldiers hustled off the Taiwanese crewmen, who were charged with smuggling. The passengers were escorted down gangplanks, their first shaky steps on land in three months. At dawn, the first fleet of buses and about fifty highway police cars with flashing lights rumbled out of the port into a heavy fog shrouding the coastal road. The Chinese immigrants were freeze-frame images in the clammy bus windows: young women ducking away from the cameras, their hair braided down their backs, young men holding up their wrists to display plastic handcuffs. Not only were they manacled, their Mexican police captors had taken the peculiar step of spraying a glow-in-the-dark substance onto their hair so that they could be spotted in case of an escape. As if dozens of Asians fleeing through the armed camp superimposed onto Ensenada would be hard to track down.

The strange convoy wailed north on the highway that runs alongside rocky beaches and cliff-top tourist resorts. The buses sped to the Tijuana airport, whose runways parallel the international border a few hundred yards away. Within hours the planes were loaded, with agents of National Security and Grupo Beta, the elite border police unit, accompanying the prisoners. As they took off and soared up over the Pacific, the immigrants caught their first and last glimpse of the United States.

In the following months, Mexico's National Human Rights Commission issued a report denouncing the secretive handling of the episode and the treatment of the Chinese. Top Mexican immigration officials were arrested or fired for alleged links to smugglers. As a joint message from Mexico and the United States to the smugglers, the Ensenada operation seemed to fulfill its goal. After intercepting a record eleven vessels carrying more than 2,500 illegal immigrants in 1993, the Coast Guard stopped only five boats with 490 people the following year. Chinese smuggling continued to thrive on the border, but more quietly.

The total number of passengers in the smuggling vessels intercepted during that period was not much greater than a single weekend of arrests on land by the Border Patrol in San Diego. But the boat people attracted national and international attention in a way that Mexican illegal crossing rarely did. Like the televised scenes of the freeway-runners, the Chinese smuggling episodes were pivotal moments: they briefly revealed the workings of an underworld that threatened to overwhelm the legitimate power structures on both sides of the line. On the U.S. side, the politics of the border hardened. The smuggling mafias were challenged by the new defenses, but their business benefited because it became harder—for Chinese, Mexicans and anybody else—to cross illegally without the help of organized crime. The migrants were caught in the middle, hostages of opportunistic politics and gangster economics.

CHAPTER THREE

Border Cops: The American Foreign Legion and the Dog That Bit Other Dogs

Afternoon roll call at Imperial Beach, the Fort Apache of San Diego, the busiest station of the U.S. Border Patrol. Young agents in green uniforms assemble at rows of tables, adjusting wraparound sunglasses, cracking jokes. Half the agents are Latino, with short black hair and dark features evoking immigrant ancestors. The agents are a hard-charging fraternity forged in the trenches of "the Line." Their worknights blur into a never-ending chase: sprinting through pitch-dark canyons, four-wheeling down hillsides, catching dozens of immigrants single-handed.

A commander gives a pep talk. He says the agents have produced excellent results in the five miles between the freeway and the beach. If they keep it up, perhaps management will shift part of the workload to the neighboring station. The commander urges his troops to arrest a lot of illegal immigrants.

"So the word is, catch as many tonks as you guys can," he says. "Safely. An alien is not worth busting a leg."

Tonks: the commander uses the word matter-of-factly, with no apparent malice. But the onomatopoetic term, used by agents for years, refers to the sound of an agent's flashlight hitting an immigrant's head. The word speaks volumes about the harsh, insular world of the Border Patrol.

After roll call, Agent Matt Madore wheels a Ford Bronco through the station parking lot filled with rows of junked Broncos and Chevrolet Blazers, casualties of budgetary neglect. The dilapidated vehicles are known to break down during chases; more than half the fleet is unusable. Madore drives past a tall, leering statue of a Border Patrol agent clutching a net and a chicken, a reference to the nickname for immigrants: *pollo.* The statue reflects the humor of the workplace, as does the name of the station softball team, a tribute to the death penalty: "the Fryers Club."

Madore was born in upstate New York, where the Patrol is a familiar presence. He majored in criminal justice and minored in Spanish at a state university. He is of medium height, athletic and jaunty, a member of the sector's elite tactical unit. At twenty-six he is a four-year veteran and one of the old hands at Imperial Beach—a sign of the attrition that gnaws at the Border Patrol. The shift starts gradually on this summer afternoon in 1992, a few hours of warm-up before the real chase begins. Madore scarfs a burrito behind the wheel and returns to the station to replace a defective portable two-way radio. Then he points the Bronco south into the Tijuana River Valley. Rabbits scurry across the dusty road. The setting sun pours through a tattered crimson rampart of clouds over the Pacific as the Bronco cruises through open fields toward the border foothills. It is twilight on the Line, the frontier between day and night. It is the time when the deals go down and the action starts: the migrants make their break, the drug smugglers start their engines, the cops check their weapons. It is the time when the guardians, marauders and survivors on both sides of the line head out into the glow of dusk and go to work.

The radio drones. The numbers are picking up. They soon escalate into an insistent babble. "Group of nine coming

through at Stewart's Bridge. . . . Got five bushing up south
of Holister . . . got traffic in the Gravel Pit."

"It's tag," Madore says. "If I touch you, you gotta sit in
jail for eight hours. Then you go home."

Madore makes arrests at a brisk pace. He collars a youth
walking down Valentino Street in the Robin Hood Homes,
the street where Harold Ray Bassham killed Humberto
Reyes for running across his lawn. The youth turns and
blurts out "I'm *mojado* [illegal]," then climbs into the vehicle without protest, without the agent moving from behind
the wheel.

Madore joins converging agents on all-terrain scooters,
futuristic apparitions in goggles and helmets, to intercept a
group of migrants from Toluca. The captured men crouch
next to the road. Frisking prisoners, dumping cigarette
lighters and identification cards on the hood of a vehicle, an
agent finds $400 wadded in a prisoner's sock. "He's bandit
bait," the agent says, urging the migrant in laborious Spanish
to be careful. "That's probably his life savings."

Madore catches a group of four hiding behind a ridge.
The mother looks trim and fashionable in designer jeans,
blond-tinted curls, careful makeup. She hugs two frightened
boys. After searching the man, Madore ushers them into the
caged back of the Bronco. The man swigs water from a bottle. He works with the woman's husband in Downey, an
industrial suburb of Los Angeles, and is taking the family to
rejoin the husband. The older boy, who is seven, recovers
from his fright and introduces himself as Walter. He says he
has to get to Downey. "I start school next week."

Madore grins. He knows that Walter and his family will
try again and maybe even make it tomorrow.

"The kids are the ones I really feel sorry for," Madore
says.

Once Madore delivered a prisoner's baby. Once, when

Madore had a Spanish test coming up, he made a deal with a Salvadoran prisoner: I buy you lunch, you help me study. They rode and talked for the rest of the shift. "It was real interesting. He was a pretty decent guy."

Madore is a cheerful Sisyphus. He makes $46,000 with overtime, not bad for a single guy. He is content to focus on the minority of border-crossers who are hard-core criminals. Back at the station, agents stand behind counters interviewing lines of bedraggled prisoners and filling out forms used to grant voluntary release back to Tijuana. Madore marches up to a crowded holding cell and gestures elaborately at a wild-looking youth with a backwards cap and a baleful stare.

"Now look at this guy," Madore says. "This guy is NOT going to pick strawberries."

Another agent growls: "He's going to pick pockets, that's where he's going."

Later, Madore drives to a cricket-infested plateau where agents man a nightscope. The infrared device protrudes, humming and swiveling, from the roof of a vehicle. The scope operator stares at the monitor, the images so precise that he can identify a woman border-crosser by the outlines of her dress. He murmurs into his radio, choreographing the chase in the brush below: tiny frantic figures glowing on the screen. The other agents watch absently, like teenagers at a video arcade, discussing their efforts to escape the drudgery at Imperial Beach. They have requested transfers and applied to other agencies: the Secret Service, the Bureau of Alcohol, Tobacco and Firearms.

The agents' world is rife with menaces: snakes, stray dogs, toxic waters, rock-throwers, drug gangsters with AK-47s, and "Mátames," the raging unarmed drunks who charge you screaming the ultimate macho challenge: *"Mátame!"* (Kill me!). But all the agents hear are allegations that they kicked the hell out of some defenseless alien. They are forever looking over their shoulders for the feds, local and Mexican cops, local and Mexican journalists, and political activists skulking in the bushes with video cameras.

"We hear so much crap," Madore says. "The people shouting 'Let 'em go, let 'em go. They're just here to work.' I like to catch the guides and the gangbangers: the little thugs sitting on the fence just waiting to steal your car."

Joel Alcaraz stands in the shadow of the border fence, watching his fellow Mexicans head north. He is a commander of Grupo Beta, a plainclothes police unit that works the border. He holds his walkie-talkie inside his leather jacket near his shoulder holster, concealing the little red light on the radio. He scans the wraithlike figures appearing out of the billows of fog that have settled on the riverbed, the silent faces pressing around him. The migrants trudge up the steep embankment, their furtive progress lit by bonfires, ribbons of city lights speckling the Tijuana hills, high-intensity spotlights on the north riverbank. The migrants scrabble up the ten-foot fence. They perch at the top—suspended between a desperate past and an uncertain future.

Alcaraz has worked the border for more than a year, but the sight of the nightly exodus never fails to affect him.

"Every one of these migrants is a story," Alcaraz says, his breath steaming in the cold below his mustache, his wire-framed glasses glinting. "They sell everything—the little house, the cow, the chickens—to come north. And then they get robbed."

Alcaraz's own story tells a lot about the contradictions of the border. He is a shepherd and a hunter. He does not stop illegal immigrants from entering the United States. Instead, his orders are to protect them from smugglers, robbers, rapists and crooked fellow cops.

Alcaraz is wry, talkative, easygoing. His favorite epithet

is the word *canijo,* which means "little loser" or "wimp." He
is a skilled detective and deadly marksman. And he knows
about crooked cops. Before coming to Grupo Beta, he spent
twelve years on the Baja California state police. He worked
on the homicide squad alongside strutting thugs and torturers who drove stolen cars and rode shotgun for drug lords.
But there were good cops, too. They kept their heads down,
ignoring the temptations, and worked their cases. On the
Tijuana homicide squad, though, it is inevitable: No matter
how honest you are, one day you get the wrong case. The
commander calls you in and says, We need to be careful on
this one. We need to go slow. And you know exactly what he
means: dangerous interests are involved. The case will never
be solved. So you reach a point where you take the money.
Or you leave. Or they kill you.

Alcaraz left. He found redemption in Grupo Beta. He
belongs to an elite group of forty agents formed in 1990. He
earns about $1,000 a month, a hefty salary for Mexican law
enforcement. He is paid to do what a policeman is supposed
to do: protect people. Unfortunately, that makes him a pari-
ah. Grupo Beta routinely gets into confrontations at gun-
point with city, state and federal police officers. Grupo Beta
arrests fellow cops, shutting off what used to be a lucrative
source of income: preying on migrants. When Alcaraz picks
up his paycheck at state police headquarters, he is greeted by
a handwritten sign near the clerk's window that says, "Beta
Is a Dog That Bites Other Dogs." Rival security forces tap
the unit's phones and make threats. "Beta is not well regarded by other police," Alcaraz says. "So we have become more
united."

Alcaraz makes his rounds on foot and in an aging Ford
LTD, jouncing over canyon trails. He commands plainclothes three-officer teams who melt into the crowds at the
fence and tramp through hills and back streets. At first, the

migrants cringe when the piratical-looking men in army
jackets materialize out of the night. The officers crouch next
to the migrants to survey the landscape, the gleaming-wet
silhouettes of U.S. Border Patrol vehicles gliding through
the mist. The officers pass out business cards. Don't worry,
compa, we're the police. Beta, Gobernación (Interior
Ministry). We are here to help. Any problems? Seen bandits
around? Any police bother you? Let us know.

Alcaraz says hello to an informant, a chubby and sleepy-
eyed seventeen-year-old who charges $50 to guide clients
over the fence to the fast-food joints of San Ysidro. Alcaraz
sweeps his flashlight beam across a dark, narrow lane in
Colonia Libertad, where migrants advance through a jumble
of low houses. He confiscates a bottle from a drunk. He
stops and frisks a shaggy, flat-faced man in a long embroidered sweater who claims to be a bricklayer. With a lupine
smile, Alcaraz tells the man to show him his hands. "Those
are some pretty clean hands," he says, dangerously mild,
cocking his head. "Those don't look like a bricklayer's
hands to me. We are going to keep an eye on you."

Alcaraz's radio crackles. U.S. Border Patrol agents are
chasing a car south on the Interstate-5 freeway in San Diego:
another fugitive making the proverbial run for the border.
Alcaraz rushes back to his LTD, plunks a revolving red light
on the roof and speeds downhill toward the port of entry.
Beta cars converge, nosing like sharks through traffic on
ramps and bridges. Alcaraz takes a breath and the LTD
lunges the wrong way into the busy southbound lanes
departing the Mexican Customs booths. Bent forward
behind his glasses, Alcaraz urges the car through the dark,
flashing his headlights at the oncoming headlights, hugging
the left edge of the road.

By the time the fleeing sedan blows past the customs
booths onto Mexican soil, Alcaraz has set the trap. The Beta

cars cut off the sedan and box it in. Alcaraz and his agents haul out a smuggler, his girlfriend and two clients, whose faces register surprise as they are spread-eagled against the car: it is February 1992, and the rules have changed at the border. It used to be unthinkable for Mexican police to team up with the Border Patrol and catch suspects fleeing south.

Alcaraz says: "That's as far as you get, *canijos.*"

The book *Lines and Shadows,* by Joseph Wambaugh, told the story of an undercover unit created by the San Diego Police in response to rampant crime at the border. In 1976, illegal immigrants were being robbed, raped and murdered with impunity. The U.S. Border Patrol and Mexican police did little to stop the slaughter. Some Mexican officers competed with bandit gangs for victims. So a sympathetic San Diego police lieutenant—a former Border Patrol agent—led a group of predominantly Mexican-American officers on a noble mission. Disguised as border-crossers, the Border Alien Robbery Force went into the canyons and offered themselves as bait. The undercover gunslingers racked up arrests and engaged in shoot-outs with the robbers and occasionally the Mexican police. The squad reduced crime and got a lot of press. But the bandit body count reached alarming proportions and the so-called BARF was disbanded in 1978. It was eventually replaced by a more conventional squad who patrolled in uniform and were known at the border as "los SWATs."

In 1990, crime and chaos at the line were as bad as ever. The San Diego Police recorded as many as eleven homicides a year there. No one kept precise statistics for the Mexican side because of a jurisdictional vacuum among largely indifferent agencies. But migrant advocates and police agreed that the numbers were grim. Three or four rapes of migrant women were reported to the office of José Luis Pérez

Canchola, the Baja ombudsman, each week. Pérez's office identified seventeen murders linked to border-crossing activity between 1989 and 1990. And most crime went unreported. Drug sales, extortion and stabbings happened out in the open. Unruly crowds spilled through the tattered chain-link fence. Shootings, fights and riots involving outnumbered U.S. Border Patrol agents provoked diplomatic quarrels at a time when the two governments were trying to build closer ties.

The border mocked commonplace notions of law and justice, chewing up many of the Mexican and U.S. officers who tried to police it, burning them out, corrupting them. Grupo Beta and the U.S. Border Patrol were two very different agencies with different personalities and missions. They were hard to compare because the Tijuana squad was a small, handpicked unit with a focused task, while the U.S. agency was a paramilitary police force guarding a vast and singular territory. The two forces had a wary relationship. Their parallel, sometimes intertwined experiences were full of turmoil and defeat. But for a period in the 1990s, their stories also went against stereotype, showing that disarray and bloodshed were not inevitable. The Line became a laboratory for experiments in police work which produced a measure of hope.

Grupo Beta was the Mexican version of the *Lines and Shadows* story. In 1990, Mexican President Carlos Salinas de Gortari ordered the Interior Ministry to create a special police unit to get the border in Tijuana under control. The project had the blessing of Governor Ernesto Ruffo Appel of Baja California, who had been elected the first opposition-party governor in the nation a year earlier. The idea appealed to Ruffo because the anarchy hurt his state's image and the border was under federal jurisdiction. The governor agreed to a novel setup: the squad would consist of officers from the Tijuana municipal police and the Baja state judicial police, as well as the Mexican federal immigration service. The presence of three agencies was a commonsense antidote to corruption. It opened the unit to oversight by the rival political forces of the PRI and the PAN. They would keep an eye on each other.

The leader of the new unit had a thorny task. He had to confront institutionalized corruption that made fellow police more dangerous than the bandits. He had to build an outpost among outlaws. He had to walk a political tightrope between working with U.S. law enforcement and the Mexican laissez-faire policy toward immigration. It was, on a regional level, nothing less than the most urgent challenge to Mexico today: reforming a legal system that is antiquated, brutal and corrupt.

The man who got the job was not a gunslinger or an "iron prosecutor" in the mold of Mexican movie heroes. He was Javier Valenzuela, thirty-nine, a psychologist and a former academic from Mexico City, who joined the immigration service after working in Mexico's equivalent of the Bureau of Indian Affairs. In the 1970s, Valenzuela had participated in the leftist university protest movement in Mexico City. Later, he worked as a psychologist for the National Indigenous Institute in the Tarahumara mountains of Chihuahua and in the troubled state of Chiapas. He immersed himself in indigenous languages and culture. He was profoundly affected by the despair and dignity he encountered among the indigenous groups, the most abandoned of all in a nation where half the population lives in poverty. Valenzuela's career brought him into one of those unofficial fraternities that trail in the orbit of powerful figures in Mexico. His mentor was Miguel Limón, an urbane deputy minister in the Interior Ministry. Limón became the godfather of Grupo Beta. He felt Valenzuela's experience lent itself to leading an unorthodox project that called for an outsider.

"My main experience with the police was keeping my distance from them," Valenzuela said in 1993. "I felt terrible arresting people at first. It went against my training as a psychologist that people are not to blame for their social conditions. I felt I was taking part in a repressive action. My attitude changed when I had contact with the victims, the migrants, who were the most vulnerable of all: the focus of all the parasites."

Valenzuela was cultured, subtle, somewhat melancholy-looking. He was slight, with large eyes in a furrowed, wide-mouthed face. He exuded workaholic intensity, an ability to read people and situations. He was intrigued by the spiritual disciplines of Asia. And he could talk. He shifted at high speed from professorial analysis to bureaucratic discourse to the slang of the streets. The social-worker tone gave way to a steely edge when necessary. Compensating for his inexperience, Valenzuela preached ideas and ideals.

"I was a neophyte in police matters, so I did what I could with what I knew: psychology, communication, dialogue, working in groups. This implied overcoming resistance in the personality of the policeman, who generally is not a person trained to express himself. They tend to be individuals accustomed to giving and taking orders."

Valenzuela assembled his troops. From the immigration service came Gilberto Castro, nicknamed Toba: beefy, bespectacled, his bushy beard and hair riddled with gray. Toba's command of street-cop English made him the liaison with U.S. law enforcement. Bringing expertise in tactics and the smuggling mafias was Felipe Forastieri, a former chief of the SWAT team of the city police. Forastieri had the aquiline features of his Italian immigrant ancestors and a fierce hearty character to match. Francisco Venegas also came from the city police, an eighteen-year veteran and an expert on street gangs. Intense and wary, a man of humble origins who chose his words with care, Venegas became a fervent disciple of the philosophy of Beta. Along with former homicide detective Joel Alcaraz and a handful of others, these officers in their late thirties and early forties were the nucleus of the experiment—Valenzuela's Untouchables, his musketeers. At first they sat and listened, dumbfounded, as their leader outlined a vision that defied the macho, paramilitary attitude customary to police work in Mexico—and elsewhere. Valenzuela said he had as much to learn as they did. The group would emphasize communication. Like a family. Each officer was expected to talk about himself, his past, his hopes and aspirations, and discuss cases and problems. All the officers would rotate into command positions. "The rule is absolute solidarity," Valenzuela said. "But if you betray us, you become an enemy of the group. And we will show you no pity."

The welcoming ritual alone was like nothing the recruits had experienced. The group greeted a newcomer with applause, listened to his presentation on what he expected from the job, and explained what was expected of him. It felt like therapy, disconcertingly sensitive, vaguely subversive. The agents were not sure what to make of the relentless little psychologist with the intimidating Mexico City accent and flowery vocabulary. But Valenzuela was not the usual haughty *licenciado* (university-trained bureaucrat) bossing around a bunch of working-class cops. His evocation of the mission enthralled them. The group would serve the public with respect and professionalism, he said. They would be the guardian angels of a defenseless population of fellow Mexicans. He appealed to ideals that had not been completely devoured by the Tijuana streets.

"Look, the custom of the police in Mexico was, the first thing after you arrest someone you smack him around," said Jaime Alberto Avila, one of the original officers. "What I learned in Beta was respect for human rights, whether migrants or criminals. Beta was based on respect for the law. I did not believe it could be possible at first. It was a policeman's dream. It represented what you think about when you are a child, and you dream, as all of us have, of becoming a policeman when you grow up."

The dreams had foundered in a rapacious justice system; the opportunities at the border add a huge source of illicit income to the national underground economy created by law enforcement corruption. As in the rest of Mexico, the official division of duties works like this in Baja: The uniformed municipal police patrol the streets. Investigations of felonies, the role of detectives in U.S. departments, are handled by the state judicial police, a separate plainclothes force. The federal judicial police enforce laws involving drugs, guns and other select crimes. To varying degrees, all the forces remain underpaid, poorly trained, ill equipped and publicly despised.

There was a joke told among journalists and detectives at the Big Boy diner on Agua Caliente Boulevard which summed up the cynicism of the public about the police and the police about themselves. It is a joke told about police in other Latin American countries as well; in the Big Boy version, the Mexican federal police are invited to a contest with the FBI, Scotland Yard and other elite investigators from around the world. The judges set loose a rabbit and explain that whoever catches the rabbit first will be declared the winner. Only fifteen minutes after the pursuit begins, the Mexican federal police return triumphantly, dragging a handcuffed elephant covered with bruises. "We caught the rabbit and he confessed," the Mexican federal police announce. They growl at the elephant: "What did you say you were, you bastard?" And the battered and frightened elephant stammers: "I'm a rabbit! I'm a rabbit!"

The officers who came to Beta had seen the degradation firsthand. Torture was standard procedure. The money and influence of political machines and organized crime permeated the system and dictated hiring, promotions and enforcement. The municipal police traditionally protected the vice and immigrant-smuggling rackets of the Zona Norte in exchange for $100,000 monthly payments split among the brass. The state and federal police took millions from drug cartels to ensure the smooth functioning of one of the most lucrative smuggling corridors in the world, the northwest Mexican route connecting Colombian cocaine producers to California consumers. The money guaranteed that illicit Tijuana warehouses unloaded cocaine shipments and sent merchandise north unmolested, that investigations of drug-related murders went nowhere. As a result, the FBI, the DEA, the San Diego Police and other law enforcement agencies in San Diego operated in a haze of contradictions at the border. The U.S. agencies took pains to show respect for Mexican sovereignty, but dedicated increasing amounts of resources and agents to working cases, gathering intelligence and investigating organized crime in Baja. Mexican counterparts worked closely and routinely with them, pursuing fugitives and prosecuting in Mexico common crimes committed north of the border—a procedure permitted by Mexican law. But the partnership had definite limits. Police chiefs and prosecutors were transferred, fired, arrested or killed in Tijuana at a revolving-door pace, hampering continuity or cooperation with U.S. agencies.

The sins were more than passive. Officials from all three Mexican agencies routinely drove Jeep Cherokees, Chevrolet Suburbans and other upscale vehicles stolen in

Southern California by high-volume auto theft rings. In several incidents that enraged the San Diego Police, Mexican police agents or their enforcers were caught stealing vehicles north of the line. Thefts surged in San Diego when special brigades of the Mexican federal police were dispatched to Tijuana because the agents took advantage of the visit to the border to place orders with auto thieves. Police officers served as bodyguards in the swaggering entourages of fugitive mafia barons, who made the rounds of flashy nightclubs with names like Baby Rock and Yuppies' Sports Bar. A clandestine coalition of state and federal officers, known as El Pelotón (the Firing Squad), reputedly worked as hired killers for the traffickers.

A Baja police veteran who served a few months as chief of the state force in Tijuana painted a hopeless picture during a secret meeting with U.S. investigators working in Tijuana for a San Diego law enforcement agency. The former chief told his cross-border counterparts that he had been virtually paralyzed by "a situation that has drug traffickers in control of the state judicial police," according to the intelligence report prepared by the investigators. The informant explained that "when he was chief, he received several offers of large sums of money, most in the neighborhood of $50,000. [He] said these officers came from various subjects involved in drug trafficking. . . . [He] said he did not accept these offers [and] feels that this may be a reason that he did not remain long as chief." The real power, the former chief said, rested in the hands of longtime commanders aligned with the mafias; the commanders called the shots even as they were transferred among different squads and cities. He identified a typical example: "a squad chief in the La Mesa sector [who] is heavily involved with drug traffickers. He is well-known and has held a variety of high-profile assignments, including chief in Tijuana, Mexicali, and Ensenada. . . . [He] is kept in these high-profile assignments because he is the main link to drug traffickers and provides a buffer for the assistant attorney general in dealing with these individuals."

The officers who joined Grupo Beta had survived by looking the other way, rationalizing, compromising. The new chiefs had to correct years of ingrained bad habits. The animated Forastieri was among those who initially balked at the philosophy of restraint: how could the Licenciado expect such good treatment of such bad people? A reluctant convert, Forastieri recalled: "This is what we were up against. I had to teach a veteran of the state judicial police who didn't know how to handle his gun properly. He had had a big .45 pistol for years, and he didn't know how to clean or dismantle it safely. What he did know was how to hit a suspect on the head with it during interrogations!"

Nonetheless, the collective enthusiasm to leave the past behind showed that good and decent officers could be molded into a disciplined force. It was a cautionary note to those who dismiss the problems of the police in Mexico as beyond repair. In the early weeks, Valenzuela dressed down and accompanied his men on expeditions into the underworld. They encountered a feeding frenzy of smugglers, robbers and police victimizing migrants and each other. For police officers, it amounted to casual moonlighting; they cruised the international line after work, shaking down migrants and smugglers. No one controlled the area, but everyone exploited it. Grupo Beta's first task was to define and reclaim the turf. Word spread through the grapevine of vendors and frequent crossers. The mysterious new cops were different: quiet, smooth, gliding out of the shadows to slap on the handcuffs. With drawn guns, they interrupted rapes and robberies. They rousted surprised stickup artists and indignant drug dealers. "We are Beta, we are the law here," they told them. "Stay off the border."

"It had to be distinct from the traditional police," Valenzuela said. "It had to be a professional, honest project with a mystique of protection and service. In the moment that we gave in to temptation, we would become just another group like all of those who prey on the people at the border."

On the other side of the line, the U.S. Border Patrol agents regarded the experiment with a healthy caution bred of experience with Mexican police. They also provided an accidental christening. On the radio, U.S. agents referred to the Tijuana "antibandit" team as "Bandit." The Mexican officers changed the designation to Beta, for the letter B, and it stuck.

While Mexico was planting a small seed of reform with Grupo Beta, the United States government was coming to grips with a history of neglect of the Border Patrol.

The Border Patrol has one of the strangest missions in law enforcement. Most of the more than five thousand agents of this paramilitary arm of the Immigration and Naturalization Service guard the U.S.-Mexico boundary. The agents make more arrests than any police force in the nation. They labor in anonymity, literally on the margin of society. In other nations, the police stop people on the street and demand immigration papers. In the United States, city police take pains not to get involved. Like immigrants, the Border Patrol agents are pawns. They are sent into a lawless world to fend for themselves. They catch the same people over and over again; the job is a metaphor for futility.

"Most of the country doesn't have a clue," said former agent Ralph Hunt. "The Border Patrol is a Band-Aid on a hemorrhage."

Hunt, an air force veteran of Irish-Portuguese descent, had a Rhode Island accent, the build of a linebacker and the mustache of a genial walrus. His vocabulary reflected his graduate studies in Soviet affairs, an unusual credential for an agent. After seven years at Imperial Beach, he said the Patrol was in crisis because it was "the stepchild of a stepchild." The immigration service, historically a poorly funded, low-rung agency, suffered from deep-rooted problems with hiring, management and internal policing. Inspector General Richard J. Hankinson of the Justice Department testified before congressional hearings in 1993: "Not only is [the INS] not managing its employees well, but it also, by this neglect, is fostering a climate in which corruption can occur."

In the 1990s, Border Patrol agents were prosecuted for murder, rape, beatings, unjustified shootings, drug smuggling, theft, embezzlement and perjury. Most Border Patrol sectors experienced scandals: from New Orleans, where a supervisor and two agents pleaded guilty in 1995 to covering up an assault on a handcuffed prisoner, to Tucson, where in 1995 the chief agent was replaced as agents were being investigated for a double murder, rape, child molesting and wrongful shootings. The record drew criticism not just from immigrant advocates but from other police agencies and the Patrol agents and commanders themselves.

In the opinion of a chief at the Patrol academy, the Border Patrol is a kind of American Foreign Legion: a forgotten army fighting a remote war. In 1924, the Patrol was created in the Department of Labor. According to an official history, the first Border Patrol agents included "former mounted guards, policemen, sheriffs, gunslingers of various types." The cowboy mystique endures; elderly Latinos still call agents "rinches"—Spanglish for rangers. The agents fought gun battles with tequila smugglers and arrested boatloads of Chinese entering Florida from Cuba. Shifting to the Department of Justice in 1940, the Patrol developed during economic and political cycles that dictated immigration policy: prosperity encouraged immigration, while harder times combined with political intolerance to produce a backlash. During the World War II–era Bracero Program, the U.S. government and agribusiness recruited Mexican farmworkers, establishing today's networks to Mexican "sending states." Conversely, during the infamous Operation Wetback of the 1950s, authorities summarily deported thousands of Latinos, including U.S. citizens. By the 1980s, Mexico's economic crisis combined with Central American political upheaval to stoke illegal immigration. In 1986, when Congress passed the Immigration Reform and Control Act (IRCA), the Patrol made a record 1.4 million arrests and came to play a frontline role in the war on drugs. As part of IRCA, the Reagan administration promised to secure the border and mandated a 50 percent increase of the Patrol. Struggling with roller-coaster budgets and attrition as high as 40 percent, the agency launched hurried hiring pushes. Therein lie the roots of the kind of corruption and brutality scandals that hit Miami, Washington, D.C., and other cities that expanded their police forces too fast. Mike Hance, president of the agents' union local in San Diego in 1992, put it bluntly: "They went through a binge where they hired everyone that walked. And now they are paying the price."

During one hiring "frenzy" in 1989, a temporary academy was created at a military base to help train a record fifteen hundred new agents. Recruits with dubious pasts and criminal records slipped through the overburdened screening process when the numbers were lower as well. One was accepted despite a conviction for impersonating a police officer. After a week at the academy, he started acting strangely and announced that he had to leave because a man named Guido was going to kill his family. He turned up in a New Jersey mental hospital. Another rookie tested positive for marijuana use and his background investigation unearthed an allegation that he was a drug dealer. But he remained with the agency and served on an antidrug task force, according to an internal 1992 study that discovered a generalized breakdown in Justice Department background investigations. Thousands of law enforcement officers finished their one-year probation period and were locked into the bureaucracy while their investigations languished. This resulted in the hiring of an officer whose report described him as a "walking time bomb, a pathological liar . . . unfit for law enforcement."

Border Patrol recruits needed little more than a high school diploma and a driver's license. The Patrol did not use psychological testing, polygraphs or other tools that were used to screen prospective FBI agents or big-city officers. And the job is at least as stressful as city police work, judging from the emotional and drinking problems among agents. In 1994, a Border Patrol pilot was sentenced to eleven years in prison for engaging in a bar fight in San Diego in which he slashed three men with a knife.

The Line takes its toll. Agents from inland regions feel marooned. Even agents from border towns suffer from low morale. Rookies in San Diego share apartments in bland shoe-box complexes near the border, where aliens occasionally run past sunbathers at the pool. The border is hard to escape. The border seethes on the edge of your sleep. It's like being at the beach when you close your eyes and keep seeing the waves. When agents close their eyes, they keep seeing the waves of faces coming at them. It is blue-collar, assembly-line law enforcement; it breeds a fierce and frazzled culture. The credo endures: We are on our own. We can only trust each other. And we have to do what it takes to hold the line. "There's a fortress mentality," said Hunt. "That's one of our failings. We are very insular."

Hunt left Imperial Beach for a desk job at the INS because

"it wasn't fun anymore. All you do is catch, catch, catch." The stress on arrest totals derived from the need for funds. Commanders appealed to Washington by rattling off statistics about the lopsided odds. To keep numbers up, agents periodically pulled back and let runners breach the line.

Tactics are often improvised in this manner. After a string of amiable arrests, a rookie looks up to see fifty charging border-crossers led by a smuggler. The rookie might respond as taught—screaming and cursing like a madman. It's called command presence. If it works, you don't lay a hand on anyone. If not, you decide how much force to use on an offender who will probably spend no more than eight hours behind bars.

"It's a large problem," says a former supervisor. "You've got these people. You know the guy is a guide. How much do you want to catch him? Is it worth injuring someone? If you've got a bunch of people that are running, you try to scare them enough. . . . Either you are going to yell 'Stop' or decide what is it worth to stop these people. I was more aggressive when I could identify the guide. Momma and the kids, I'm more concerned about running them off the edge of a cliff."

Until 1994, the San Diego sector commonly fielded fewer than one hundred agents per shift against several thousand border-crossers lining the riverbanks and canyons. The sector recorded as many as three thousand arrests on busy Sundays. Every night was a potential riot, a journey into a battle theater of the absurd. The steel fence on the river levee had not yet been built, so agents routinely used their vehicles to herd back crowds, speeding at them, churning up clouds of dust. Technically, it was against the rules, but the agents say they were ordered to retake the turf. There were injuries and deaths.

"Run them off the levee, that's all we heard," Ralph Hunt

said. "It was absurd. I refused to do it. I'm not going to endanger myself and I'm not going to endanger them."

Pressured by chiefs and provoked by migrants, some agents felt there were times when the rules cried out to be broken. An Imperial Beach veteran gleefully recalled the ultimate transgression: chasing a suspect into Tijuana. The hell-bent foot chase zigzagged back and forth into hostile territory as far as the median of Calle Internacional. The agent knew he was risking diplomatic uproar, scandal, maybe a lynching. But as he pounded fearfully close to the gloomy houses and graffiti-stained walls of the Zona Norte, he fancied himself an implacable green avenger. He showed he was not to be messed with; he got away with it; he felt good. "I was mainly worried about getting caught by a *judicial* [Mexican policeman]," the veteran said. "If the guy draws down on me, I'm not going to give up. . . . We get rocked and spit at. These people taunt you. Then, if you cross the line, it's like you violate their national honor."

While brutality occurs in many police agencies, the Patrol was especially vulnerable because of the difficulty of substantiating complaints against agents, the volume of arrests, the exasperation. "The guy sees so many people get away with so much that he starts administering street justice," says Randy Williamson, a thoughtful and gregarious supervisory agent who retired after twenty years in the trenches. Williamson said he refrained from abuse, finding that the best strategy was to keep things peaceable. But in explaining the mentality of agents who become "thumpers," he said: "You catch the same guide, and you catch him again, and you know he's a guide, and he keeps walking. And he maybe even sits up there and laughs at you. . . . And there are some people that, under the circumstances, just get carried away. If they get away with it a few times, then OK, it becomes a way: I'm the judge."

Physical abuse, primarily "payback" beatings after chases, is the most frequent allegation against the Patrol. Border-crossers say agents hit them with fists, feet, flashlights and batons. Victims with bruised faces and broken arms allege that agents released them on the spot, warned them to shut up and even pushed them back into Mexico. Human Rights Watch, the international watchdog group, has accused the Patrol of having "one of the worst police abuse problems in the nation." The Patrol responds that most accusations turn out to be unproven and that complaints are low in proportion to the huge number of arrests. The response among some veterans is more schizophrenic. They complain about trumped-up accusations but acknowledge the existence of excessive force. When Agent Ralph Boubel was a rookie, some old-timers encouraged young agents to punish suspects with beatings—a practice Boubel disdained. "If somebody ran, you were supposed to thump him," Boubel said, "It was expected by the journeyman agents."

Punishment for agents tends to be slow and spotty. The cumbersome internal investigatory system can drag on for years, casting a cloud over wrongly accused agents and enabling the guilty to elude justice. Rogue agents are also protected by a code of silence. Agents have testified about their fear of the code; whistle-blowers have been hounded into transferring across the country. In El Centro, a heat-stunned city near the Calexico-Mexicali border, Agent Kyle Ray felt the wrath of the code when he reported fellow agents for roughing up prisoners. One hard-drinking night, Agent Raymundo Chavez found Ray at a bar and taunted him into stepping outside. A brawl ensued. Chavez clenched Ray's left ear in his teeth. When the combatants were separated, Chavez sat up on the sidewalk, spat out a bloody chunk of Ray's ear and, according to the police report, snarled: "There you go, fucker."

Ray lost one third of his ear. Chavez was prosecuted. In the strange aftermath, Ray obtained a restraining order against his fellow agent, alleging "a clear and present danger of armed aggression by defendant in the workplace"— the Border Patrol station. The judge ordered Chavez to stay 150 yards away from Ray. Chavez was convicted of assault and sentenced to four months in jail. The Patrol suspended him for thirty-one days. Upon his release from jail, he went back to work at the Line.

That episode exemplified the upside-down world of the Patrol. But Charles Vinson was the worst-case scenario, as far as police and fellow agents were concerned. Shortly after he started at Imperial Beach in 1988, other agents complained about his behavior. They accused him of taking liberties with women prisoners when he frisked them. "It was common knowledge that other agents didn't want to be around him when he was around women," an agent said. "The troops brought it to the attention of the supervisors." Vinson was removed from the horse patrol, a coveted assignment, but no formal accusation was filed. In 1990, Vinson set off an international uproar when he killed Victor Mandujano, seventeen. Vinson said he chased Mandujano on foot to the fence near the pedestrian crossing, then shot him as they struggled for the agent's gun. The circumstances were strange: Vinson was in plainclothes and working an antismuggling assignment. Agents said he should not have been at the fence chasing people solo in the first place. Investigators' photos of Vinson taken after the shooting showed a pale man wearing a camouflage-type jacket and jeans. His mustache, droopy eyes and swept-back sandy hair gave him the look of a biker.

Grupo Beta got involved in the case on the Mexican side, finding witnesses who alleged that Vinson had yanked the youth off the fence and shot him when he was down. Beta's objectivity was questioned, however. A witness told San Diego Police that a Mexican detective, presumably from Grupo Beta, pressured him to incriminate the agent. Vinson was cleared and a civil case was decided in his favor. Later, he was absolved of charges of using excessive force on another suspect.

But Vinson made headlines again, five years after the Mandujano shooting, when the San Diego Police charged him with an on-duty rape. A twenty-five-year-old woman from El Salvador said the uniformed agent confronted her on a lonely trail at dawn. At first, she thought he was a robber; when she saw the green uniform, she thought she was safe. Then Vinson sexually assaulted her in his vehicle. Vinson pleaded guilty to a lesser charge and was sentenced to ten years in prison. His lawyer said the case was a nightmare for his churchgoing family. It was certainly the nightmare of every woman border-crosser—and every humane border agent.

"They are out there without supervison," said Roberto Martinez of the American Friends Service Committee, a veteran advocate for immigrants. "Who knows how many of these cases go unreported?"

In 1992, Javier Valenzuela was in perpetual motion: firing off cellular phone calls, interviewing recruits, shaking hands with visiting dignitaries and journalists. The experiment attracted so many visitors that agents joked about renaming themselves Beta Tours. The small headquarters next to the San Ysidro pedestrian entry to Tijuana overflowed with projects. A computer analyst assembled crime statistics and migratory trends into a data bank. Felipe Forastieri was named chief of a spin-off team focused on big smugglers. Concerns reached Valenzuela about prostitution and drug use among the cross-border street kids of Balboa Park in San

Diego; he assigned officers to identify the youths during their returns to Tijuana, interview them and take them to their homes or social service agencies. A few officers reacted dubiously to the role of counseling boy prostitutes; Carlitos, the fourteen-year-old from Balboa Park, recounted how a Beta officer mockingly asked him his moniker: "So what do they call you, Gloria Trevi?" (a Mexican female pop star). But other officers, like the paternal Venegas, ended up acting as informal mentors for the street kids.

The nonchalant self-destruction of the boys of Balboa Park disturbed Valenzuela. Working with them was the kind of humanistic policing he envisioned. And the tight-knit atmosphere among his officers inspired him. Transcending differences of rank and social class, Valenzuela became a mix of teacher, student, advisor and friend—a "paternal, or maternal, figure," he joked. He counseled officers on family matters, shared off-duty bottles of tequila. "I never imagined the transformation—of sensitivity, of attitude and conduct—that was possible among police officers," he said. "Taking into account the factor of discipline, it showed the possibility for profound change."

The changes brought a rare consensus in both nations and along the ideological spectrum. The watchdogs who regularly dug up police misconduct—the press corps, human rights groups, other police forces—concluded that for once the promises were credible. Beta's record stayed relatively clean during the first three years, especially compared to the deluge of scandal at other Tijuana agencies. "Grupo Beta is demonstrating that with political will, with interest on the part of the government, you can have a police force free of corruption," said Víctor Clark Alfaro. "They are doing good work. They are cleaning up. They have a good image."

Belonging to Beta could be harsh and uncertain. Internal pressure compounded external dangers. After a string of death threats—presumably from other police—Valenzuela took to carrying a pistol, tutored by the marksman Alcaraz. And Valenzuela showed his stern side after he got a tip that three officers had beaten two handcuffed prisoners who were high on drugs and resisted arrest, cutting an agent. "There was no formal complaint," Valenzuela recalled. "But we went to this person's house to talk to him face-to-face and, in fact, he had been beaten. Despite the context in which it had happened, there was no justification."

The three officers were fired after an excruciating meeting in which the accused were interrogated in front of their coworkers—"the group acting as jury," in Valenzuela's words. He hammered away at the officers, encircling them with their own inconsistencies, until they broke down. On another occasion, a middle-class Tijuana family showed up at headquarters complaining that their two sons had been roughed up by Beta agents in a traffic altercation. Valenzuela ordered an on-the-spot lineup. The scene was visible through a window from the sidewalk: like suspected criminals, the agents trooped into an office in front of the accusers to face front, turn to the side, put on and remove a cap.

"In the moment that we let down our guard, that we give in to the possibility of a bribe or abuse, we lose moral authority," Valenzuela said. "That would be lamentable. Also, it would be known immediately: Beta lives in a glass house."

Valenzuela appeared to welcome scrutiny. He opened Grupo Beta to human rights groups on both sides of the line, inviting them to give lectures and ride with the officers. He won allies at the College of the Northern Border, a Tijuana think tank on border issues, and Casa Scalabrini, the migrant shelter run by Italian priests, where Beta housed victims and witnesses. The alliance that coalesced around the unit generated unusually solid information. Experts, whether INS intelligence analysts or Mexican scholars, did not always know as much about the inner workings of the milieu as they let on. Beta had a unique advantage, combining street presence and intellectual curiousity. Beta knew first when the smugglers' prices went up. Beta discovered that, due to longtime confusion about jurisdictions near the border, the slalom-speed traffic on Tijuana's poorly lit Calle Internacional killed migrants on foot at a rate comparable to the deaths on Interstate-5 in San Diego.

While migrants and small-time smugglers became a crucial intelligence network, the unit dealt sternly with minor offenses such as disorderly conduct. This strategy of cultivating trust and order mirrored the "community policing" techniques that are gospel in U.S. law enforcement. "All this stuff we talk about here, Problem-Oriented Policing, Valenzuela brought that approach with him without anyone having taught him," said Sergeant Vicente Villalvazo of the San Diego Police, who worked as a liaison with Beta and other police in Baja. "He was ahead of his time down there."

Grupo Beta mapped uncharted geographic and sociological territory. Roster books filled with photos and files of repeat offenders. Many had gone north in the past, like the young marauders whom the agents encountered on the river levee fresh from Los Angeles County Jail: outfitted for trouble in close-cropped gang haircuts, baggy pants and crucifix necklaces knit from thread, still carrying crumpled deportation papers. Valenzuela called them "failed migrants" who fed off the vulnerable newcomers. The border even spawned its own gang. The members lived on both sides of the line and splattered their name over the U.S. and Mexican inspection stations: Linea 13. In the lexicon of Latino street gangs, the numeral 13 represented the letter M, for marijuana. But where a Southern California gang would use the name of a street or barrio (such as Pacoima 13), this gang substituted the word Linea (Line)—proclaiming the very boundary between the Third and First Worlds as its turf. With better understanding of these subcultures came gradual control. Grupo Beta tolerated minor smugglers unless they mistreated migrants or absconded with money, a swindle known as a *quemón* (burn). Shutting down the *polleros* would cut lines of communication to the migrants. But smuggling is against the law in Mexico; the agents targeted major rings.

Beta brought down walls of suspicion. The relationship with the San Diego Police came full circle from the days in the 1970s when Tijuana police and San Diego officers of the antibandit unit shot at each other in the badlands. Grupo Beta and the Border Crime Intervention Unit of the San Diego Police, the uniformed descendants of the 1970s undercover unit, shot together at a San Diego firing range. Beta shared radio frequencies with the San Diego Police. The two squads held routine strategy sessions and coordinated searches and captures. Lieutenant Adolfo González of the San Diego unit became a believer because his officers interviewed numerous migrants without hearing a complaint against Beta. For years, criminals had used the line to escape justice, jumping back and forth with an agility that mocked the bureaucracies. The joint operations dealt a blow to that impunity; Mexican law enabled Beta to prosecute crimes committed in the United States.

"The gang members, the dope dealers, they committed a crime here, we didn't have to worry about them escaping to the south side," González said. "It was extraordinary. I don't think it's ever been repeated anywhere. It was the most exciting thing I have ever been a part of. It was police work of the twenty-first century."

The partnership also extended to the Border Patrol, which donated radios and other surplus equipment to help Grupo Beta get its start. Responding to Border Patrol alerts about rowdy groups and rock-throwers, Beta defused cross-border skirmishes. Assaults on U.S. agents declined sharply, as did murders: from nine on the U.S. side in 1990 to none in the following years. Other crimes dropped as much as 70 percent. Beta's rapport with the San Diego Police grew from a shared calling—protecting migrants. In contrast, the relationship with the Border Patrol was inherently more complex. Mexican and U.S. agents hurried to each other's aid in emergencies and went drinking after work. But it was a curious interplay of teamwork and mistrustful vigilance. Beta agents investigated accusations against the Border Patrol as they would any other crime. This led to the peculiar spectacle of the undercover Mexican officers spying on their counterparts through binoculars and over fences and accusing the U.S. agents of roughing immigrants up, running them down with vehicles, unleashing dogs on them. In one case, two Beta agents among a group of migrants watched a Border Patrol agent alight from his vehicle on Stewart's Bridge as two men ran south in the stream bed below the bridge into Mexico. The agent, apparently feeling menaced by the crowd, fired a shot into the stream bed and fled. Running parallel to the fence, the Beta agents spotted the number on his departing vehicle and put in an urgent call to the Imperial Beach station. Patrol supervisors promptly rounded up the agents in the vicinity, ordered them to stand facing Tijuana and turned a spotlight on them so the witnesses could identify the shooter. The agent received a seven-day suspension. The idea of U.S. agents conducting an improvised public lineup of their own colleagues at the request of Mexican police showed how times had changed. But many Border Patrol agents found it humiliating and outrageous.

Command-level relations were cordial, but tense. The Patrol commanders' praise was genuine, but privately they resented Beta for accusing U.S. agents of mistreating immigrants. The commanders felt betrayed, particularly since they had given equipment to Beta and had refrained from comment about their own suspicions. They saw Beta's help in the delicate area of drug interdiction as noticeably limited and noted that a commander of Beta had been found murdered execution-style, raising questions about whether he was connected to drug mafias. Moreover, Valenzuela and his Mexico City bosses struck the Border Patrol chiefs as sneaky bureaucrats and anti-American leftists. The Mexicans, meanwhile, tended to see the Border Patrol chiefs as two-fisted cowboys in the Yankee imperialist mold.

The Patrol said that most allegations by Beta proved unfounded or lacked details. Nonetheless, Valenzuela became increasingly vocal. In April 1993, he testified before the U.S. Civil Rights Commission about more than two hundred cases of alleged abuse by Border Patrol agents documented by Beta. Adding the voice of a police force to those of the usual critics, he caused a stir.

"In many cases, there is a tendency to identify the migrant as a criminal and treat him as such, with excessive force and little consideration," Valenzuela said in an interview at the time. "We see them as workers, people whose economic situation has pushed them to the brink. . . . There has been an extraordinary increase in arrests by the Border Patrol and an extraordinary decrease in crime. That means that migration in itself does not cause crime."

All the talk about brutality enrages Border Patrol agents. Even if some allegations are true, agents say, such misconduct pales in comparison to the mayhem that Mexican police perpetrate on a daily basis against their fellow citizens—especially migrants. The more candid Mexican diplomats admit that migrants choose to run north and take their chances with the Border Patrol if they find themselves trapped between U.S. agents and Mexican police—other than Grupo Beta. And the difficulty of establishing the truth of skirmishes between Patrol agents and aliens is a legitimate reason why many allegations go unresolved. Paradoxically, the archetypal hardworking migrant (agents call them "Guanajuato Joes") is more likely to take an undeserved beating and keep silent. Thugs, on the other hand, complain and lie. Former supervisor Randy Williamson calls it "loading up."

"The guy loads up so much that he destroys his own credibility. If the guy said, Yeah, I ran: When he caught up with me, he smacked me in the back with a flashlight and knocked me down. That's probably true. But then he says he kicked me fifty-three times in the ribs, three times in the face and broke my nose. And he doesn't have a mark on him."

Williamson was a burly, wise old warrior. He defied the caricature of a "Green Gestapo" painted by ardent critics of the Patrol. Williamson represented a far more complex and interesting reality. He belonged to that singular breed of Border Patrol agents who have been consumed by the lure of the border and the culture of their nominal adversaries. He peppered his vocabulary with Spanish words like *pistolero* and *cuate*. Like many Anglo agents, he married a Mexican woman. His retirement left him time to travel extensively in Mexico, where he made no secret of his former profession and was well received by all. "Those people know how to party, man," Williamson chuckled, sipping a beer in the pleasantly cluttered patio of his suburban house a few miles from the Line. "That's a fun group."

During his years at the Chula Vista station, Williamson told his trainees the secret to preserving their sanity: "You can't take this too seriously. If you are the kind of guy who has to see concrete results for your work, get out of here. If you can look upon this as a game, enjoy it. It is the greatest game in the world. . . . Before I came on the Border Patrol,

I used to save up all of my vacation, my money, and go big-game hunting. For the last twenty years, I got paid to hunt the wiliest game that there is. And I didn't even have to bag 'em out. The people coming in are pawns. The game is between you and the smuggler."

Williamson's approach to the job mixed ferocity, stoicism and humor. He recalled his preferred tactic during standoffs with menacing crowds on the other side. "You pick some-body out, some *cholo,* the leader over there, and just turn your [vehicle] spotlight on him. He'll walk away, you just follow him with the light. Pretty soon he's yelling. People start laughing at him. You are making the time go. Everybody's having a good time but him, and I don't care what he thinks. Or you can sit there and let them screw with you. Well, some of these guys haven't learned: it's more fun to screw with them."

Williamson dabbled at compiling his war stories in mem-oirs. Among the unforgettable characters: a supervisor named Lester. His repertoire of pranks featured fake "exe-cutions" inspired by the garish Mexican movies that depict bloodthirsty U.S. agents machine-gunning immigrants. Lester would prop a realistic, rag-stuffed dummy, dressed like a migrant, in a bush ahead of time. Then he would drive up with a vanload of prisoners, order the dummy to surren-der and feign eye-popping rage at the lack of response. Finally, to the horror of his passengers, Lester would draw his revolver, fire several rounds into the lifeless figure and drive off, muttering, "That'll teach him."

Lester was vintage "Old Patrol," the term veterans use to describe the days of head-busting good ol' boys. But the best agents are unusually talented police officers: they are bilin-gual, steeped in Latin American culture, experienced at tac-tics and survival in extremes of climate and landscape, conditioned by the unpredictable. The barrage of despair moves them to acts of compassion and heroism. Pursuers turn rescuers: pulling drowning migrants from waterways, thwarting robbers and rapists, forcing unscrupulous contractors to pay employees before the agents take them away. Agents learn to think and talk like migrants. No one else quite understands the bond between the hunters and the hunted—not the activists, not the politicians. Look at the industrious Guatemalan Indian laborers of San Diego County, a Chicano agent exclaims. "They have good jobs and live in nice apartments. They work hard. If they can succeed, what's wrong with our country, what's wrong with the citizens? Why are there all these homeless Americans? They take citizenship for granted."

The Border Patrol has been subjected to shrill and unfair invective. Some detractors seem to think that the very existence of the agency is an abuse. The stereotype of agents as white-supremacist storm troopers is fundamentally inaccurate because almost half the force is Latino. For every brawler, there are benovolent agents who tell stories like the one that Agent Art Apac tells about the dazed and dirty children he encountered on a Greyhound bus in Texas. The eight-year-old-boy and his five-year-old sister were traveling to join their parents in Miami and had crossed the Rio Grande on their own. In his lilting Tex-Mex accent, Apac recalls: "When they got to the border they were robbed. The smuggler only left them with bus fare. They were crying, they were just kids. They were hungry as hell. They hadn't eaten for three days. You're sitting there, it burns me up. The boy had a busted lip, a little knock on his head. The smuggler had started messing with his sister and the kid defended her, fought him off. I left the checkpoint and bought them some food with my own money. They were very nervous. They had been assaulted. Anything that came close scared them. After hearing that, I was heartbroken. God. That's what makes the job tough. Because that's only two aliens out of the hundred you'll see in a day."

After Apac caught the children, the Patrol did what it often does in such cases: it relented for humanitarian reasons. The children were sent to Miami to be reunited with their parents. Apac left the Patrol after a year in the hope of becoming a commercial pilot, but then returned to the academy for a second shot at the career. Trainees undergo a challenging eighteen-week regimen at the academy. The setting is a long way from the border: Glynco, Georgia, on the Atlantic coast. The sprawling Federal Law Enforcement Training Center resembles both boot camp and college. Amid pine trees and gnats, the hype of Patrol recruiting videos—agents on galloping horses, agents in snowshoes reaching across the Canadian border to shake hands with Mounties—gives way to a real-life grind: the intricacies of immigration law, the alphabet soup of visa categories.

Many recruits are idealistic and excited about the job. Sitting in an auditorium behind a pile of orientation folders, Haydee Carranza of Arizona, a twenty-six-year-old with flowing black hair, told a typical story. She was a daughter of Mexican immigrants and had two brothers in the Patrol. She worked five years as a guard in the Arizona prison system, guarding death-row inmates from a gun tower. She came off as polite, sharp and eminently capable of pulling a trigger. Like most Latino agents, she scoffed at the notion that ethnic sympathy makes the work painful.

"I always looked up to the Border Patrol," she said. "People ask me, How can you do that job? How can you do that to your *raza*? I say: They're breaking the law."

The Patrol is one of the few uniformed law enforcement agencies in the world which requires trainees to be proficient in a foreign language. This causes trainees grief and spurs attrition. Agent-instructors teach a Spanish designed for survival which does not always conform to the classical prose of *Don Quixote de la Mancha*. Small circles of agents strain forward in Spanish class, close-cropped heads almost touching, and bellow phrases like "I know that Juan is a smuggler," and *"Ponte truchas!"* (slang for "Look sharp!"). Rookies also acquire a remarkable command of profanity; even the lamest Spanish speakers can spew curses during arrests.

The academy has tried to respond to the problems in the field. The chiefs were vocal critics of the failure to screen recruits properly. The curriculum has expanded to cover Latin American culture and human rights. Mexican diplomats give lectures. Philosophy professors lead ethics discussions. Trainees see the movie *El Norte,* the compelling story of Guatemalan refugees in Los Angeles. The instructors and students seem keenly aware of the Patrol's harsh reputation. "You hear a lot about the negative aspect, " said six-week trainee George Gibson. "They've been really honest. They've told us, We want responsible people out there making responsible decisions."

Gibson was from Yuma and his grandfather's career in the Border Patrol inspired him to sign up. Before arriving at the academy, though, Gibson spent two years as a Mormon missionary in the slums of Atlanta, working with illegal immigrants. Gibson's solemnity and prematurely receded hairline made him look older than twenty-three. He saw no contradiction between his past and present callings; he planned to be both aggressive and sensitive on the streets of Imperial Beach.

"I have talked to some of my friends who were illegal and said I was going to join the Border Patrol," he said. "And that's something that they brought up: Hey, you are a good person, we know you. There are some bad [agents] out there. Maybe you can help some people out."

Javier Valenzuela's criticism of the Border Patrol came at a bad time. U.S. officials complained to their high-ranking counterparts in the Mexican Interior Ministry, which had experienced a traumatic shake-up. The removal in early 1993 of the imposing Interior Minister Fernando Gutiérrez caused an exodus from the ministry that left Valenzuela without his mentors. New immigration officials arrived at the border; coincidentally or not, they were accompanied by the wave of Chinese smuggling in Baja in the spring. Valenzuela was demoted and isolated by the new officials. In June, he left Grupo Beta. He accepted a job as vice-consul in charge of protection of immigrants at the Mexican consulate in Los Angeles. On Valenzuela's last day at Beta, the mood was somber. Shortly before the group sat down for a final meeting, a young boy came running through the truck yard of the Mexican customs station to the Beta office, breathless but surefooted in the dusk. The boy's mother was a vendor of sandwiches. She had just been mugged near the river levee by a low-life smuggler known as Pulpo (Octopus). By now, everyone knew that if you were in trouble, you ran to Beta for help. A team was dispatched to hunt for Pulpo. Valenzuela, dressed in a suit and tie, his expression tired and distracted, paused for a long moment looking at the boy, as if contemplating the finished and unfinished business he was leaving behind.

Valenzuela discussed his departure with discretion. He said: "Beta has demonstrated the possibility of a new police in Mexico: the humanity of police in Mexico with proper incentives, recognition and respect to the figure of the police officer. It has demonstrated the real possibility of this kind of policing at a decisive moment in this nation. A change for the worse would have a high cost for Mexico."

The new chief of Beta, Mario Arturo Coutiño, had worked for new Interior Minister Patrocinio González in Chiapas when González was governor. Coutiño adopted a stern style with officers and migrants. Dissension spread. Veterans complained about a purge of Valenzuela loyalists. They said new orders to lock up small-time smugglers were ruining years of hard-won trust, causing migrants to scatter in panic when Beta pulled up. Simultaneously, the agents said, big-time smugglers flourished. A disgusted Felipe Forastieri resigned. "I am upset by this change in attitude," Forastieri declared, thumping a table in a south San Diego coffee shop. "Beta required a lot of sacrifice, working twenty-four hours a day, and now it's being lost. This strong card that the Salinas administration had with the United States in the area of reform, they are throwing it in the garbage."

Abuse and crime crept back up. José Luis Pérez Canchola, whose access to information was blocked by the new regime, said: "The smugglers were under control with Valenzuela. Now there has been a resurgence, permitted or aided by the federal authorities. These are people from elsewhere who do not know the world of the smugglers and the migrants. And the officers from Chiapas are characterized by a hard line toward migrants."

Coutiño argued that he was toughening up a squad that had deteriorated into an attitude of "passive contemplation." He also suspended the meetings with the San Diego Police and the Patrol, saying Beta's Mexican identity had been "diluted." The chill made Valenzuela look pro-American in comparison and worried U.S. officials. In October, most of the Beta officers signed a letter expressing their discontent and faxed it off to Mexico City. A high-ranking immigration administrator rushed to Tijuana for an extraordinary meeting. He listened to the agents give impassioned speeches about how Beta was disintegrating. Within days, a new chief was appointed.

The untouchable image never fully recovered. The internal disputes continued. Beta agents were accused of protecting smugglers, and of possessing stolen guns and vehicles—the classic vices. But Beta survived. It was contradictory: the international line remained a safer place for migrants even while drug wars heated up in Tijuana and brought it a new kind of notoriety. As justice reform became a top priority of the Mexican government, Grupo Beta offered an example of professionalism and a rare point of consensus in the polarized debate at the border. Other Mexican police agencies similarly found that bringing in outsiders—human rights activists, academics, military officers—was the best hope for reform.

On the afternoon of October 1, 1994, Gustavo De La Viña stood outside the Imperial Beach station wearing a dark suit. He looked tired. The Border Patrol chief with the rumbling Texas drawl and chiseled lines around his eyes had held his ground all evening. His cowboy boots were planted firmly. And still they kept coming at him in the dusk: CNN, Los Angeles television crews, the Tijuana press corps asking for the Spanish-language version.

De La Viña, chief of the San Diego sector, had been an agent for a quarter of a century. He hailed from south Texas, one of the many Mexican-American agents from that region. Known as Tejanos, the agents have a reputation for being hard-nosed and patriotic. De La Viña was also gentlemanly and colorful. He could say things like "Jeepers, fellas," and "Shucks" and not sound corny. He came off as a plainspoken sheriff, the shrewd pitchman for a force that had traditionally been stolid and uncomfortable with attention. Today, the news was good.

"Operation Gatekeeper goes full blast," De La Vina said. "We are tying together everything we have been working on for the past eighteen months: personnel, fences, lights, technology. We are starting to roll."

The title and concept of the operation was slapped on hurriedly: a gambit to weaken the Republicans' hold on the anti-immigration banner in the November elections of 1994, in which the GOP won control of Congress for the first time in half a century. On one level, the launch of the operation was pure hype. Nonetheless, during the previous eighteen months the Patrol had begun a transformation, bringing to an end what Alan Bersin, the U.S. attorney in San Diego, called a "generation of neglect." Instead of old junk heaps, a new fleet of shiny Jeep Cherokees and Ford Broncos rolled past De La Viña into the night. The number of agents soared: a record two thousand agents would ultimately be assigned to San Diego. Instead of agents logging arrests with pencils, a computerized fingerprint-identification system flashed photos and records on overhead screens. Extra prosecutors targeted smugglers, criminals and persistent repeat crossers. Construction crews built new lights and metal fences arrayed in rows of two and three in volatile areas such as the riverbed. And finally the Border Patrol deployed an extraordinarily large concentration of agents along the westernmost five miles patrolled by the Imperial Beach station. They hoped to discourage crossers and push them east, away from the city, into the mountains and deserts that were easier to police.

The crackdown in San Diego was hastened by the audacious initiative in El Paso of Chief Silvestre Reyes. Reyes decided that his agents were racking up meaningless arrests and rousting innocent Latino citizens in the streets of El Paso. It made no sense to hang back and chase people once they crossed. Instead, he put all the agents he could muster along a twenty-mile strip of the narrow Rio Grande, where migrants waded between the two downtowns with ease. The blockade was an overnight success. Arrests plummeted. Frustrated crossers went elsewhere. Agents sat around barbecuing and strumming guitars behind the wall of green vehicles. Reyes retired and was elected to Congress as the man who shut down the Line in El Paso.

Nonetheless, De La Viña resisted pressure to copy the El Paso strategy. He did not want to put a row of agents eyeball-to-eyeball with migrants. He opted instead for a three-tiered deployment. In contrast to El Paso, where half the crossers are day laborers who do not venture farther inland, Tijuana had rough terrain and desperately determined immigrants bound for Los Angeles and points north. De la Viña was convinced that if he moved too aggressively, there would be violent clashes. He cared about the agents, the migrants and his career.

"My main concern would be riots," De La Viña said. "I'm concerned for their side and I'm concerned for ours. It's not going to be a happy situation. . . . I'm afraid of the scenario of people dying on this border."

Initially, the Clinton administration had paid as little attention to the border as its predecessors. But soon the Patrol went from being a forgotten Foreign Legion to everybody's favorite crusade. Politicians competed to see who could come up with more money, equipment, agents and help from the military. The agency's woes had generated increasing concern at the Justice Department and in Congress. After the 1992 presidential elections, the political obsession with immigration spread. There were the episodes of Chinese boat smuggling, the footage of the freeway "Banzai Runs." NAFTA focused attention on Mexico. De La Viña and other chiefs found a receptive ear with the new INS commissioner, Doris Meissner, a scholar on immigration.

The turnabout was dramatic. In an era of shrinking government, the Clinton administration and the Republican Congress pumped funds into the INS, whose budget more than doubled in five years to $2.5 billion in 1996. At the Border Patrol academy, the chiefs who had complained about hiring frenzies prepared for a 40 percent expansion of the force. As in the past, the overflow of recruits required the creation of a temporary academy at a military base. But the Justice Department claimed that, this time, the recruits would be properly investigated and trained.

Despite political rhetoric about illegal immigration gone wild, San Diego became comparatively calmer thanks to the fences, more agents, the cooperation with Mexican police and the intensified scrutiny of the Patrol and other border agencies. The Patrol's buildup redirected smugglers into rural land and into new strategies, such as using fake documents at legal ports of entry. In a larger shift, the crackdowns in San Diego and El Paso pushed more crossers to Arizona. Posturing aside, no one realistically thought the border would shut down anytime soon. Voices on the left warned that beefing up the Line would push Mexico into social implosion. Voices on the right demanded a "real" blockade, sending in the marines if necessary. Instead, the Patrol achieved the modest results that were permitted by the self-imposed restraints of a democratic society. The border could not be sealed, but the illegal flow of people could be managed and discouraged. And the Patrol was being treated like a professional, serious agency. The question was whether it would avoid the mistakes of the past—and whether the cycle of neglect and backlash would recur.

As De La Viña departed for a promotion to western regional director of the immigration service, he looked back on four years at the Line in San Diego and pronounced himself cautiously pleased.

"The basic thing back then was the killings, the shootings, the altercations, the bandits, masses of people right at the international line," he said. "There was just a great deal of massive confusion and disorder and violence that slowly, with time, brought the national attention. And we were able to control it, to a degree. I think it's under better control now than it was four years ago. And hopefully it will remain that way."

Eventually, Javier Valenzuela returned to Tijuana and served briefly as director of a new Mexican department of immigrant protection. He gathered a handful of trusted veterans—Toba, Venegas, Alcaraz. They traveled to the other corner of the border, the rowdy town of Matamoros on the Gulf of Mexico, and built another Grupo Beta. The long-term plan called for the creation of tripartite police squads along the length of the border in the cities of Tecate, Mexicali, Nogales and Ciudad Juárez, as well as the southern border in Chiapas, where Central Americans entered illegally from Guatemala.

But Valenzuela's return to the line did not last long. There were too many leftover animosities. He became the target of criticism and vague accusations among rivals in Mexico and INS officials in the United States, though he retained the admiration of San Diego Police commanders, human right activists in both nations and other allies in the community that formed around the squad. Gabriel Székely, a political scientist at the College of Mexico, concluded that Beta had made a breakthrough.

"Beta represents a model of what it is possible to achieve in response to one of the principal political demands of the people: preserving the security and tranquillity of the citizens with the actions of the police," Székely wrote in *Cuaderno del Nexos,* a monthly scholarly journal published in Mexico City. "The necessary legitimacy has been gained in order for U.S. police agencies that share the goal of reducing violence and protecting immigrants to collaborate with Mexico."

Commander Jaime Avila put it more succinctly: "Beta is the seed of what the police could be in Mexico."

Bowing to the inevitable, Valenzuela definitively abandoned the world of pistols for the world of books. He accepted a job as administrator for the secretariat of education in Mexico City.

Valenzuela left behind a mix of achievements and disappointments. His hopeful legacy was summed up by the name he chose for the Matamoros version of Grupo Beta: Grupo Ébano. The name came from a tree called the *ébano*, or ebony, which grows along the banks of the Rio Grande. Carpenters there use the wood of the tree for making cradles because of its special symbolic properties. In the folklore of the region, the sturdy tree shades and protects weary travelers: a guardian of the weak against the forces of fear.

CHAPTER FOUR

The Gang and the Cardinal

Cougar, Charlie, Popeye, Puma, Spooky: the home-boys made names for themselves in Logan Heights, the old Mexican-American neighborhood southeast of downtown. Hemmed in by docks and industry, drawn and quartered by freeways, dominated by the towering Coronado Bay Bridge, Barrio Logan has been the first stop for Mexican immigrants in San Diego for decades. One of the toughest patches of landscape in the city, it nonetheless presents contradictions. Drug dealers and crackhound prostitutes roam warehouse wastelands, which give way to tidy restaurants and shops, surprisingly solid schools, a model public health clinic that has been visited by the president of the United States. On a side street winding alongside Interstate-5 past the murals of Chicano Park, the Our Lady of Guadalupe church keeps busy with anniversaries, funerals, weddings. Even those who have left the neighborhood for better jobs and bigger houses return, like the woman who just started working at IBM and held a reunion of her Catholic youth club. The small church has a sky-blue cupola. The white walls are untouched by the graffiti that rages across nearby schools, fences, telephone poles and defaced traffic signs that pledge allegiance to the gang: "Can't STOP 30."

As in Thirtieth Street. As in the Thirtieth Street gang, or Calle Treinta.

"I know a lot of gang members and they are always respectful to me," says Father Richard Brown, who has been pastor of the church for twenty-five years. "No matter how far a Mexican boy or girl will go, they have great respect for the priesthood. Just because he's a gang member doesn't mean he doesn't have a soul."

The homeboys were a mix of U.S.-born citizens and legal and illegal immigrants. Some dropped out of school. Others worked sporadically as welders, mechanics, security guards. The turf, and generations of gang tradition, united them. Whether a muscle-bound diehard like Spooky or a laid-back hanger-on like Cougar, whether smart or thick-headed, polite or vicious, they automatically shared enemies from adjoining neighborhoods. Unless you were blessed with exceptional academic skill, athletic talent or survival instincts, it was hard to avoid joining the Thirtieth Street gang.

"I got involved when I was fifteen," said Cougar. His real name was Jesús Zamora Salas. The attributes he shared with his predatory namesake were a lean frame and a quiet watchfulness. Otherwise, he looked peaceful and a little sheepish compared to his boyhood cronies. His mustache was neatly groomed, conservative. His forehead furrowed morosely below buzz-cut hair. He talked slowly and was prone to long sighs. At twenty-one, he was one of the few homeboys who did not have a criminal record.

"I wasn't a full-time gang member," Cougar said. "There was always enemies around because you live in that area, people who don't like you. Gangs from Barrio Sherman, Shelltown. So you and your friends watch out for each other."

The homeboys hung out at the corner of Thirtieth and Martin. A lot happened within those few blocks, where the homes are barred little forts surrounding Memorial Park and the oases of the junior high school and the Boys and Girls Club. Popeye saw his brother get killed in front of his house. The police busted Spooky for dealing PCP, one of a string of arrests that kept him in juvenile hall and prison. Puma survived a shotgun blast fired into his legs from a passing car. The gang ruled by terror, shooting at witnesses, burning down houses. They did not stray far. Occasionally they ventured north to the ghettos of Los Angeles to buy angel dust for resale. To the south, Tijuana was familiar territory; some of the homeboys had lived there or had family there. They liked to party on Avenida Revolución, but the Mexican police were mean. Except for fistfights when rivals bumped heads, the homeboys avoided trouble south of the border. In short, the universe of the gang was harsh and narrow. They were a violent but generally unremarkable gang during the 1980s, comparable to dozens of other Latino street gangs in Southern California. In the 1990s, however, the gang underwent a metamorphosis that made history. Recruited by the Tijuana cartel, the homeboys became the first U.S. street gang to join forces with a Mexican drug mafia. They became mercenaries for the feared Arellano brothers, plunging into a cross-border war with political dimensions beyond their understanding. "People get a picture of gangs very much located in pockets within a city," said Julius Beretta, special agent in charge of the Drug Enforcement Administration in San Diego. "This gives a whole new implication to gangs in America. This gang is international now."

The combat left a trail of more than two hundred bodies from San Francisco to Tijuana to Venezuela, engulfing politicians, police forces, business magnates, rich kids, priests and, of course, migrants. In Mexico and increasingly in the United States, migrants were cannon fodder in the drug wars, a huge and natural employment pool for cartels that paid fistfuls of hundred-dollar bills for driving a load car through a port of entry or pulling a trigger.

The homeboys lived a rookie thug's high-rolling dream, a whirl of cash, luxury and bloodshed that was the stuff of gangster melodrama. At the end of the movie, though, the gangsters tend to fall hard. The homeboys landed in the middle of one of Mexico's most mysterious and explosive crimes of recent years, the first major salvo in the crisis of "narco-politics" which would help topple the "miracle" of modernization touted by President Carlos Salinas de Gortari and his admirers. The homeboys escaped the gunfire, but some did not survive the aftermath.

"I think if they had known the predicament they were going to get into, they wouldn't have done it," said a detective from the San Diego Police gang unit who charted the trajectory of Thirtieth Street with grim relish. "But maybe it was like a big game to them. You get people throwing money at you, you start thinking you're invincible."

The game was too big. The homeboys or their families had come from Mexico like many other immigrants. Their parents worked hard and improved themselves, even those who remained poor by U.S. standards. Logan Heights was as mean as San Diego got, but it was not unescapable or hopeless. Like the boys of Balboa Park or the failed migrants who robbed new migrants on the Tijuana River levee, the homeboys fell between cultures. Maybe if they had lived in Fresno or Chicago, a few might have grown out of it, survived scrapes with the law, seen the error of their ways. But they were too close to the line.

The man who led them across, the nexus to the Tijuana cartel, was David Barrón Corona. Born in 1963 in San Diego, Barrón was five to ten years older than the others, a legendary *veterano* who had done some boxing in prison. He accumulated nicknames: D for David; C.H. for the deferential Spanish title "honorable citizen"; and Charlie, because he resembled the actor Charles Bronson. The precocious Charlie was first charged with taking a life at age sixteen. Weeks after completing a juvenile sentence for robbery, he went to a house party. He and two friends stepped outside late at night and relieved themselves against a car, reeling in a cloud of marijuana and alcohol. The owner of the car—oddly enough, a seventy-year-old transvestite wearing a dress—appeared and rebuked them. Charlie ended the argument by shooting the old man in the chest. Charlie fled to Tijuana, but the San Diego Police retrieved him with the help of the Baja state police, whom his attorney accused of torturing a confession out of the youth. Charlie was convicted of voluntary manslaughter. In 1980, the judge sent Charlie to prison as an adult, declaring: "He wasn't out of the California Youth Authority two months before he killed a human being." The judge bemoaned Charlie's "history of violence. He comes out and drifts back into the same setting, the same element and becomes a leader."

Charlie served a six-year sentence. During that time, the drug underworld in Tijuana and the rest of Mexico began a profound evolution. Mexican traffickers had historically produced and smuggled marijuana and heroin. Sophisticated Colombian drug lords dominated the cocaine trade along air and sea smuggling routes in the Caribbean. The Colombians made Florida the gateway to the U.S. market in the late 1970s and 1980s; Miami became a battle zone. Then geography and politics forced a landmark shift. The U.S. poured interdiction resources into Florida. The Colombians responded by expanding their partnership with veteran Mexican smugglers, who offered a long and vulnerable land border and pipelines of transportation and corruption. Initially, the Mexicans were junior partners and transshipment specialists. They received planeloads of cocaine—small aircraft were replaced ultimately by 727s and

Caravelle jets—shipped the merchandise overland in cars, trucks and trains, and smuggled it across the international boundary. Some U.S. law enforcement officials estimated that at least half the drugs entered through legal ports of entry, camouflaged by commercial and passenger traffic and an extensive network of paid-off U.S. inspectors. Then the Mexican transporters turned the merchandise back over to Colombian distributors in the United States.

The realignment of routes produced a transitional generation of Mexican drug barons. They began receiving payments from the Cali and Medellín cartels in cocaine instead of cash. The Colombians ceded lucrative sales turf—in Los Angeles, Houston, the East Coast—to the Mexicans. The resulting explosion of profits elevated the Mexican groups to the level of full-fledged mafias with the financial might to overwhelm political, legal and economic systems at both the state and federal levels. Soon the Mexican mafias were supplying 70 percent of the cocaine consumed yearly in the United States, were earning between $10 billion and $30 billion a year in profits and, according to a study by the University of Guadalajara, were spending an estimated $500 million a year exclusively on the bribery of public officials in Mexico. That figure was roughly double the entire budget of the Mexican federal attorney general's office and federal police. "The mafias have taken the concept of corruption to its maximum expression," said Víctor Clark Alfaro, the Tijuana human rights advocate. "Their talent has been to convert corruption into a practice that overwhelms everything. And it is all based, of course, on money."

Independent voices like Clark and other activists and political figures in Mexico had warned of the dangers of the mafias for years. North of the line, though, the concern did not extend far beyond law enforcement circles and conservative politicians who tended toward indiscriminate

Mexico-bashing. There was a certain well-meaning reti-
cence among U.S. journalists, academics and diplomats to
harp on the problem and play up clichés, even though the
warning signs dated back a decade. In 1985, traffickers in
Guadalajara tortured and murdered DEA agent Enrique
Camarena, causing a diplomatic crisis between Mexico and
the United States. The Mexican government officials who
were implicated in protecting the killers included Governor
Enrique Alvarez del Castillo of the state of Jalisco, a cartel
stronghold,as well as the interior minister and the defense
minister. Federal court testimony in Los Angeles detailed
the allegations of their links to gangsters, but the three officials were not charged. The Mexican government
denounced the testimony and condemned the DEA for kid-
napping a suspect in Mexico and bringing him back to the
United States for trial. Upon taking office, President Salinas
alarmed U.S. law enforcement officials and some Mexican
critics by appointing former Governor Alvarez of Jalisco as
his attorney general.

The Salinas administration made early gestures toward
reform by arresting Old Guard traffickers, mostly those
working with the Medellín cartel of Colombia. But the
business of other Mexican drug lords—tied to the increasingly dominant Cali cartel—grew. In a pattern that repeated
itself in the byzantine milieu of Mexican drug enforcement,
some of the investigators who made the big arrests of those
years were later accused of working for rival drug lords on
the rise: self-styled untouchables such as Javier Coello
Trejo, the "iron prosecutor" who was the first federal
antidrug chief of the administration, allegedly earned more
than a million dollars a year in bribes from the Gulf cartel
for clearing the competition out of the way, according to
court testimony. Halfway through Salinas's term, the
panorama looked like this: On the eastern end of the border,

Juan García Abrego's Gulf cartel reigned supreme over the cocaine route along the Gulf of Mexico. Chihuahua, roughly at the center of the border, was the fiefdom of Amado Carrillo Fuentes. In the northwest states of Baja California, Sonora, Sinaloa and Jalisco, two mafias were fighting for control of the lucrative Pacific corridor. At stake: California, the prize market in the world's most drug-hungry nation. Tijuana acquired vital strategic value as the hub of the corridor, the Miami of the 1990s. The border's biggest city belonged to the Arellano Félix brothers—at least as far as the Arellanos were concerned. The legendary trafficker Miguel Angel Félix Gallardo, known as the "godfather," set up the Arellanos in their Tijuana empire. The Arellanos, who are thought to be Félix Gallardo's cousins or nephews, also inherited his feuds. Their nemeses were Joaquín Guzmán, known as Chapo (Shorty), and Héctor Palma, known as Guero (Whitey), who had broken away from Félix to form the Sinaloa cartel. The godfather was jailed in 1989, but he exacted revenge on his former protégés for their disrespect.

"Félix, like the twisted old man that he is, sends a group of Venezuelan narcos, led by a guy named Clavel, to infiltrate Guero Palma's family," recalled a veteran Mexican antidrug investigator. Rafael Clavel ran off with Palma's wife and her two small children. After persuading her to withdraw $7 million of her husband's money from a bank in San Francisco, the Venezuelan hit man killed the wife and sent her severed head to Palma in a package. Then he took Palma's son and daughter to Venezuela and threw them off a bridge. "After that, Guero Palma is ready to kill anything that he thinks has any relation to an Arellano," the Mexican investigator said. "And the Arellanos know that it is kill or be killed."

The Palma-Guzmán alliance retaliated by killing Félix's

lawyer and three others. Norma Corona, the director of the Sinaloa human rights commission, dug up evidence implicating the mafia's allies in the federal police in the quadruple murder, so she was killed too. The public outcry over her murder spurred President Salinas to create the National Human Rights Commission in 1990, but the warfare persisted. Even by the standards of the underworld, the four Arellano brothers earned a reputation as reckless renegades. They caroused and machine-gunned their way through desperate escapades that a screenwriter would have dismissed as unbelievable. "They are crazy," a DEA official in Mexico said. "Completely paranoid." Another agent described a small massacre in Tijuana—in which rampaging gunmen in military-style uniforms stormed a house, kidnapped six rivals and dumped their bound, tortured and executed bodies around town—as "real Arellano stuff."

The Arellanos were from the green and violent hills of Sinaloa, the northwestern state that has been fertile ground for gangsters. They started as southbound runners of contraband U.S. goods into Mexico. Gradually, they made the transition into smuggling U.S.-bound heroin and marijuana, which grow in abundance in Sinaloa, and then cocaine transshipment. The few available photos showed dashing thugs with new-money flash: long hair, scorpion-shaped jewelry, big-shouldered jackets, champagne glasses in hand. The brothers looked like pop music stars, or, more precisely, stars of the *banda* music genre from Sinaloa which has immortalized drug cowboys. The leader was Benjamín, a pudgily handsome kingpin in his forties who liked expensive restaurants and kept a mansion in the exclusive San Diego enclave of La Jolla. In the early 1980s, Benjamín was arrested on several occasions in joint antidrug stings teaming the Mexican federal police and DEA. Benjamín was just a wealthy up-and-coming punk at the time; DEA agents unfail-

ingly found him in the company of stunningly beautiful
women. The eldest brother, Francisco, laundered money and
jet-setted at his disco in Mazatlán, Frankie Oh's: a palace of
hoodlum chic featuring with a small plane on the roof, a
waterfall, laser shows. Francisco was a self-proclaimed
friend and reputed business partner of boxing champion Julio
César Chávez, a Sinaloan whose fervent following among
gangsters has led the DEA to assign surveillance teams to his
U.S. fights in the hope of catching a big fish.

The craziest Arellano brother was said to be Ramón, a
pugnacious, baby-faced warlord in his late twenties and a
devotee of the martial arts, sports cars and motorcycles.
Ramón commanded security and combat operations for the
cartel. As a result, Ramón Arellano hired David (Charlie)
Barrón and his crew. Just as the Colombian kingpins recruited Mexican partners, just as the godfather Félix Gallardo
groomed the Arellanos, Ramón brought the homeboys from
Barrio Logan into the big leagues.

Upon his release from prison in California, the veteran
homeboy named Charlie racked up an arrest record in San
Diego—possession of a machine gun, speeding, burglary. He
stated in probation documents in 1987 that he worked as a
deliveryman for a carpentry shop. He also hung out in
Tijuana, where it is believed he had relatives active in politics and related by marriage to the Arellanos. His connections paid off; Ramón Arellano made Charlie his chief
bodyguard, according to law enforcement. Charlie joined the
Arellanos' swaggering entourage of state and federal cops
and a remarkably vicious group of youths from Tijuana's
wealthiest families who had developed a taste for the gangster life. Rich kids in Mexico are known as "juniors"; these
kids were known as "narco-juniors," and they were shielded
by the double impunity of the underworld and the social
elite. They evolved quickly into full-fledged, hard-core hit

men, carrying out crazed daylight attacks that left their rivals
bleeding in bullet-shredded vehicles. The Arellano social circuit included the fast-cash nightspots of the glass-and-steel-
lined avenues of the Río Zone, the new downtown: Plaza
Fiesta, a faux-Mexican village of restaurants and bars
designed for the tourist trade; and the Rodeo de Media
Noche, a cowboy music club in a mall near the border. The
gangsters' forays into high society were duly chronicled in
gossip columns and, when the festivities ended with gunplay, in the police pages. From their home base in Tijuana
the Arellanos jetted to Mexico City and the northwest states
that were contested and risky territory.

During a trip to the coastal resort of Puerto Vallarta,
Charlie won his badge of honor. He accompanied Ramón
Arellano and another brother, Javier, to Christine's dis-
cotheque on November 8, 1992. While the Tijuana drug
lords were drinking, the federal police chief cleared his
agents out of town for the night so that the Sinaloa cartel
could send a truckload of forty gunmen in a commando
assault on the disco. The dance-floor firefight left six dead.
But the Arellano brothers escaped through a bathroom window thanks to an impressive display of combat reflexes by
Charlie, who held the assassins at bay, scooping up and firing the guns of fallen thugs. His bosses rewarded him with
a mansion in Tijuana and a place in the inner circle. He carried himself accordingly. A soldier later told the FBI about
working security for Charlie on a Sunday outing in a downtown Tijuana mall. Gunmen stood by while Charlie's family cavorted in a children's entertainment center that was
"reserved for the entire day only for [Charlie] and about
forty of his family members, including grandparents, to celebrate the birthday of his one-year-old son," the FBI report
said.

When Charlie was instructed to hire shooters for the

mafia, he went to a familiar stable of talent: Thirtieth Street. His recruiter was another *veterano* in his early thirties, Alfredo (Popeye) Araujo, who had shuttled back and forth between Logan Heights and working-class neighborhoods in Tijuana all his life. Popeye was about five eleven, with a long face and a roguish mustache curving below the corners of his mouth. He had spent a couple of halfhearted years in junior college. He had progressed from a beach brawl in 1983, in which he took on fourteen drunken rivals, to battles against neighboring gangs from Shelltown and Barrio Sherman. In his new assignment for the Arellanos, he hooked up with the younger homeboys on street corners in the barrio, over cheap drinks in the deafening dance clubs and nonstop happy-hour joints of Avenida Revolución. The gang members were impressed by his new cars and his gold badge identifying him as a squad chief in the Baja state judicial police. Popeye's recruiting rap was slick, his offer generous: the mafia paid weekly retainers of $500, plus food and a place to live. "They just said you're going to make some money, easy money," Cougar recalled.

During 1992 and early 1993, about thirty gang members from Barrio Logan went to work for the Arellanos as watchmen, hired guns, flunkies. They were as young as fourteen. Most had reached the stage when a gang member outgrows teenage turf wars and faces a fork in the road between a career in crime and straight life. One of the youngest homeboys whom Popeye ushered into the underworld was his childhood friend Juan Enrique (Puma) Vascones, one of four children of Mexican immigrants. Puma's father was a fumigator who divorced Puma's mother, a maid. Puma liked baseball and studying—at least that was what he later said during a brutal interrogation by the Mexican police. Puma said he accepted Popeye's offer of employment in early 1993 because his sixteen-year-old girlfriend was pregnant, he had turned eighteen and, he claimed with somewhat peculiar logic, he wanted to clean up his act. During the previous summer, Puma worked at the Boys and Girls Club in Memorial Park. A counselor who tried to convince him to go back to school recalled a thin-faced, long-limbed youth with eyes that looked hard and lost at the same time. She described how he kept coming to work at the Boys and Girls Club after he was wounded in a drive-by shooting, hobbling around on crutches. The counselor found that image hard to reconcile with that of an international desperado. "If he was involved, how could he be involved in something so big?"

But a neighbor saw disturbing changes. Puma would disappear from the 2900 block of Imperial Avenue for a while, then reappear in full high-roller regalia. "He was an OK kid," the neighbor said. "But I knew he was not going in the right way. I used to tell him, 'What's up, lowlife?' 'What's up, hoodlum?' He was going to Puerto Vallarta, Cancún, Mazatlán. He had his little cellular phone, a pager, people with nice cars coming over. I thought, This guy's getting into it big time."

The first time Popeye drove Puma down south, he told him to close his eyes so he would not see the route. Their destination was the steel-doored garage of a three-story pink mansion occupying half a block in Colonia Chapultepec, one of the choicest addresses in Tijuana. The Arellanos had a dozen safe houses—outfitted with secret basements, cast-iron vaults, high-tech equipment for telephonic eavesdropping—in the exclusive hillside enclaves overlooking the Agua Caliente racetrack. Puma bunked at the houses and was soon joined by a dozen homeboys. Unlike Popeye and Charlie, the younger gang members were foot soldiers: they did maintenance, washed cars and bought groceries. Puma later told interrogators: "I used to call my mother to let her know that she shouldn't worry, that I was fine, but I never told her what I did or where I was. Then I would go back to my work."

Among Puma's workmates was the easygoing Cougar, aka Jesús Zamora. His Spanish was rusty, though his parents had emigrated from Tijuana and Guadalajara. Cougar's mother had collected welfare to support him and his two sisters. After graduating from Point Loma High School, Cougar avoided trouble and studied to be a security guard. In Tijuana, he dutifully completed his tasks for his new employers: "taking care of houses, cleaning cars, odd jobs. It seemed fairly easy." After some prodding, Cougar admitted with a sigh that, yes, he did carry a .38 for protection. Yes, he saw rifles in the mansion. But he insisted that he never heard of the Arellanos or knew his bosses' line of business. "I had kind of an idea, but I was not sure. It seems kind of wierd, but it's true. It's like they want to keep you ignorant about it, like not to know anything, not to know any names."

Even if Cougar truly managed to stay ignorant, many of the others did not. They received training in the use of heavy weapons. Equipped with police radios, they rode shotgun for the bosses, chiefly Ramón. The gangsters tooled around town in convoys of pickup trucks, sport utility vehicles and luxury cars, holding meetings and receiving drug shipments in fast food-joints and shopping centers, where the big parking lots provided cover. The entourage occasionally repaired to a ranch on the mountain road to Tecate, a colossal spread with a menagerie of ostriches, kangaroos, peacocks and other exotic animals. The parties filled the night with the sounds of trumpets, drums and gunfire.

As imported *pistoleros,* the homeboys were obedient and had the advantage of being able to float between nations. "It makes apprehension and prosecution difficult when you have people running across borders," said William Esposito, special agent in charge of the FBI in San Diego. Some gang members became international hired guns, traveling to assignments in other Mexican states and California; Puma and Spooky boasted about having killed a lawyer in Los Angeles, according to testimony. An unusual series of murders occurred in Logan Heights and the U.S. border suburbs of Chula Vista and National City. Not the drive-by shootings that are standard fare among street gangs, but mafia-style executions. Gang detectives found a survivor in a Barrio Logan alley: one eye bulging out, his tattooed torso punctured by nine bullets, sprawled in the thickest, darkest pool of blood the detectives had seen a living person lose. The victim had been messing with someone's wife and drinking and talking too much, so the bosses ordered the hit. In the hospital, the wounded gang member boasted obliquely about his exploits in Mexico. "You wouldn't believe what's going on down there," he grunted. He had nothing to say about who shot him, though. As soon as he could walk, he checked himself out of the hospital.

The violence was intoxicating yet workmanlike, matter-of-fact. A henchman named Paisa recounted how Popeye was giving him a ride in Tijuana one day and announced he had to make a stop. Popeye parked his Volkswagen Jetta on La Mesa Boulevard and got out to talk to a man in front of a junkyard. "Having talked to him for a half hour, they went around the corner out of my sight and I heard three shots," Paisa told interrogators. "Then Alfredo [Popeye] came back around the corner and started walking casually towards the car where I was waiting for him, got in and continued to drive without saying anything. . . . Later on I heard on the news that a man had been murdered in the same place . . . and I realized that Alfredo had killed this man."

On this new battlefield, the homeboys discovered, the police were either allied to mobsters or keeping their heads down. Drug money had cast a spell over the feared *judi-*

ciales of the federal and state police, turning them into fellow employees who guarded loads and carried out contract killings. A bodyguard recalled that when officers pulled over the ostentatious convoys, "my bosses called the people who worked for them in the judiciary police and they would get us out of trouble, telling these agents that we also worked for the judiciary police." The defensive cocoon was thickest among state officials: the Arellanos owned prosecutors, commanders, key divisions such as the all-important homicide squad, geographically strategic districts such as the southeast La Mesa station, an area where the gangsters tended to live and do business. The drug murders fit a pattern: brazen gunmen piled out of vehicles in public places, sprayed their victims with automatic weapons and fled. Even when bystanders died, when a stray bullet felled the daughter of a leader of the National Action Party in 1991, the murders went unsolved. Or unresolved: the day after a boxing promoter and three others died in a fusillade that tore up their taxi, Attorney General Juan Francisco Franco identified the suspects as three brash rich kids linked to the Arellanos. Subsequently, the case fell apart; the "narcojuniors" went right on killing.

Murder files piled up; criticism weighed down the attorney general. Paradoxically, the Ruffo administration succeeded in cleaning up other sectors of the government, but the rapacious ways of law enforcement worsened. Governor Ruffo at one point brought in army officers to lead the state police; this is a frequent reform move in Mexican law enforcement because the military is considered disciplined and resistant to temptation. But the soldiers succumbed too. An army major who commanded the police was linked to the Arellanos after hundreds of thousands of dollars in cash turned up in his house.

"Despite the presence of a political party distinct from

that which has traditionally governed Baja," said Víctor Clark, "corruption and torture are . . . a structural matter, which does not appear to distinguish between parties in power."

Just as the border transformed police into gangsters, Clark was transformed into a reluctant sleuth. It was not his intention to dig up drug corruption. But his human rights work gained him well-placed informants in state and federal law enforcement who were disgusted with what they saw all around them. During this time, Clark operated in a modest building on a side street across from a supermarket loading dock; his no-frills, weakly ventilated office was routinely packed with journalists prowling for news. And the soft-spoken activist had plenty to tell them. His lone-wolf investigation of corruption in the state judicial police brought him threats. The federal government provided him with bodyguards and followed up some of his leads. In a stinging report in 1993, Clark used photos, internal police reports and inside sources to document the sale of police badges to gangsters for $8,000 each. He accused the chief of the attorney general's security detail of being the go-between with the gangsters. Indignant state officials took legal action against Clark; Attorney General Franco claimed the identification cards were falsified. But much of what Clark alleged was graphically confirmed by events. The attorney general suffered through a scandal after the discovery of Baja police credentials on henchmen killed in the gunfight in Puerto Vallarta on the night that the veteran homeboy named Charlie saved the Arellanos' lives.

After Charlie's heroics at the disco, a DEA agent said, "They were making up songs about him." The homeboys appeared to regard the cliff-hanging escapes and labyrinthine corruption with the simultaneous enthusiasm and detachment of youth. It was faintly unreal, a world of action movies and folk ballads. The popular music of northern Mexico which chronicles the drug wars is comparable to the "gangster rap" of America's urban underclass. Topical songs known as *corridos*, whose protagonists were once heroic revolutionaries, celebrate gangsters and offer a running account of drug wars, assassinations, the rise and fall of desperadoes. The impact of drugs on the culture of Mexico has not received as much attention internationally as the infiltration of the justice system, politics and economy. But the "narco-culture" phenomenon helps explain the damage done to a generation of Mexican young people, and the cross-border reach of that threat to places like Thirtieth Street. Consumption of heroin and cocaine has surged in Mexico, led by Tijuana and other border cities exposed to the vices of the United States, after years in which drugs passed through on the way north but drug use was minimal. Interviewed by *Proceso* magazine, Emilio Goicochea, a former opposition candidate for governor in Sinaloa, lamented "this drug culture that is transforming the youth. This *banda* music, these songs that commemorate fallen narcos . . . the abductions of girls in the countryside; the ambition of becoming a legend by way of vice and violence; crime in all its splendor, accompanied by impunity and corruption in the justice system. . . . When you ask them the cause of this attitude and tell them they are endangering their lives, most of them respond the same way: 'Well, if we get killed, they'll make up a song about us.' "

Goicochea's warning suggested that the allure of the Arellanos and those like them goes beyond money and politics, beyond the poverty grinding down half of Mexico's population. It also grows out of the mythology of gangsters and cops, who are symbiotic to the point of being interchangeable. It is about icons such as cowboy boots, sunglasses and assault rifles: the name of the AR-15 rifle has

been appropriated by a musical group. The Jeep Cherokee
and the Chevrolet Suburban have attained cult status. In the
United States, these upscale sport utility vehicles are popular with yuppie families; in the border underworld, they are
war wagons whose mystique blends menace and style.
Traffickers and cops like the elevated view of the road, the
cargo space, the durable frames built for the topography of
places like Tijuana, where potholes can resemble small
canyons. A band called the Pioneers of the North sing an ode
entitled "The Suburban of Death" about a truck stocked with
guns and gadgets: "The Suburban of Death / Is what they
call it everywhere / And Customs and soldiers can't stop it /
When the *federales* see it, they better beware."

This was the force that swept up the homeboys; they did
not know it, but more songs were yet to come. The war for
the northwest border was rushing toward a showdown.

The Arellanos and the Guzmán/Palma alliance had dueled
for years with car-bomb attacks and street ambushes in
Culiacán, Guadalajara, Tijuana, Guerrero and Mexico City,
where, in April 1993, the former attorney general of Sinaloa
was gunned down while he jogged in a park: payback for
defying Guero Palma. The gangsters used clandestine allies
in the police to strike blows at each other by proxy. In April,
federal police in Tecate busted seven tons of cocaine concealed in a load of canned chili peppers transported by a Los
Angeles import-export company tied to the Reynoso brothers, three millionaire Southern California grocers who were
allegedly a front for Chapo Guzmán. Even the seeming triumph had a cynical explanation: the Tijuana commander
who supervised the seizure was soon dismissed for suspected collusion with the Arellanos.

There were drug wars elsewhere in Mexico, of course.
But the other mafias also worked together federation-style,
sharing routes and resources. The Arellanos' proprietary

defense of Baja California against incursions from the
enemy strongholds of Sonora and Sinaloa was extraordinary, as was the bitterness of the rivalry. "There is still a very
strong hate relationship that will not go away until one kills
the other off," said Craig Chretien of the DEA, a chief agent
in San Diego who went on to direct the agency's international operations. "It's personal more than business.
Business they could work out."

Pinned to the wall of the homeboys' spacious crash pad in
Colonia Chapultepec was a photo of Chapo Guzmán. Don't
forget this face, the gang members from Barrio Logan were
told. If I see him, I'll kill him, Popeye said. In late May, the
word came down: We're going to Guadalajara to do a big
job. Curiously, the team of about fifteen gunmen assembled
for the trip consisted largely of green recruits such as Puma,
Cougar and Ramón (Spooky) Torres Mendez. Spooky was a
sullen, flat-nosed, jailhouse weight lifter, brawny as a bull,
his neck, arms and stomach emblazoned with Logan mottos.
"The type that thought he was tougher than everybody," a
fellow homeboy said. Spooky, twenty-four, had not spent
more than a month at a time out of custody during the past
ten years. In April, he had been released from state prison
and deported to Tijuana; Popeye ran into him at the Magic
Oh's disco and hired him on the spot. A month later, Spooky
boarded a plane to Guadalajara, presumably inspired by the
promised bonus of $30,000 to the man who shot Chapo.
Arriving on separate flights, the homeboys rendezvoused at
a house with a team of professional killers headed by a
hoodlum known as the Frog—older, local talent based in
Guadalajara. From an armory containing gas masks, an M-
60 machine gun, flak jackets, grenades and military uniforms, the bosses passed out .38 pistols and AK-47s. Spooky
later told the FBI that he had never fired an AK-47 before.

For several days, the assassination squad headed by

Ramón Arellano stalked the enemy, riding in the camper shell of an armor-plated pickup truck with tinted windows that obscured the driver and the street. The plan was simple: when you get the order, jump out and shoot. But the order never came. One night, the young gunmen dutifully waited outside in the pickup while Ramón attended a house party featuring entertainment by a Sinaloan band. Between patrols, they kicked back at the safe houses. Cougar claims that he did not participate in the hunt or know the target. He stayed inside and did as he was told. "I did not jump in no truck with guns looking for anybody to kill. I'm pretty sure nobody else knew what was going on, because I didn't know what was going on. Nobody says anything about anything. Very quiet days. Then we get the word, somebody at the house says I got tickets to go back to TJ. Nothing's going to happen here."

On this point, the accounts agree: On the morning of Monday, May 24, Ramón Arellano declared that the job had been called off. The bosses distributed plane tickets and spending money for the homeboys to go shopping, with orders to meet at the airport for a four o'clock flight to Tijuana. Spooky, Puma and Cougar wandered around a mall, ate lunch and bought shirts, gym shoes, a souvenir silver sombrero. A Tijuana henchman named Jesús Bayardo spent the day sucking down a bottle of cognac. By the time they reunited with Ramon and Javier Arellano at the departure counter of the airport's national terminal, Bayardo was staggering and snarling. The ticket clerk refused to issue him a boarding pass. Puma tended to Bayardo and the rest gave him hard looks. Popeye had warned Bayardo about his drinking.

At that moment, the other actors in the imminent drama converged on Guadalajara's Miguel Hidalgo International Airport, completing a lethal triangle that the official version attributes to coincidence. In front of the terminal, an entourage entered the parking lot led by a green bulletproof Buick carrying three bodyguards and their short and stolid boss: Joaquín (Chapo) Guzmán of the Sinaloa cartel. He planned to catch a plane to Puerto Vallarta, according to the police.

As Chapo's men opened the doors and trunk, a white Mercury Grand Marquis stopped a few yards behind the Buick by the walkway to the terminal. The corpulent passenger in the front seat of the Grand Marquis wore a crucifix over his black clerical soutane and wire-rim spectacles on a grandfatherly face. He was Juan Jesús Posadas Ocampo, sixty-four, one of the nation's two Roman Catholic cardinals, the influential prelate of a fervently Catholic city. Cardinal Posadas had begun the day with his customary morning swim. He said Mass, put in a few hours at his desk and, after lunch, departed with his driver for the airport. The cardinal planned to pick up the Vatican's ambassador to Mexico, Girolamo Prigione, who was flying in from Mexico City.

It was 3:30 p.m.

Spooky saw the first sign of danger: lots of men wearing federal police badges on their belts. The broad-shouldered homeboy hurriedly turned away; he heard shots; he ducked among the taxis in front of the terminal and fired back, blindly. Reaching under his shirt for his pistol, Puma spotted Chapo Guzmán—the face from the photo on the wall in Tijuana. Chapo brandished a rifle, surrounded by a phalanx of his henchmen. Puma later testified that he squeezed off a few rounds, lobbed the .38 into a bathroom and ran for the plane. Cougar, meanwhile, says he had already boarded the plane. Outside the terminal on the front sidewalk, another homeboy watched, frozen in place and still holding a soft drink, as Charlie charged, AK-47 chattering, into the gunsmoke, exploding glass and whirling combatants in the sun-lit parking lot. Crowds stampeded for cover.

Just before the first shots, according to a witness, some-one shouted, "There he is, there he is." About twenty-five seconds elapsed until the moment when three gunmen aimed their weapons at the cardinal's Grand Marquis from the back and both sides. Cardinal Posadas had started to get out, one foot on the asphalt. He was confronted by a gun-man, identified by police as one of the older hoodlums from Guadalajara, whose nickname was Guero. The two may have struggled momentarily. Then the gunman mowed down Posadas with a scorching close-range volley. Riddled with fourteen bullets, the cardinal slumped back into the seat toward the lifeless body of his driver. Three bystanders and two gunmen were also killed in the free-for-all. But Chapo Guzmán, supposedly the intended target, survived once again. His Buick careened out of the parking lot, shots flat-tening tires and cracking the windshield. Chapo and his gun-men abandoned the Buick, accosted a pair of taxi drivers—flashing badges and shouting that they were feder-al agents—and made their getaway in a commandeered cab.

On the runway behind the terminal, Aeromexico flight 110 to Tijuana sat waiting. The airport authorities mysteri-ously delayed the flight for twenty minutes—there are sus-picions the order was given by someone connected to the Arellanos. The final busloads of passengers to board the plane were shaken by the shoot-out. Among the stragglers were at least half the members of the assassination team. The homeboys were disheveled and sweating. Settling into his seat in the coach section, Puma turned to Spooky and, according to testimony, exulted in Spanish: "We gassed Chapo Guzmán" (roughly equivalent to "We blew him away"). The two Arellano brothers sat in the almost empty first-class section. During the flight, the homeboys trooped from the back of the plane to hover around the bosses. A flight attendant remembered Ramón Arellano as an agitated young man wearing a fat gold bracelet. He spat repeatedly on the carpet and stared her down when she asked him to stop. At the Tijuana airport, the Arellano brothers were met immediately by men who looked like cops and sped off, bypassing security checkpoints. Ten airport security guards were arrested on charges of helping the fugitives leave through an unauthorized exit. Despite immediate indications that the suspects had fled on a commercial plane, despite the two-hour duration of the flight, no alert was issued to federal police in Tijuana to be on the lookout. Perhaps it would not have mattered. The henchmen who met the plane included federal cops, according to a senior Mexican investigator, but they worked for the Arellanos.

Left to fend for themselves, the homeboys scattered to both sides of the border. The news caught up to them at cheap hotels, at the homes of their families and girlfriends. Around midnight, a friend came to see Paisa in Tijuana and told him to get out of the house fast. "He told me that Guero had made a mistake," Paisa testified. "He had killed the cardinal of Guadalajara. I asked him who the cardinal was and he answered that he was a father. And I asked him if it was Chapo's father and he told me no, a priest from the church." Meanwhile, Cougar sat mesmerized in the glow of the televised images of the butchery he had escaped hours earlier, the images that stunned Mexico: the shattered bodies in the shattered Grand Marquis. He realized that he was in enormous trouble. "I saw the car with the windows broken. I panicked. It was a shocker, you know?"

Cougar had been drifting emotionally for months, plagued by doubts. While working for the heaviest hitters in organized crime, he had been dabbling more and more in Christian religious ideas. He says the death of the cardinal caused his epiphany; he found God. Upon seeing a newspaper article identifying him as a wanted man, the born-again Cougar hit the road. He ran as far as Lompoc, a little town near a military base north of Santa Barbara. "I was keeping low, trying to keep away from the police. I had a religious experience. God told me to go to Lompoc."

Alone among the homeboys who were caught, Cougar showed considerable remorse about the death of the cardinal. Though his religious conversion might appear dubiously convenient, it convinced more than one hard-bitten U.S. federal agent. The agents regarded the gang members as incorrigible punks, but they felt kind of sorry for Cougar. "He had a lot of guilt," an investigator said. "He was the only one who had guilt about what happened." Guilty or not, the homeboys were going to pay. The police and the press trumpeted their names. They were now the gang that killed the cardinal—pawns on an international chessboard.

When a grim-faced President Salinas attended the cardinal's funeral in the cathedral of Guadalajara, throngs of mourners shouted "Justice!" The symbolism and timing could not have been much worse. Drug traffickers had killed Mexico's highest-ranking church official at the airport in its second largest city and escaped with the acquiescence and assistance of the police. It was a grave blow to Salinas, who had reinstated church-government relations after decades of official anticlericalism decreed by the revolution. He was entering the final stretch of a difficult campaign to win approval of NAFTA in the U.S. Congress. Simultaneously, he was overseeing an arcane process within his Institutional Revolutionary Party: the ritual of negotiation and manuevering that culminates in the president's selection of a candidate to succeed him, an appointment known as the *dedazo* (big finger). No one doubted that corruption and violence persisted, but the image makers and power brokers in both nations had hammered away at a message of stability: the Salinas administration was purportedly cracking down, cleaning up, establishing control. The airport carnage was a graphic rebuttal to the NAFTA sales pitch.

The government quickly pronounced the cardinal's death an accident. He supposedly had entered the airport just as the Arellanos ambushed Guzmán and got hit in the crossfire. This explanation did not impress the media, the political opposition or the public. Critics declared that the cardinal was the intended target. "He was shot fourteen times . . . so I find it hard to believe it was an accident," said José Luis Pérez Canchola. "The politics of this government have centered on economic development and NAFTA. Everything that has to do with public security, corruption, the police, has been neglected. . . . We are confronting a situation of grave danger."

Planeloads of federal police descended on Tijuana. Raiding houses, riding around in Suburbans with gun barrels sprouting from the windows, they brought along a captive with a black hood covering his face—Jesús Bayardo, the alcoholic henchman of the Arellanos. He had missed flight 110. He stumbled away from the airport in Guadalajara and got himself arrested by regaling a bartender with his story of the shoot-out. Under interrogation, Bayardo gave up the Arellanos, Charlie, Popeye and several dozen other names and street monikers. Federal Attorney General Jorge Carpizo announced a multimillion-dollar reward for the arrests of the kingpins of the Tijuana cartel, Benjamín, Javier and Ramón Arellano. Carpizo also embarked on the most sweeping anticorruption purge of the Salinas term, locking up or firing more than one hundred police officials in the northwest and Mexico City. Within weeks, investigators captured Chapo Guzmán with the help of Guatemalan troops after he fled across Mexico's southern border. The kingpin was paraded before the cameras in a prison-issued cap and coat, a rich and astute mobster with a fourth-grade education. He professed innocence, describing himself as a simple farmer. The police seized millions of dollars worth of properties, vehicles and armament from Chapo and his rivals.

The police also rounded up Puma, Spooky and Paisa. The fanfare in both nations about the arrests did not impress Sergeant Vicente Villalvazo, a veteran cross-border liaison officer for the San Diego Police, who said it was just a diversion. He compared the gang members to "throw-down" guns dropped at a shooting scene to fool investigators. "These are throw-down guys," Villalvazo said. "They don't know anything." The capture of Puma and Spooky, according to investigators, was prearranged: a sacrificial display of obedience and loyalty, what gang members call "heart." Hoping that arrests would ease the pressure, the bosses promised the two homeboys that they would only spend a few years in jail and that their families would be handsomely compensated. Puma was young and cocky; Spooky was an expert at doing time. They agreed to return from San Diego to Tijuana and let themselves get nabbed. Before walking intentionally into a police stakeout at the Tijuana airport, Puma called his mother. A friend recalled: "His mom was totally blown away. Shocked. My understanding was that he called her from Tijuana and told her this is what's happening. Basically, he said good-bye."

Puma and Spooky were hustled to a military prison. For the next week, their questioners subjected them to the full repertoire of interrogatory techniques, according to defense lawyers and relatives who later visited them. They were stomped, beaten, starved, hog-tied, terrorized. Puma's eardrum was ruptured. When he pleaded for a drink of water, they drenched him with a barrel. At one point, according to court documents, "they placed him in a truck and drove him to a hill. He was thrown out of the truck and told he was going to be killed. The Mexican officers covered his face and placed a gun next to his head. They pulled the trigger several times and he could clearly hear the sound of the hammer. . . . [T]he men laughed at him because he was scared and crying." A homeboy named Tarzan later put it this way: "He was just a little kid. He had to talk quick."

The confessions of the gang members, combined with Guzmán's statement, were key to constructing the official version of the cardinal's death. Attorney General Carpizo presented the conclusions in a 106-page bound volume. Carpizo was a rare credible figure at the helm. Steely and temperamental, the third and most effective of five attorney generals who served during the Salinas administration had a reputation for integrity. He left a university law career to direct the National Human Rights Commission before accepting the top federal enforcement job. He minced no words, estimating that half the police force was compromised and declaring himself "surrounded by traitors."

Unfortunately, the investigation suffered from the very defects that Carpizo had criticized in the police. Manipulation by drug lords and the routine use of torture cast the most basic facts into question. The official account strung together inconsistencies, coincidences and mysteries. The thesis—that the gunmen did not kill Cardinal Posadas on purpose—had not changed. The authorities now explained his multiple point-blank wounds by saying that the Arellano forces thought the cardinal was part of the enemy entourage. Citing testimony that the hit team was told Chapo drove a white Grand Marquis, the police suggested that the gunmen mistook the cardinal for Chapo himself. This seemed unlikely, given the difference in age and size (Posadas was tall; the nickname Chapo means Shorty), and the cardinal's priestly clothing and recognizable face. "It is impossible to confuse two people who look so different," objected the bishop emeritus of Ciudad Juárez, Manuel Talamas. On the other hand, some investigators who had lived through the blur of instinct and adrenaline that is a shoot-out accepted the notion of mistaken identity—especially considering the caliber of the shooters. "You aren't talking about a military strike force," said a San Diego Police gang detective. "You're talking about a bunch of gangsters."

There were more problems, though. The official version relied on the confessions of Puma, Spooky and other Arellano soldiers, yet skirted around their consensus that the Arellanos had no plan to ambush Chapo at the airport. The testimony made it clear that the hit had been called off and that the gang members had gone drinking and shopping. Without explaining the contradiction, the authorities said that Arellano henchmen (presumably from the Guadalajara contingent, clearly not the homeboys) had assembled five vehicles full of weapons in the parking lot for a "carefully organized, maximum-security operation." More discrepancies emerged in the account of a federal police commander, Edgardo García, an admitted boyhood friend of Javier Arellano. García testified that he met with Javier shortly before the incident. The drug lord said an operation would be carried out against Chapo, according to García, and instructed the police commander to guard the entrance to the airport. If there was a plan for an assassination at the airport, the Arellanos did not inform the very gunmen they had brought from Tijuana for the mission.

The homeboys' stories could have been coached, of course. But the most disturbing part of the case for most Mexicans was the fundamental weakness of the premise that all three forces—the Arellanos, Guzmán and Cardinal

Posadas—arrived at the same place at the same time without any connection to one another. A history of governmental deception made the magic of coincidence hard to accept. Church leaders became outspoken in their dissent, demanding justice and joining the press in speculating and investigating on their own. The theories were mostly political in nature. Church officials in Mexico, to quote the scholar Jorge Castañeda, "have been members of the elite in this country since the first days of the conquest." Posadas had socialized with President Salinas and other politicians.

Analysts focused on the theoretical beneficiaries and casualties of the cleric's demise. Some felt the cardinal posed a threat to gangsters allied with factions of the ruling party because he supposedly favored the opposition National Action Party, which was gaining dominance in Jalisco. Others believed he was murdered because he had spoken out against drug trafficking—though it was hard to believe that his preachings alone would compel gangsters to eliminate him and bring certain outrage upon themselves. Another possibility surfaced in intelligence reports that were handled gingerly by U.S. and Mexican antidrug agents. There was speculation that the cardinal had arrived at the airport in the company of one of the gangs because he was somehow in contact with traffickers. Posadas had previously been bishop of Tijuana. It was possible, analysts said, that the cardinal was negotiating between the rival mafias or between the mafias and the government, just as other clerics in Latin America have mediated between the state and guerrillas and outlaws. The gangsters, after all, were devout. The Arellanos reportedly socialized with priests, donated generously to the Tijuana archdiocese and held private baptisms for their children, rolling up to the seminary in limousines. Church corruption was not unheard of, as exemplified by scandals in Italy involving the Vatican. No hard evidence surfaced to support the very delicate scenario of a link between the cardinal and the underworld. But events soon provided new details about contact between other clerics and the traffickers.

The most intriguing and insightful theories about the murder ventured into the terrain of "narco-politics." This term came to define the shadowy forces suspected in the Posadas case and two political assassinations in 1994. Analysts of the power structure saw more than a drug feud; the gangsters allegedly had links to the political factions competing for supremacy in the selection of the ruling party's presidential candidate, a decision scheduled for the end of the year. In that context, party strongmen allied to gangsters could have ordered the murder so as to send a terroristic message to President Salinas. The well-sourced editor of *Zeta,* Jesús Blancornelas, suggested that the conspirators had struck at a key moment for NAFTA, the issue that would define the president's success or failure. Their aim, he wrote: to "destabilize the Salinas administration and extort it with a view toward the [presidential] succession. . . . In this hypothesis the principal goal is to guarantee the arrival in power of a political group within the system; this group has strong interests and connections with drug trafficking." Mexican and foreign analysts portrayed the potential aggressors as the "dinosaurs," or Old Guard wing of the PRI, pitted against the modernizing "technocrats" led by Salinas. The passage of time confirmed the existence of factional struggles. But the revelation of bonds between Salinista "technocrats" and the most prehistoric of the dinosaurs blurred the distinctions drawn between the two sides, of young versus old, tradition versus reform: the political mafias were too complicated and pervasive for facile labels.

A spectacular discovery in Tijuana after the cardinal's

murder suggested apparent connections between the political mafias and the drug mafias. Federal police found a cross-border smuggling tunnel in the final stages of construction. The tunnel had been commissioned by the Chapo Guzmán organization. Like another Guzmán cocaine tunnel detected a year earlier in Arizona, it was an impressive feat of engineering: a ventilated, lighted passageway extending more than fourteen hundred feet under the border from a Tijuana warehouse to the site of an Otay Mesa cannery being built by the family of Southern California grocers named Reynoso. Investigators had previously linked the Reynosos to the seven-ton load of cocaine concealed in jalapeño pepper cans in Tecate. The three millionaire immigrant brothers had allegedly commissioned the smuggling tunnel which began in an industrial compound on the Tijuana side and led to an unfinished cannery in San Diego, where the smugglers planned to conceal cocaine in cans of peppers and other Mexican food products to be trucked north. Executives José, Antonio and Jesús Reynoso operated an import-export empire in Los Angeles that ranked in the top fifteen minority-owned companies in Los Angeles County. Newspapers and television had chronicled the triumphs of the family business. But there was an untold side to the story. In 1992, José Reynoso's son, René, fled to Guadalajara after ordering the murder of a rival in a business dispute in Los Angeles. He resisted extradition, allegedly with the complicity of Mexican officials, until he was finally sent back to California and convicted.

As for the three elder Reynosos, the U.S. government charged them with posing as upstanding businessmen while making an illicit fortune with a silent partner: Chapo Guzmán. The drug lord allegedly used the Reynosos' cross-border network of grocery companies, canneries, warehouses, truck fleets and Learjets to camouflage a mammoth

cocaine-smuggling-and-distribution operation stretching
from Mexico to California, Arizona, Illinois and New Jersey.
Federal prosecutors called it a staggering example of the
capacity of the cartels to infiltrate nominally legitimate
businesses—export-import companies, currency exchanges
specialized in wiring money to Mexico—north of the border
as well as south. The case showed the dark side of the economic integration envisioned by NAFTA.

The narco-tunnel led into the political underworld as well.
In 1993, a high-placed informant in the Guzmán mafia told
U.S. investigators during a conversation north of the border
that influential drug lords would play a role in the selection
of the ruling party's presidential candidate for the 1994 elections. The informant predicted that President Salinas would
choose Luis Donaldo Colosio, a party leader from the state
of Sonora, with the blessing of the drug lords for whom the
informant worked, according to several U.S. officials familiar with the meeting. The officials assessed his words with a
mixture of interest and healthy skepticism, the correct attitude toward unconfirmed "intelligence." Subsequent events
would make them think back to the conversation.

Soon after Colosio launched his candidacy in November
1993, a U.S. federal wiretap picked up further indications
that the mafias were trying to infiltrate presidential politics
and that Colosio's ascent might benefit the Guzmán/Palma
camp, which remained strong in Sonora despite Guzmán's
arrest. The wiretap recorded the conversations of a reputed
gangster named Enrique Avalos, who allegedly worked as
Guzmán's go-between with the Reynosos. During a telephone conversation in late 1993, according to court documents, "Avalos expressed satisfaction" that "Colosio had
been announced as the next presidential candidate." Avalos
boasted that executive Antonio Reynoso and Colosio were
"very, very good friends," and that Colosio's designation

would "bode well for the future of the organization." Avalos predicted, according to the court documents, that Colosio "would be in a good position to grant the organization favors in the future." Moreover, informants told U.S. investigators that "Colosio was a friend of the Chapo Guzmán organization" and that "the Reynosos contributed large amounts of money to his campaign," according to the documents.

José Reynoso was arrested in the lengthy narco-tunnel probe. At first, he insisted that he was an upstanding businessman and knew nothing about drugs. Later, he pleaded guilty. His fugitive brothers, Antonio and Jesús, took refuge in Tijuana, where Antonio owned a mansion yards from the border in the Playas de Tijuana area. The U.S. government requested their extradition, but the fugitives did not seem worried.

Despite the boasts of the gangsters, it has by no means been shown that the drug lords influenced President Salinas's choice of the candidate or that presidential candidate Colosio approved or knew of attempts by drug lords to gain influence with him. In fact, some say Colosio angered drug lords by resisting their overtures. But the murder of the cardinal revealed to Mexicans a labyrinth of drugs and politics which would become increasingly convoluted and hazardous over the next year. The aftermath of the cardinal's death suggested that somone powerful wanted the case to stay unsolved. There had been an apparent reconfiguration of power in the drug trade and among its official protectors. The legendary Guzmán, who had painted himself as the hapless victim of a murder attempt, had been toppled. The Arellanos emerged comparatively unscathed, even though they were supposedly less influential, even though they had been branded as the killers of the cardinal.

And the testimony of two stewardesses on Aeromexico flight 110 to Tijuana introduced into the official record another politically prominent name. Describing how the Arellano brothers had sat in the almost empty first-class section, María Guadalupe Flores told police that her supervisor had told her "that the passenger of the seat 2A was the son of Hank González." When the plane landed in Tijuana, coworker Angela Africa Sánchez testified, "there were a lot of judiciary police because they were waiting for the son of Hank González." The mention was tantalizing. The clan headed by Carlos Hank González, billionaire former cabinet minister and a leader of the ruling-party dinosaurs, had been the subject of accusations of links to drug mafias. High-ranking U.S. and Mexican officials confirmed later that the Hanks were being investigated on both sides of the border. Jorge Hank was the controversial owner of the Tijuana racetrack whom the magazine *Zeta* and others had accused of ordering the murder of editor Hector (Gato) Felix in 1988; Jorge's brother, Carlos, had headed the airline Taesa. Other than two cases in which Jorge Hank was fined or charged in connection with the smuggling of exotic animals and furs, however, the Hanks were not charged with a crime. Sources close to the Hank family denied that the policitian's son was on the flight with the Arellanos, according to the newspaper *El Financiero*. But the questions did not go away: Was one of the Hanks traveling with the drug lords? Where was he during the shoot-out? If he was not on the plane, did someone use that name in connection with that flight on that day and why? Why did police and prosecutors avoid mentioning the Hank references?

Emilio Goicochea, the opposition politician from Sinaloa, summed up the mystery of the drug lords' elusiveness this way: "The Arellanos are not the kingpins, they are the midlevel bosses. The real bosses are figures connected with national politics. Their names are known in the United States. Those who show their faces feel protected; that is why there is so much impunity."

The fall guys kept falling. During the summer, the DEA, the San Diego Police and other U.S. and Mexican agencies tracked down five more homeboys accused of participating in the Guadalajara hit squad. Fittingly, the end of the line for Cougar came in a little church in Lompoc. The arrest team set up outside; a youthful agent slipped inside and padded through the pews to Cougar, who was praying. "They didn't go in with no guns," Cougar recalled. "They just came up and tapped me on the shoulder." Cougar and two other homeboys who were U.S. citizens underwent extradition hearings. (The gang members who were illegal immigrants were quickly deported.) To preempt defense challenges on the grounds that the evidence had been obtained through torture, FBI agents flew to Guadalajara to question the jailed soldiers. Their stories lost color and inculpatory details, but the names and places were the same.

Cougar spent more than a year in San Diego's Metro-politan Correctional Center. After the judge ruled against him, his attorney staved off his extradition with appeals, giving Cougar more time to worry about the reception that a reputed priest-killer could expect from police and convicts in Mexico. Soon there was more bad news: Spooky was found dead in his cell in Guadalajara. Police immediately called it a homicide, saying the killers struck him on the head and suffocated him. Then came a bizarre reversal. The Jalisco state attorney general announced that further study had determined that the strapping youth had died accidentally. The cause was "broncho-aspiration"—something to do with swallowing vomit. The bruise on Spooky's forehead was explained as another accident, inflicted by a dropped barbell during weight lifting. In a derisive response, the newspaper *Siglo 21* announced a contest among readers to see who could come up with a more creative explanation.

Spooky was the second alleged triggerman to die. Police

in Sinaloa had already cornered and shot to death a gun-wielding fugitive who turned out to be the older Arellano henchman from Guadalajara known as Guero. His death precluded a definitive answer to the mystery of whether he had really shot the cardinal. Nonetheless, the danger was not enough to break the captured homeboys, who declined offers from U.S. agents to cooperate. Their street training told them to shut up and take it. This fatalistic creed was expressed by the imprisoned Tarzan, a rock-muscled homeboy with a shaved cowl of a head and a Mephistophelian grin, who seemed at ease behind the bars of San Diego's federal jail. "When you get arrested, you keep quiet," Tarzan said. "There's no reason why I should be afraid as long as I'm right here. When I get down there, then I'll be scared."

Cougar was not grinning. He had never even done prison time. Sooner or later, the U.S. marshals would come for him. They would shackle his arms and legs, bundle him into a van and deliver him to the Mexican police. "I know I'm gonna get tortured," he said slowly. "I know that. That's 100 percent. They are going to want me to confess to something, anything." Sitting in the interview room of the high-rise federal jail, a rectangular wedge of afternoon sky framed behind him, Cougar did not cry. He anticipated his ordeal pensively; he seemed sheepish and apologetic about the whole affair.

"I didn't think I was going to get involved in anything like this," Cougar said. "I feel like a scapegoat of some kind. I mean, I don't understand. There's no evidence whatsoever that I shot the cardinal or that I attempted to shoot anyone. Yet somehow the U.S. attorney on the case has found me extraditable. I don't understand that."

The Arellanos were similiarly adamant about their own innocence—and in a better position to defend themselves. They contacted Father Gerardo Montaño, a trusted veteran of the Tijuana archdiocese. Montaño was Benjamín Arellano's alibi for the day the cardinal was killed; the drug lord claimed in a phone interview with a Mexican newspaper that he was at the baptism of one of his children officiated by Father Montaño at the time.

Montaño arranged for a sit-down with the papal nuncio himself, Girolamo Prigione. The Vatican's emissary was the person whom Cardinal Posadas had come to pick up at the airport. In December 1993 and January 1994, Benjamín and Ramón Arellano traveled to the residence of the ambassador of the Vatican in Mexico City. The brothers pleaded their case to Prigione: they claimed they had not shot the cardinal and that Ramón was actually the intended victim of the fracas. Ambassador Prigione said later that President Salinas was aware of the meetings; the Arellanos later claimed (in an interview from hiding by questionnaire with the newspaper *El Financiero*) that Salinas and Prigione discussed a possible rendezvous between the president and the drug lords. Ambassador Prigione's public admission that he had held summit talks with the accused killers of his colleague provoked consternation. The nuncio declared that it was his priestly duty to hear the fugitives' side of the story and to refrain from turning them in.

"I am calm," Prigione told the press. "My conscience is clear. I have not acted outside of the law."

In Tijuana, the admitted mediation of Father Montaño cast a shadow on the archdiocese. A priest would no more have acted without the approval of higher-ups than a sergeant without orders from a colonel, critics said. Bishop Emilio Berlie of Tijuana indignantly denied wrongdoing. But it raised further questions about the possibility that the church was not immune from the vices infecting other institutions. Most of all, Mexicans marveled at the monumental impunity. The most-wanted fugitives in the nation had met

twice with a prominent diplomat in the nation's capital without being intercepted. "No one in the country accepts the
idea that they cannot be found, when this country has an
impressive apparatus of domestic espionage," said José Luis
Pérez Canchola. "This has been a science-fiction search."

At least one small group of federal agents was searching
in earnest, though. Attorney General Carpizo created an elite
secret unit in Mexico City with the mission of bringing the
Arellanos to justice. In December, the unit culminated
months of surveillance by scooping up Francisco Arellano,
the flamboyant discotheque-owning brother, at a house in
Tijuana. Francisco, who offered his captors a million dollars
to let him go, was not a suspect in the Posadas murder. He
was a consolation prize. Nonetheless, his presence in the
border city effectively debunked various reports that the
kingpins had taken refuge in Spain, Canada, Chile, Florida.
In fact, the Arellanos never stopped supervising their vast
smuggling machine, which never stopped pumping drugs
north. They had nothing to fear; they owned Tijuana.

The secret federal team hunting the brothers learned that
lesson once and for all on the night of March 3, 1994. Seven
federal agents riding in two Chevrolet Suburbans stopped a
stolen red Suburban on a side street just short of Boulevard
Díaz Ordaz, the city's busiest thoroughfare. Two officers of
the state judicial police were in the front seats of the red
Suburban. And as the federal agents had suspected, one of
the Arellano brothers was among the passengers in back. His
guards unleashed a wild barrage, shooting out their own
windows and sending an errant slug through the roof. Reinforcements, in the form of an Aerostar van and a Volkswagen Jetta, zoomed into the intersection and ambushed the
federal agents. Another episode of desperate, close-quarters,
Arellano-style combat ensued. Muzzles spewed hundreds of
rounds, scarring the walls of an adjacent flea market painted

with the giant face of a clown. Police converged from around the city to join the fray, encountering epic confusion about who was fighting whom. The agents from Mexico City were overwhelmed by the gangsters and their police allies, both state and federal. A turncoat officer administered the coup de grâce to the prone commander of the search unit, according to a Tijuana cop who observed the scene from a distance. His arms jumping in imitation of the recoil of an assault rifle, the Tijuana cop recalled, "One of his own supposed comrades finished him off."

Commander Alejandro Castañeda died, having come fatally close to his prey. A state officer and three gunmen were also killed. The Arellano drug lord in the red Suburban was allegedly taken into custody, but released within the hour. The state police blamed the escape on the commander of their homicide squad, charging that he sneaked two prisoners out the back door of state headquarters. The enraged federal authorities filed charges against a host of officials, including Baja's deputy attorney general, the top-ranking state official at the scene. Grainy footage of the incident startled the television viewers of the trans-border metropolis: echoes of the slaughter in Guadalajara, closer to home. Gathered around their television in the pristine San Diego suburb of Poway, a family named Rogers recognized, to their amazement, the Chevrolet Suburban in which the state police had chauffeured the drug lord. The Rogerses' wagon had been stolen from outside a San Diego–area restaurant two weeks earlier and still bore the California plates. It was now the Suburban of Death: a hulk of shredded metal and pulverized glass. Bodies sprawled beneath the open doors. Armed officers argued over prisoners, shoving and cursing. Ambulance crews carted off the wounded. And a stately, black-clad personage could be seen moving through the landscape of guns, blood, stretchers, cartridges, discarded medic's rubber gloves. Coincidence is apparently a strong force in the narco-universe: Bishop Emilio Berlie of Tijuana had been walking nearby when the shooting began. Now the bishop attended to the dead and dying. He crouched, silver-haired and benevolent, his fingers tracing ritualistic shapes in the air, and dispensed the last rites to the latest casualties in the unholy war for the border.

The next day, a platoon of grim federal agents armed with heavy weapons marched into state police headquarters and took custody of the remaining prisoners from the gunfight. They were not polite about it. The detectives of the homicide squad of the Baja police had been eating lunch in a Chinese restaurant across the street from state police headquarters. When they saw the federal agents arrive, the worried state police detectives—whose squad chief would be arrested months later in an Arellano safe house—turned off the lights in the restaurant and hid in the kitchen.

In the aftermath, the FBI and the DEA said that Ramón Arellano had been at the scene of the shoot-out, though at first the Mexican authorities announced that the fugitive was a high-ranking Arellano lieutenant. (And there were later versions, based on a videotape of the prisoners at the crime scene, that identified the Arellano brother in the red Suburban as Javier.) It is also likely that the Logan Heights homeboys were represented on the night of bloodshed which came to be known simply as the Third of March. Popeye and Charlie were Ramón Arellano's shadows; they had gotten too close and too big. As long as the Arellanos kept dodging death and capture, their imported triggermen would be at their side. During the coming years, a public clamor for reform brought about the arrests in Mexico of suspected political assassins, top drug lords, fabulously wealthy businessmen, formerly untouchable political boss-es. But no one laid a glove on the Arellanos for the next three years. The phantom kingpins kept ordering the murders of prosecutors and police, running drugs and frequenting trendy Tijuana restaurants with police escorts. Ramón Arellano was sighted at the wheel of a Ferrari, cruising the Río Zone. Their whereabouts were not a mystery to the chiefs of the DEA, the FBI and the Mexican federal police. "They know exactly where the Arellanos are," a senior U.S. law enforcement official said. "But every time they try to put together an operation, there's a leak. [The Mexican attorney general] just throws up his hands." Until the brothers fell, it would be difficult to know for sure how much of their good fortune was due to patrons in the highest circles of power and how much to old-fashioned, ground-level graft.

The March 3 clash between federal and state police in Tijuana dominated the headlines for several weeks. Back in Barrio Logan, though, nobody talked much about the gang and the cardinal. Not the priests, not the youth counselors, not the cops. The killing of Cardinal Posadas struck a deep cultural nerve. Only a few junior gangsters who loitered in the park where Martin dead-ends at Thirtieth bragged about the notoriety. They threw hand signs and proclaimed: "If the mafia needs us, we're here." Certainly, the mafia had a prodigious reach: federal judges in Guadalajara would later issue orders releasing several homeboys from prison. The judicial writs were based on deficient evidence. A youth named Lalo, who apparently had not seen the light, hurried north and promptly got busted with half a kilo of heroin in Chula Vista. And someone sprayed this message on the wall of the recreation center in Memorial Park: "Fuck the Cardinal. We're Back."

Police suspected the crazy teenage homeboys of painting the sacrilegious graffiti. The older guys knew better, especially those who had seen action in Tijuana. Drawing that kind of attention was a good way to get shot. As for the unexpected liberations in Guadalajara, the U.S. and Mexican investigators who hunted down the suspects were disgusted. What does it say about this case and the system in Mexico, they wanted to know, when even the foot soldiers get away?

Barrio Logan went about its business. People woke up early, worked hard, went to Mass. Memories faded. But every once in a while, the Tijuana radio stations played one of the ballads about the Posadas case which appeared in Mexican record stores during 1993. The melodies were lively, the words mournful and sarcastic. A verse in "The Death of the Cardinal," by the band Los Plebeyos, expressed the lingering suspicion on the street: "They say it was mistaken identity / But nobody's swallowing that trick."

CHAPTER FIVE

The Mysteries of
Lomas Taurinas

Mario Aburto Martínez is in a rush.

He glances periodically at the wall calendar near his workstation, behind the machine that cuts up lengths of audiotape. He has drawn a cross on the calendar marking today's date: Wednesday, March 23, 1994,

Mario has worked as an industrial mechanic at the factory Camero Magnéticos for six weeks. The factory manufactures cassette tapes and occupies a low gray landscape of industrial complexes, miles of *maquiladoras* spreading south from the Otay Mesa border crossing. It is Mario's sixth job at a *maquiladora;* he has changed jobs a dozen times in six years. He works hard, but he is moody and restless. At a toy factory, they fired him when he got involved in organizing a union. At the Hyundai plant, he lasted only a week. His new coworkers at Camero Magnéticos don't know quite what to make of him. He carries himself like a tough guy and reads books about Marxism. He strikes some people as solitary and taciturn, others as mature and polite. He has few friends, but he brags that he has lost count of his girlfriends. Once he starts talking, he has a big vocabulary and ideas spill out of him. Strange talk: about the secret "project" he is writing in a notebook. About the old soldier who tells him tales of adventure and revolution. About the secret political meetings

Mario claims to attend with mysterious *licenciados* (college graduates) and *delegados* (delegates).

Mario drops vague hints about his politics. He confides in female coworkers when he is on the prowl for companionship, which is often, and wants to impress them. Like María Elena, who borrowed his black leather jacket once when it was cold on the shop floor and found the two bullets in the pocket. He handled it as best he could, shrugging off her questions. A few days later, they got to talking again during a midnight shift and he could not resist mentioning his mission: how he works undercover in politics and will soon risk his life to make a lot of money. He told her she would find out about it on television. He would make his mark on the system. He would strike a blow for the laborers, the exploited, the migrants from Sinaloa like her, from Michoacán like him.

Mario did not tell María Elena what the two bullets in his jacket pocket were for. And he did not tell her about the pistol. Very few people know about the pistol, only those he trusts most. Recently he showed the gun to his teenage cousins, Mauricio and Marcelino, pulling it from beneath a mattress at his house: an old Taurus .38 revolver. Brazilian-made. I need it for a big score I'm getting ready to pull off, Mario told them. It's going to be risky, but then I'll be rich. The deal goes down on March 23.

During the 11:30 a.m. lunch break at the cassette factory, the conversation centers on sports. Mario forces himself to join in, calm and casual. The others don't seem to notice anything strange. But on his way out of the cafeteria, Graciela González buttonholes him. She wants to know what's wrong, why he looks so agitated. Mario brushes her off, returning quickly to his machine. Graciela is only sixteen, one of the young migrant women who predominate in the *maquiladora* workforce, dark angelic rows of them

perched at long assembly tables in smocks. She came to
Tijuana from Mexico City a few weeks ago. Mario asked her
out on her first day at work. Maybe it was her youth and vulnerability that made Mario open up to her during their date.
She will later say that he told her about the gun range where
he practices shooting and about his political group. He did
not identify the group but told her they were sick of how the
Institutional Revolutionary Party wins all the elections all
the time. After lunch at a Chinese restaurant, Mario and
Graciela strolled the hustle-bustle streets of the old downtown to the Tijuana wax museum, his favorite excursion on
dates. He showed her the statue of the Aztec warrior: the
Eagle Knight.

"That's what my friends call me in my political group,"
Mario said. "I am the Eagle Knight. One day you will come
back to this museum and see a statue of me."

The shift ends at 2 p.m. Mario hurries through the crowd
of departing workers, a solidly built twenty-three-year-old
in a black leather jacket and off-white jeans. Mario exercis-
es with weights and avoids alcohol and cigarettes. He struggles to keep the fat off, eating nothing but a candy bar on
days when he feels chunky. He has an incipient mustache
and tangled black hair that he combs back. Above a sunken
chin, his mouth protrudes slightly, tight with defiance. He
looks drawn and puffy-cheeked, as if he has not been sleeping well. But now he moves as if propelled by an invisible
force. At the security booth in front of the factory, he asks
the guard for directions to Lomas Taurinas, the neighborhood where they are having the big campaign rally this
afternoon.

The company shuttle van drops Mario off downtown.
From here he will grab a sandwich, then catch a bus to
Lomas Taurinas. On the sidewalk he starts to run, a book
clutched in his hand. He shoulders aside a fellow employee,

María Cristina Alcazar. She watches the black-jacketed figure sprint across Avenida Constitucíon and disappear into
the crowd.

Later, the bosses at the factory will discover that, on what
turned out to be his last afternoon at work, Mario Aburto did
not punch out.

The campaign jet touches down at Abelardo L. Rodríguez
airport just after 4 p.m. The candidate of the Institutional
Revolutionary Party for the presidency of Mexico, Luis
Donaldo Colosio, disembarks into the applause and back-
pounding hugs of a welcoming committee of congressmen
and PRI leaders. Grinning, Colosio presses the flesh on the
tarmac and outside the terminal. The crowd is unexpectedly
large and raucous. Colosio steps up on the running board of
a waiting Chevrolet Blazer and waves: a forty-four-year-old
in a beige Burberry windbreaker, open-collared blue shirt
and casual brown slacks. He has a hearty man-of-the-people
appeal: thick mustache and very curly hair, expressive and
rather sad-looking eyes, an athletic vigor. He hails from a
small border town in Sonora, the desert state east of Baja.
Unlike President Salinas and other stiff-mannered sons of
the oligarchy, Colosio comes from a middle-class family of
ranchers. He likes baseball. He did graduate work at Penn,
rather than Harvard or Yale, and his scholarly achievements
are less impressive than his political ascent. In six years, he
has climbed from the Congress to the party chairmanship to
a cabinet post to the presidential candidacy.

Colosio ducks into the Blazer. His five-vehicle convoy
cruises across the industrial flatland of Otay Mesa. The first
stop of the two-day swing through Baja will be a rally in the
shantytown of Lomas Taurinas. Though the campaign is
four months old, this visit represents a new beginning.
Yesterday, Manuel Camacho, the former mayor of Mexico

City, announced that he would not run for president. Camacho has haunted Colosio since their discreet intraparty competition for the candidacy last year. Mayor Camacho, a longtime ally of President Salinas, had a power base in the capital and among young party activists. But Colosio bested him in the internal maneuvering by walking a tightrope among the increasingly divided factions of the ruling party. As minister of social and urban development, Colosio honed an image of sympathy for the average Mexican. His adherence to free-market policies and his loyalty to Salinas make him a Salinista. The dinosaurs of the Old Guard find him palatable because he is a gregarious regular guy. In November, President Salinas exercised his time-honored privilege to anoint Colosio to run to succeed him in the elections of August 1994. While the opposition parties have put up more of a fight in recent elections, the nomination is still tantamount to a coronation.

Soon after the jubilant *destape* (unveiling), the candidacy stumbled. In a momentous break with tradition, also-ran Camacho refused to join the usual adulatory ritual required of loyal PRIstas. He dared to voice his displeasure at having been passed over and hinted that he might still run for president. Then came the unpleasant surprise of the guerrilla rebellion in the state of Chiapas on New Year's Day, when everyone was supposed to be celebrating the birth of the North American Free Trade Agreement. Camacho's shadow candidacy acquired sudden viability when President Salinas named him the government's negotiator with the guerrillas in Chiapas. Colosio was stunned. With Mexicans' attention riveted on Chiapas, the assignment amounted to a calculated elevation of Camacho and a slap at candidate Colosio. Rumors rumbled: The president was dissatisfied with Colosio's lackluster campaign. The president was grooming Camacho as a replacement candidate. Something was going to happen to Colosio. Perhaps he would be forced to "get sick" and step down.

Riding in the Blazer, Colosio watches the scenery change. The caravan toils up a hill, the streets curving and rising through an old, middle-income residential area of white-walled, closely packed houses. The past month has been grueling. The campaign has tried to sharpen its message by emphasizing the unfinished business of democratization and of extending the benefits of the Salinas economic "miracle" to the millions of downtrodden. On March 6, Colosio gave a landmark speech promising clean elections and the dismantling of the authoritarian PRI-government monolith. Some analysts interpreted (and others exaggerated) his words as a declaration of independence from his mentor, the president. The infighting has been intense. In addition to Camacho, Colosio's relationship with President Salinas and the president's formidable chief of staff, José Cordoba Montoya, has reportedly deteriorated. But Colosio has persevered: after a private meeting, Camacho agreed to step aside. Camacho's announcement came yesterday, while Colosio was campaigning in Sinaloa. Aides urged Colosio to refrain from immediate comment, but the candidate insisted on expressing his happiness to the press. He told his aides: "Tomorrow anything could happen and then my words won't have importance. You see how the country is, things happen every second, and tomorrow who knows what will happen?"

The Blazer rolls down the steep ramps on the other side of the hill. The cement underneath gives way to the dirt landscape of poverty. Colosio's name and face stare back at him from walls, light poles, blankets draped on rooftops, bobbing signs, balloons. It is ironic: Baja was Colosio's baptism of fire in 1989. When President Salinas decided to uphold the election of Ernesto Ruffo Appel of the National

Action Party in the governor's race in Baja, Colosio was president of the ruling party. Colosio dutifully went on national television to announce a historic rejection of one of the PRI's tenets: tolerate the opposition, but don't let them win. His gracious concession speech enraged his fellow party stalwarts in Baja, an outpost of graft and electoral chicanery. Emotions boiled over and there were shouted curses and threats against Colosio. Some local bosses still bear a grudge.

Today, five years later, Colosio hopes his fortunes will be reborn in Tijuana. He must heal the internal party conflicts and gather his strength for challenges from the opposition candidates during the electoral home stretch this summer. He is still the front-runner.

The Blazer falters to a stop on the crowded street that is the sole entry to Lomas Taurinas. Double-parked cars and spectactors block the way. After a moment's hesitation, Colosio gets out and starts walking. His habit of diving into crowds has become a trademark ("bathing in the masses," the press calls it) and drives his bodyguards crazy. They scramble to catch up as the candidate strides into the cauldron of noise and humanity in Lomas Taurinas.

The name, "Taurine Hills," evokes a sense of spectacle: the drama of the bullfight. Lomas Taurinas sprawls across a half-hidden canyon created by the miniature mountain ranges that stratify Tijuana's geography and socioeconomics; the poor live in the gulches and ravines where the asphalt ends. In Lomas Taurinas, terraced dirt streets, interlaced with staircases, ring the steep hillsides. The houses are hand-built affairs, boxlike structures piled on top of each other, propped up by wooden poles. The architecture is graced by the improvisational flair of self-taught artisans: vivid colors, carefully carved balcony facades. The popu-

lous canyon walls form a natural amphitheater around the
sloping dirt arena that serves as the plaza of the urban village: center stage. The community was born as an illegal
encampment of shacks built by migrants from the south, a
classic Latin American squatter colony. Through the mediation of a neighborhood boss, the squatters became loyal voters and foot soldiers of the PRI. City Hall responded with
electricity, running water, police patrols. Lomas Taurinas
evolved into a tiny gear in the nationwide party machine.
Although the local strongman was supplanted by operatives
of Solidarity, President Salinas's patronage and public
works agency, little has changed. It is an election year; the
party needs help; Lomas Taurinas says *"Presente."* The
spectators number about three thousand, bolstered by busloads of obedient PRIstas from around the city.

Cheers engulf Colosio as he crosses a footbridge to the
dirt plaza. Below the rickety wooden bridge runs a creek
whose waters mix human and toxic waste, giving off a
burnt-rubber stench. The ancient splintered bridge is among
the reasons that local cops questioned the choice of the site
for the rally. The area has high crime, difficult terrain, poor
access. And these are dangerous days in Tijuana: the war
among drug mafias for the border, heralded by the murder of
the cardinal of Guadalajara ten months earlier, has escalat-
ed. Three weeks ago, federal antidrug agents shot it out in
the street with state police guarding "one of the Arellano
brothers," who escaped. Despite the tensions and the warn-
ings, the organizers of the Colosio rally have insisted on the
site—orders from Mexico City—and have informed the
municipal police that they want no help with security, except
a few traffic cops. Nonetheless, Federico Benítez, the city
police chief, has stationed the Special Tactical Group, the
municipal SWAT team, outside the canyon. Just in case. The
Tactical Group is in radio contact with a supervisor in

Lomas Taurinas, where there is no shortage of plainclothes law enforcement. Colosio makes his way across the jam-packed plaza through a human corridor formed by more than fifty guards. Two dozen have been supplied by the local branch of the ruling party and call themselves Grupo Tucán: a collection of veteran cops, many of whom lost their jobs after the PRI lost power in 1989. They have dubious reputations and solid connections in the gritty milieu where police and politics converge, where you show up at the rally, squeeze into a photo with the candidate, maybe collect a favor someday. Also working crowd control are fifteen civilians, about half of the private security men who travel with Colosio. Another fifteen plainclothes officers, the highly trained military men of the Estado Mayor, the presidential guard corps, form the inner circle around the candidate. The entire force is commanded by the balding General Domiro García, a handpicked veteran of the presidential guard, the future president's shadow. General García follows Colosio up onto the podium, which is mounted on the back of a pickup truck parked against the brick wall of a house.

On the rooftop of the brick house behind the podium, federal police commander Marco Jácome Saldaña and another federal agent crouch behind a video camera. They have been ordered to film the event. Just in case.

Mario Aburto stares up at the candidate. Mario stands in the sea of bodies about fifty feet away from the pickup truck/podium. He arrived in Lomas Taurinas between 3:30 and 3:40 by bus. Soon afterward, there was an altercation between PRI sympathizers and a group of young protesters who unfurled a banner criticizing Colosio and the government. Some witnesses will later say Mario made signals at the protestors, as if he knew them. Mario watches the podium as the microphone is passed among four representatives of the "urban sector" of the party, who praise the beaming candidate and expound on their needs and hopes. During the speeches, Mario stands near two volunteer plainclothes guards from Grupo Tucán, a tall young man with black hair and a tall old man with a baseball cap.

Colosio's speech is brief and upbeat. He thanks the other speakers. He promises that he will not forget them. "We are going to bring the power of the citizenry to the presidency of Mexico," he declares. He predicts victory in August, both nationwide and in this opposition-run state. And he ends with a rousing "Viva Baja California!" The event has lasted thirty-five minutes from start to finish.

The candidate descends into the crowd to the right of the podium. Mario presses forward. Somebody cranks up the music on the sound system—loud. The tune is "The Snake," a *cumbia* of the dance style popular in the north: "Beware the snake / He will bite your feet." The lilting melody and bouncy beat serve as the soundtrack as Colosio and his guards slog toward the footbridge on the other side of the plaza. The going is slow. The closely packed crowd buffets the candidate, jostling, shoving, stumbling on the sloping dirt floor of the plaza. The guards shout "*Valla!*" (Form a wall, let him through!), but the security strategy has disintegrated into pandemonium. People grasp for Colosio's hand. They brandish papers asking for autographs, slip him letters asking for favors. They reach out to touch the physical incarnation of power and history for an instant.

Head low, half-crouched, Mario glides through the crush of bodies, voices, music. He blots it all out, bearing down on the moving target. He grips the Taurus .38 in his right hand, beneath his leather jacket. He follows in the wake of the old campaign security guard in the baseball cap, who lumbers up behind Colosio, flailing and pushing with long arms. Someone snarls, "Get out of the way, bastard!" Someone else (Mario?) declares: "I want to shake his hand!" A little sandy-haired man in a sport jacket appears to stumble, falling at Colosio's feet, blocking his advance. Mario emerges from behind and to the right of Colosio. Mario is very close. The gunman grabs the candidate's right shoulder with a sinewy left hand. For an instant, the tableau suggests a citizen accosting a politician to make an earnest and familiar entreaty: Listen for a minute, look at me. I have something to say.

Then the long barrel of the pistol rises into view. With his right hand the gunman places the muzzle deliberately, delicately, against the side of Colosio's head. It does not appear that Colosio has time to see the gun. Colosio's head turns right, toward the muzzle, and then slightly left again, perhaps reacting to the touch of the metal. At approximately 5:10 p.m., the assassin pulls the trigger.

Haníbal Colosio, a dignified gray-haired cousin of the candidate, had traveled from Sonora to see his famous relative on the campaign trail. After the speech, Haníbal Colosio managed to clutch the passing candidate's hand above the heads of the crowd. They exchanged hurried, bellowed greetings. Colosio asked after the health of Haníbal's elderly mother, the candidate's aunt. Then the entourage swept him on.

"There was so much pushing I was afraid they were going to knock him down," Haníbal Colosio recalled two hours later, his voice drained by shock. "Then I heard the two shots. People ran. And when they clustered again he was already lying on the ground. And there was a pistol, it looked like a .38, black, on the ground next to him."

María Vidal, a neighborhood leader from El Cañón del Padre, said: "I was walking next to [the candidate]. I was telling him about the concerns of our organizations. He was paying attention to what I said, looking down as he walked. The people greeted him and he extended his hand to greet them. . . . Then came the gunshot. I looked up and all I saw was the pistol, coming out of the crowd. The crowd opened and Colosio fell to the ground. Blood started coming out of his head. We said to pick him up, because everyone was stunned for a moment. And then it was as if the daze was broken and people started shouting 'Grab the gunman, get him.' I didn't see his face, only the gun, the hand appearing. People were crying, screaming, desperate. They said: How could this have happened?"

Colosio had been shot twice in rapid succession, in the head and in the left side. The amplified music muffled the gunfire and the screams, so hundreds of people did not realize what had happened. Whirlpools of movement swirled around the candidate and the gunman. One group, led by the distraught General García, picked up the inert Colosio and rushed him across the footbridge to the Blazer. The head wound poured blood, staining the earth, rocks, bystanders, vehicles. Cars crashed into each other trying to get out of the Blazer's way. Outside the canyon, they loaded the candidate into an ambulance and sped to the hospital.

Meanwhile, at the vortex of the fury in Lomas Taurinas stood Víctor Cantú—a silver-haired, square-jawed major of Colosio's elite military guards. Major Cantú grimaced slightly, like a man in a hailstorm. He held his semiautomatic pistol in one hand, leveled against the bare chest of the disheveled Mario Aburto. The major's other hand gripped Aburto, a grip that looked impervious to a chain saw. Blood coursed from Aburto's forehead where a man had brained him with a rock. Aburto's shirt and jacket were partly torn off in the struggle after he was tackled by Vicente Mayoral, sixty-two, one of the local security guards. Despite his apparent heroism, Mayoral was also arrested because, as they wrestled in the dirt, Aburto kept yelping: "I didn't do it! It was the old man, it was the old man!"

Charging like a fullback, Major Cantú half dragged, half ran Aburto through a gauntlet of fists, curses and cameras to a Chevrolet Suburban. Other guards piled in, pummeling the captive in the backseat. The crowd chased the Suburban, shouting that the gunman might vanish or be killed. Journalists appealed for help to the black-clad municipal police officers of the Special Tactical Group, who swooped into the canyon from concealment upon hearing the report of a disturbance. Aburto's military captors found themselves confronting David Rubí, the chief of the SWAT team, the toughest cop in Tijuana. Girded for combat in his aviator sunglasses and leather jacket, Rubí bellowed at the occupants to stop and identify themselves. They refused; Rubí and his fierce young officers surrounded the Suburban, rifles at the ready. After an angry exchange, Rubí told the military men that his officers would escort them to federal police headquarters. "I want that young man to arrive alive and well," he growled at the federal campaign guards. To his own officers, Rubí barked: "If they try to get away, kill them!"

To this day, conspiracy theorists are convinced that Rubíi prevented the death or disappearance of Aburto. The suspicious reaction of the SWAT team and the crowd reflected a profound, reflexive distrust. They feared that they would never learn the truth about the assassination. Their fears were realized.

Citizens streamed through the streets to the General Hospital of Tijuana, congregating on the steps outside the lobby. They wept, prayed, scuffled, lit candles, held up placards of the fallen leader. Colosio's wife, Diana Laura, raced past them up the steps and down the heavily guarded hallway to the operating room. Her face was contorted with anguish, her slender frame showing the effects of the cancer that would kill her a year later. The lobby filled with journalists, police, bigwigs. A yellow medical helicopter landed in the street, ready to transport Colosio across the border to a trauma center in San Diego. An hour later, the helicopter left, climbing heavily like a metal vulture. Empty.

In the hospital lobby, stone-faced nurses and doctors told reporters what they needed to know with eye contact, a shake of the head. Their faces presaged the announcement at about 8:40 p.m. Liébano Saenz, a campaign press secretary in an elegant suit, climbed onto a reception counter in the lobby and raised his arms for quiet. His tone was firm, measured, official. He said: "It gives me great grief to inform you that, despite the efforts of the doctors, Luis Donaldo Colosio has died."

The crowd erupted. "No!" "Assassins!" "It's a mafia!"

From that moment on, the Colosio assassination rapidly acquired the trappings of myth and mystery that accompany crimes of state. The comparable previous crime, the murder of President Alvaro Obregón, took place in 1928, during the birth of the elaborate one-party system that would hold Mexico together for sixty-five years. The Colosio case signaled the demise of that system. And there were other portents. In 1994, Mexicans rode a roller coaster of crises: the Chiapas uprising, the kidnappings of tycoons, brazen drug corruption, the assassination of the secretary-general of the PRI and the catastrophic devaluation of the peso. The contradictions between wealth and poverty, economic modernization and political authoritarianism, reformism and gangsterism, reached the breaking point. For years, the murders of journalists, opposition politicians, human rights activists and other victims of impunity and repression had generated outrage, then faded away. The murder of Cardinal Posadas lingered longer, reverberated louder. The Colosio assassination definitively shattered the image of progress and stability that the Salinas administration sold abroad and at home.

"The assassination of Colosio did not occur in a vacuum," wrote the political scientist Jorge Castañeda the next day. He faulted President Salinas and his "modernizing and ambitious young men" for playing "sorcerer's apprentice: they tinkered with the magical, mysterious procedures of the political system built by their predecessors, had them break down, but never replaced them with new ones. . . . Because they refused to substitute the old ways with new, democratic ones, they are faced with the worst of all possible worlds: the old system in place but out of sync and no new system around to keep things rolling."

The confusion in Lomas Taurinas never really dissipated. It carried over into the investigation and public perceptions of the case. The interrogation of Mario Aburto transpired, according to a later investigative review, amid "evident disorder and lack of technique." The scene was federal police headquarters, a green, modern, three-story building in the Río Zone. More than thirteen agitated officials packed into an office: chief prosecutor Arturo Ochoa Palacios, deputy prosecutors, commanders, agents, a secretary. In addition, several prominent defense attorneys and José Luis Pérez Canchola were invited as observers. "There is no reason that justified the presence of all the people who participated in the interrogation of Aburto," concluded the subsequent prosecutor's review, "not only for the excessive number, but for the disorder [and] incoherency of the process." Aburto sat in an armchair, his head bandaged. He denied everything at first, so the federal chief in Tijuana, Raúl Loza, decided to show him the videotape that one of his federal commanders shot at the rally. (Loza later came under withering scrutiny for the convenient existence of the video; he explained that

it was his habit to film campaign events in case of trouble.)
Shot from the rooftop behind Colosio, the videotape showed
the excruciating moment in which the gunman's hand
appeared and fired into Colosio's head, blood geysering.
Then the camera jumped and the images blurred momentarily. Neither the second shot nor Aburto's face was visible at
the moment of truth.

Aburto began to talk. He paused frequently and complained of a headache. He claimed to belong to a political
group that had honored him with the title of "Eagle Knight,"
but did not name the group. The gun was given to him by
someone he preferred not to identify. During the past weeks,
Aburto had gone to a gun range for target practice. He
intended to wound Colosio, not to kill him, in order to call
attention to his own "pacificist ideas" and "the presence of
armed groups" in numerous Mexican states. Aburto said he
had spent time with those groups; he had contemplated an
attack on a president or candidate for eight years. As for the
crime itself, he said that he was pushed, upsetting his aim.
And he promised to tell all if he were allowed to talk with
the host of a lurid tabloid news program on a Spanish-language television network based in Miami.

Some of the observers came away with the impression
that Aburto was sane, lucid and part of a conspiracy. "He
talked about many people," said Xavier Carvajal, the head of
a Tijuana lawyers' association. "He never said who, but he
insinuated that others were involved. However, he gave no
reasons, no names, no places. . . . He left me with the
impression that there were others."

Pérez agreed. From the outset, the human rights ombudsman raised the possibility of a plot teaming drug lords and
politicians. He saw Aburto as the kind of triggerman who
needs to be trained and directed. "I doubt that he acted alone
because of the circumstances. For one thing, the fact that he

practiced to shoot him. He needed information to get there and be there at the right spot. We are talking about a *maquiladora* worker. . . . This is the type of act that lends itself to collective involvement."

The interrogation lasted three hours. Aburto declined to answer further questions, refusing twenty-two times in all. He shut down, receding into a near trance. Subsequently, a high-ranking federal prosecutor described the assassin as "an extraordinarily cold and controlled man. Usually, when one man has just killed another, there is at least an adrenaline rush. But he looked as if he had just returned from a day in the countryside. He was calmer than we were."

At about 10 p.m, Attorney General Diego Valadés and a planeful of top federal prosecutors and commanders arrived in Tijuana. Valadés had succeeded his friend Jorge Carpizo as federal attorney general less than three months earlier. Like Carpizo, the lanky Valadés was a legal scholar; his manner was genteel, professorial, occasionally mercurial. The federal officials considered Baja enemy territory. The wounds of the March 3 shoot-out with the state police were still fresh. Moreover, Valadés was apparently informed en route that one of the suspects was a Baja state police detective. This was inaccurate: Vicente Mayoral had retired from the state police after serving under past PRI governments. When Governor Ruffo and state Attorney General Franco greeted Valadés in the governor's Tijuana offices and offered their services, the chief federal prosecutor did not conceal his ire. Valadés rebuffed the state attorney general contemptuously, according to Ruffo, who says Valadés exclaimed: "Listen, Governor, once again your police are involved. This is disgusting." Taken aback, the governor explained that none of his officers were suspects. "The situation got ugly," Ruffo recalled. "It left me very disoriented, because we knew that there was no state police officer there and what's more, [the PRI] had asked us to keep away" from the campaign rally.

In a telephone conversation with President Salinas that evening, Governor Ruffo proposed a special state-federal prosecution unit for the Colosio case. Although the crime of murder was technically under the jurisdiction of the state, the president declined. In another apparent effort to assert the ruling party's presence on opposition turf, Governor Manlio Fabio Beltrones of Sonora rushed to Tijuana. The smooth, dapper Beltrones was considered an ambitious "baby dinosaur" of the PRI. His allies included the less savory figures of the Old Guard and the Salinistas, such as the president's brother, Raúl Salinas de Gortari. Beltrones had developed his mentors as a young Turk in the Interior Ministry. Under his rule as governor, drug smuggling and police corruption flourished in Sonora and he was forced to defend himself against the subsequent allegations.

In addition to representing Colosio's home state, Governor Beltrones and his contingent of Sonora police were there to help ensure that Aburto reached Mexico City alive, the high-ranking federal prosecutor later said. "We couldn't ask for help from the state police; after the March 3 incident, we might end up with gunplay. And we didn't want to leave him in the hands only of the federal police, who might not all be honest." The prosecutor said Governor Beltrones spoke to Aburto in police headquarters for only a few minutes, asking "Why Colosio?" Aburto responded: "They asked me that already. I'm not going to answer."

Beltrones may have had honorable intentions, but his visit ended up branding him a suspicious actor in the drama. The reason: a clandestine interrogation of Aburto that was conducted somewhere outside police headquarters after the formal declaration. The likely location was a house near the ocean; Aburto later said he had heard the sounds of water while being tortured. The interrogation probably occurred during a mysterious two-hour gap in Aburto's whereabouts before police bundled him onto a plane for Mexico City at 9 a.m. Some speculative versions placed Beltrones and/or his chief bodyguard at the grilling, causing speculation about a cover-up or a secret parallel investigation. Governor Beltrones denied those accounts. Regardless, Aburto endured a thrashing and disclosed nothing, according to a federal agent who was present. The agent later told a Baja state official that the stoic Aburto had told his captors: "If you knew who else was involved, you'd be surprised."

On March 24, Attorney General Valadés, flanked by the two governors, faced the press at federal police headquarters. He announced the logical preliminary conclusion dictated by the evidence. Aburto had killed Colosio, according to eyewitnesses and his own confession. The Taurus fired two of four rounds in the chambers. The wound to the right temple was fatal. The second bullet inflicted a superficial through-and-through wound to the left abdomen. In a perplexing detail, though, the bullet trajectories went in opposite directions. Forensic analysts concluded that Colosio had spun 90 degrees to the left after the first impact, while the shooter had moved to the left and fired again into the victim, who went down face-first. Valadés announced that Mayoral was being released because the former detective had merely tackled the gunman. The police also released an agent of National Security, the domestic espionage agency, whom a municipal policeman nabbed running from Lomas Taurinas with blood on his jacket. The hapless spy said he was en route to his car to radio his supervisors when he brushed against the guards carrying the bleeding candidate. Strangely, the agent's hands tested positive for gunpowder residue, a fact that was never convincingly explained. But he denied firing a gun and there was no evidence that he had done so near Colosio.

President Salinas quickly appointed a special prosecutor, Miguel Montes, who was an inexperienced investigator and a distingushed jurist. Montes ended up chasing a series of tangents and dead-ends which other special prosecutors inherited. Whether because of fate, blundering or a skillful cover-up, Aburto remained the mystery within the mystery.

Until the assassination, Aburto was the archetypal hard-working denizen of the U.S.-Mexico border. His family moved to Tijuana from Zamora, Michoacán, when he was fifteen. He left school after the eighth grade, a decent student with disciplinary problems. In the classic pattern, the border soon divided the Aburtos. The father and Aburto's two older brothers went to Los Angeles and landed good jobs at a furniture factory. Lacking immigration papers, the mother and four younger siblings stayed behind in the small, solid house with brick walls and a low roof in Colonia Buenos Aires. Like Lomas Taurinas, it was a migrant neighborhood: a ragged grid of muddy streets, dark nights bereft of streetlights, houses cobbled together with sweat, cast-off lumber and cardboard in the harsh foothills east of the city bus station. Aburto joined his father in Los Angeles for a while but returned to Tijuana in 1991 to help his mother. He saved enough money to buy a second house a few blocks from the first. He had no criminal record, in spite of a family history of brushes with the law: in 1967, Aburto's father killed two men, including his own brother, in a bar shooting in Michoacán. And police in Tijuana and Los Angeles arrested Mario's brothers for robbery, weapons possession and other offenses. Responsible and serious beyond his years, Aburto was a bridge between the family's cross-border worlds.

Still, copious pages of analysis by prison psychologists detailed Aburto's internal torments. They labeled him "rebellious," "frustrated," "narcissistic," "chronically delirious," a borderline paranoiac who had lashed out against the ultimate authority figure by killing Colosio. Acquaintances and friends described the mood swings and grandiose pronouncements of a fast talker who dropped names and played the big shot. "I am going to be famous," he told a coworker at the cassette factory. For an industrial laborer who never went to high school, Aburto exuded restless ambition and intellectual curiosity. He chafed at the low-paid drudgery of the *maquiladoras*. He took a vocational course in soldering and conscientiously cultivated relationships with teachers and job counselors who might be helpful. While living in Los Angeles, he looked into joining the U.S military and registered to vote, apparently in the mistaken belief that this could help secure legal residence in the United States. His political beliefs were passionate, if less than coherent. "He was a worker who tried to improve himself," said a Mexican federal official who investigated Aburto's background. "He was sensitive and impressionable. . . . But he wasn't brilliant either. He could be influenced."

His influences appear to have been older people, whose company Aburto sought out, complaining that his peers wasted their time drinking and dancing. He told friends about a wise old migrant from Aburto's native Michoacán. Referred to variously as Don Lucio and El Paisa (the Countryman), the old man supposedly had served as a soldier and a bodyguard to the beloved President Lázaro Cárdenas in the 1930s. Aburto spent hours listening to him talk about his travels, his exploits, his politics. Don Lucio seemed a significant lead to those who argued from the start that Aburto had acted out of ideological frenzy, induced by one or two radical mentors; some theorists felt that it was the old man who fanaticized Aburto and planted the seed of assassination in his mind. But Don Lucio, aka El Paisa, was never found.

Other strands of Aburto's life led to authority figures and politics. Among the assorted girlfriends, doctors and relatives in his address book, one entry stood out: the name, home address and telephone number of Blas Manrique, eighty-one, a venerable activist affiliated with the Party of the Democratic Revolution. Aburto had jotted down the place and times of meetings of Manrique's small local faction of the PRD, Mexico's main left-wing opposition party. The police, who did not get around to questioning Manrique for two months, said they found no other link between Manrique and Aburto and cleared the white-haired and courtly Manrique. A socialist since the 1930s, Manrique had decades of experience of being shadowed and harassed by the security forces. Asked in an interview why Aburto would want to gather information about him, he answered emphatically: "Maybe he was working for the police."

Conspiracy theorists point out that Aburto had the characteristics of the working-class young people whom Mexican police and intelligence services use to spy on opposition political groups. If Aburto worked as such an operative, known as an *oreja* (ear), that would explain strange details: the Manrique entry in the address book; Aburto's membership card for the Civic Committees of the People, a leftist organization that denied he was a member; the badge he flashed at a friend, saying it would protect him; his continual references to political meetings. Aburto told coworkers that he "had worked in politics" and that he was paid to attend political gatherings. And he showed interest in working for law enforcement, according to his parents. They said Mario applied to the state judicial police, where his uncle worked, in 1993, and later told his parents he was rejected.

The informant theory places Aburto in the byzantine and thuggish subculture of the government security forces which swarms with stool pigeons, enforcers and auxiliary cops. This is conceivably where a sophisticated mastermind could have cultivated a relationship with him and recruited him for a plot. But investigators never publicly linked Aburto to specific meetings, political organizations or the "armed groups" mentioned in his confession, let alone to a police force. A simpler scenario is that he exaggerated in conversations about his dabblings in insurgent politics. He spoke obsessively about injustice and tried his hand at writing. In May 1993, the publisher of *El Popular,* a Spanish-language newspaper in Bakersfield, California, got a call from Aburto, who wanted to publish a manuscript. Aburto told the publisher, Raúl Camacho, that his 120-page work was "a reflection on the need for change in Mexican politics." Camacho said publishing a book independently might be expensive. Aburto replied, "No problem." The publisher recalled: "His vocabulary was rich. He sounded quite intelligent."

The longest known piece of Aburto's writing is a seventeen-page tract in a notebook. Although the language flowed well in sections, the ideas were jumbled and misspellings abounded. Handwritten in a laborious scrawl, it was the kind of diatribe one might expect from someone who decides to shoot a politician one day. "If it's authentic, we are talking about a delirious, crazy guy," said the Mexican official who probed Aburto's background. The document was found in a trunk belonging to the Aburto family which a neighbor turned in to city police the day after the assassination. The trunk contained family papers, snapshots of Aburto's brothers posing with guns, a recruiting pamphlet for the U.S. Marines, a Bible, books on Marxism and labor law. And the handwritten tract, which predicted that its words would echo around the world. It espoused pacifism, an international

treaty against drug trafficking, more educational scholar-
ships, protection of marine life, better public transportation
and the resistance of workers against the sixty-five-year rule
of an "imperialist party."

"Many of my brothers have preferred to leave the country
in search of better opportunities," Aburto wrote, "but that is
not the solution. . . . [T]he solutions must happen in the
fatherland." Mentioning no names, he referred ominously to
a presidential candidate "who always spoke with dema-
goguery like other leaders who always left the country with
more problems. . . . [I]n this nation there are still dictators
supported by an empire formed by a political party."
Culminating with words of apocalyptic retaliation, the writer described himself as a man ready to renounce everything,
"even his family," to effect real change: "The rulers who do
not respond to the people with true justice and democracy
will pay the consequences."

The tract was signed by the "Eagle Knight," the Aztec
warrior whose image Aburto wore on a ring and whose title
he adopted as a nom de guerre. Aburto's manuscript
described a fanciful childhood encounter with an elderly
revolutionary in the countryside, in which the old man christened Aburto an Eagle Knight dedicated to fighting poverty
and oppression. The passage resembled the origin story of a
comic-book action hero; Aburto drew heroic images of himself wearing the warrior's eagle headdress, a bearded sage
gazing approvingly from the background. The provenance
of the Eagle Knight figure remains elusive. Mexican police
and the FBI found no nexus to street gang iconography,
police fraternal groups or the like.

The best lead pointed to Avenida Madero in the
Revolución district, which is dominated by bars, restaurants,
curio shops, clothing stores and storefront medical offices.
In a musty suite above a restaurant were the offices of Dr.

Ernesto G. Messina, a plastic surgeon and the founder of the
Party of the American Union. The tiny fringe group had previously incurred the wrath of authorities by proclaiming that
the remedy for tyranny in Mexico was the violent overthrow
of the government, abolition of the border and absorption of
Mexico by the United States. Dr. Messina now attracted the
attention of Colosio investigators because his office supposedly fit the general description of a building that Graciela
Gonzalez, Aburto's sixteen-year-old coworker, told police
was where Aburto said he went to political meetings. Two
more discoveries sent journalists and police trooping to
Messina's door. First, in his party's manifesto, Messina concluded a soliloquy about his dream of fusing Mexico and the
United States with these words: "This is not leaving, but
entering into glory. To consciously desire power, to be a man
of knowledge, a warrior, a gladiator, an authentic Eagle
Knight." Second, not only did the phrase and tone evoke
Aburto's writings, Dr. Messina serenely and politely told
anyone who asked that he admired Aburto for killing
Colosio.

"Aburto is a patriot and a hero," Messina told a visitor,
eyes shining. The short doctor sat low in his chair beneath
photos of Bo Derek and the Statue of Liberty. His face was
blunt-nosed and elfin; he vaguely resembled the character
actor Peter Lorre. The books on his desk included the auto-
biography of Mario Vargas Llosa, the Peruvian novelist and
political figure, in which entire paragraphs criticizing the
excesses of nationalism were underlined in bright ink. In
mild but relentless cadences, the doctor expounded on his
defense of Aburto. Messina viewed the event in Lomas
Taurinas as a rite of courage and sacrifice for which the apt
metaphor was the bullfight: Aburto, the brave matador, slays
his powerful foe, the incarnation of the dictatorship.
Messina quoted Alvin Toffler, Erich Fromm and especially

Thomas Jefferson: "The tree of liberty must occasionally be watered by the blood of the patriot and of the tyrant."

"I hope that Aburto read my book," Messina said. "It was time that someone began to act with political consciousness. It is time to take up arms when other recourses are exhausted."

It was possible, Messina said, that Aburto had attended meetings of the political party. (Messina estimated the membership at almost one hundred; a cousin told police that the doctor was the only member of the party because "nobody pays attention to him.") But Messina denied ever having met the assassin or have played any role in the crime. After interrogating Messina and ransacking his home and office, police eliminated him as a suspect. Nonetheless, some investigators clung to one of the few tangible connections in the case, convinced that the doctor's revolutionary rhetoric, directly or indirectly, had influenced the self-proclaimed Eagle Knight.

Other than the Aztec symbol, the Messina connection rested on the testimony of Graciela González. This was a problem. It is quite possible that the federal police intimidated the sixteen-year-old into embellishing her account of Aburto's statements during their dates. During Aburto's trial, she broke down in tears and admitted that he had not said some of the incriminating things she had attributed to him. Graciela seemed a peculiarly convenient witness, knowing a lot about Aburto scant weeks after meeting him. The municipal police chief of Tijuana, Federico Benítez, expressed doubt about Graciela and about the authenticity of Aburto's political screed. The chief had reviewed the manuscript and the other contents of the trunk before turning them over to the federal police. He wondered if the trunk and the manuscript were part of an orchestrated portrait of Aburto.

"This writing is full of misspellings," Benítez said in an interview in April, contemplating a copy of the manuscript with a cagey smile. "But the language reflects a good level of education. The education of someone who writes this does not correspond to someone who writes like this. I doubt Aburto wrote it. It does not correspond: someone who reads so much could not make so many mistakes. It may have been dictated by someone else."

Benítez echoed the misgivings of millions of Mexicans. It was as if Aburto had been presented in a gift-wrapped package: a lunatic with a gun. A Lee Harvey Oswald. Though Benítez stopped short of accusing anyone, the logical conjurers of this facade would be the federal police and their bosses in the slain Colosio's own party. If Aburto was really a hired gun, Benítez was asked, how would the plot function? How do you transform an unremarkable, hardworking young migrant into a kamikaze? The chief shrugged. That was the easy part, he said. "There is no shortage of people who can approach and recruit someone. Posing as radical groups, taking advantage of mental weakness, using doctrines and drugs. You can fanaticize someone in a couple of weeks."

During the weeks and months leading up to March 23, Aburto changed. Never extroverted, he became secretive and ill-tempered, according to those who knew him. In August, he took and quit three jobs. In November, a U.S. immigration inspector at the border confiscated his border-crossing card after realizing Aburto had worked illegally in Los Angeles in the past; this symbolically shut down his horizons in the north. Aburto also may have gotten mixed up in criminal activity. He talked to coworkers about buying and selling pistols. At a general store where the Aburto brothers frequently used a pay phone, the owners overheard Aburto talking on several occasions about what sounded like the

smuggling of guns by car into Tijuana from California—a
common sideline among small-time drug and immigrant
runners. He dressed better, acquiring the black leather jacket. In January, a surprised friend found the normally moder-
ate Aburto hungover and haggard after a drinking binge. He
socialized with a new set of older, better-educated friends—
"a lot of lawyers," said his father, Rubén Aburto. After starting work at Camero Magnéticos in February, the odd
conduct continued: arguments with his family, the talk about
cloak-and-dagger meetings with big shots and the money he
was about to make. The clerks at the general store in the
Buenos Aires neighborhood said that Aburto's mother,
María Luisa, had come in days before before the assassination and had asked a clerk to calculate the exchange rate on
$40,000. In good spirits, she said the family was coming
into money from a house they were selling in Michoacán,
according to the clerks. The sum seems very high for property in the rural south of Mexico; it fits in with the suspicions that Aburto received an advance payment. But Mrs.
Aburto denied that the conversation about money ever took
place.

Aburto's mother did describe a moment when she found
her son sitting alone in the house. He was crying.

His mother later recalled: "I asked him, 'What's the matter?' He said: 'Someone's following me, I don't know who.'
He was working the night shift at the time. He said: 'When
I go to the factory, they're watching. When I leave, they're
watching too. And they follow me.' "

Aburto's life seemed to gather momentum, spinning out
of control. Something was pushing him toward Lomas
Taurinas, whether his own psychological demons or manip-
ulative conspirators using money, threats, promises. As in
the case of the cardinal of Guadalajara, ambiguity and
uncertainty colored the most elemental facts. The murder

weapon, for example. For at least two years, the investigation did not confirm when and where Aburto had obtained
the ancient Taurus revolver, which is not a gun typically
used in a well-orchestrated criminal enterprise. Aburto's
version, recounted to *Zeta* in his only prison interview, was
that he had bought it for about $280 from someone he met
in a collective taxi. Two years later, another version surfaced. An inmate in the La Mesa state penitentiary of
Tijuana claimed that the gun had been provided to Aburto by
a drug trafficker who moved back and forth between the
Buenos Aires neighborhood of Tijuana and Logan Heights
in San Diego: the recruiting ground for the Tijuana cartel.
The inmate had been busted with the cross-border trafficker
with a load of cocaine; he said the trafficker who had supplied Aburto with the gun had been released on the spot.
And the inmate said federal police agents later showed up at
the prison, slapped him around and warned him not to say
anything about Mario Aburto to anyone.

This potential clue was at least as credible as others
churned out by a prolific conspiracy industry. Convoluted
theories centered on the alleged substitution of Aburto,
inspired by doubts about his appearance during his arraignment in Almoloya de Juárez Prison near Mexico City.
Undeniably, the suspect standing before the judge and the
cameras looked startlingly paler and younger than the
swarthy, battered suspect in Lomas Taurinas. The authorities
said they had merely cut his hair and shaved him before the
arraignment; they commissioned exhaustive anthropomor-
phic studies to prove Aburto was Aburto. Witnesses, including those who tackled him in Lomas Taurinas, said he was
the same man. Nonetheless, theories circulated that *three*
Aburto look-alikes had lurked in the crowd and that the real
triggerman was one of two men gunned down in a Tijuana
automotive shop hours after the assassination. Aburto's fam-

ily subscribed to this notion. They previously embraced other theories, though. Aburto's father linked his son to a series of suspects whose names appeared in the press and who were then absolved. Mario Aburto himself did not help much. The accused assassin defended himself with aplomb during his trial, dueling with prosecutors. But his rambling, evolving accounts made him seem unbalanced. This did not, of course, rule out the possibility that he had been used by plotters and was hiding the truth. Aburto's most consistent account in 1994 was that he had intended to give Colosio a scare.

"Something came out inside me, something spontaneous, no?" Aburto told *Zeta*. "And in my ignorance, I thought I would pull my gun and shoot at his feet, no? . . . In fact, on my right foot there are marks of where I tripped. In fact someone hit me in my right foot at the moment that I tripped, and that was how the gun went off, but with my arm well extended, it was extended when I tripped, and that was how the accident happened."

As if Aburto were not enigmatic enough, the investigators did not dog his trail while it was warm. The special prosecutor operated out of Mexico City, one thousand miles from the crime scene. The probe seemed passive; surprised reporters tracked down potential witnesses before the police did. Montes pursued an ill-fated, hydra-headed conspiracy theory that, in fairness, was tempting. It fairly leapt off the television screen. The presence of dozens of cameras made the Colosio assassination one of the most photographed crimes in history. Even before Montes took charge, the investigators pored over videos and photos. They saw strange things. They saw Aburto bulling his way through the crowd behind a tall, grizzled volunteer security guard, who hurried up to Colosio and flailed his arms as if pushing away the candidate's military bodyguards. Then the volunteer guard, identified as Tranquilino Sánchez, appeared to slide back and let the assassin strike. The investigators spotted a chilling juxtaposition: Aburto and Sánchez together in the crowd during the speeches before the shooting. The two appeared to huddle with a black-haired young man in a brown leather jacket, another member of the local security team. The two guards had their backs turned to the speakers, their heads inclined toward the shorter Aburto, as if deep in dialogue. Fast-forwarding to the fatal moment, the black-haired man—identified as Rodolfo Mayoral, twenty-five—reappeared a few feet from the candidate and from his father, Vicente Mayoral. The elder Mayoral was the former homicide cop who jumped Aburto after the shots and was briefly detained. Why did the three guards converge on the candidate? Seen in conjunction with Aburto's movements, the trio looked like they were clearing a path for the gun-man. Federal agents went out and arrested Sánchez, fifty-six, an infirm veteran of the municipal police, a nightclub bouncer and sometime burrito vendor. On March 28, the feisty Tijuana correspondents for the *El Universal* newspaper, Dora Elena Cortés and Manuel Cordero, served up their scoop on Tranquilino's arrest in a headline for the history books: "Colosio, Victim of a Plot."

Tranquilino's wife, María Sánchez, was small, forlorn-looking and sixty-three years old. She spoke with the humble, wary inflections of *los barrios populares*—the neighborhoods of the people. But in a display of anguish and indignation, she marched up to the front entrance of federal police headquarters and demanded to see her husband. The police refused to tell her anything. Reporters approached her and she launched into a steadfast defense of Tranquilino. "We are poor, but we are peaceful people," María Sánchez declared. "I am his wife and I have a right. And as his wife I say that he is innocent. He did not do this and he is not mixed up in this." As she spoke, her voice choked and plaintive, the clamorous knot of reporters grew, spewing questions, over-whelming her. Did Tranquilino own a gun? What did he say after the assassination? Did he know Aburto? Television lights blazed in her face. A satellite feed to Mexico City kicked in. The voice of María Sánchez boomed suddenly in the night, amplified by the sound system of a network truck parked in the street. She was sobbing now, wailing her hus-band's name to the farthest reaches of Mexico.

Amid the uproar, the special prosecutor kept studying videos and photos. He hauled in rally organizers and securi-ty men for questioning. The finger of guilt turned back on the small army of bodyguards who had failed to stop the point-blank shooting. The more that incredulous Mexicans found out about the sleazy cops, ex-cops and paracops entrusted with the safety of the nation's next president, the more the prosecutor looked like he was on the right track. Carlos Monsiváis, the writer and cultural commentator, summed up the ensuing saga of suspected treachery and gal-loping paranoia: "It seems that Luis Donaldo Colosio con-ducted his campaign surrounded by imminent executioners, and that there is nothing more dangerous than having a secu-rity force, just as there is nothing more vulnerable than belonging to a security force."

The PRI's local crowd-control team, Grupo Tucán, were ready-made villains. Their ranks included cashiered officers and suspected criminals. Their title was either a bellicose Spanish acronym for the words "Everyone United Against National Action" (the opposition party) or a nickname inspired by an imagined resemblance of the hooked nose of their chief, Rodolfo Rivapalacio, a former state police com-mander, to the beak of a toucan, a tropical bird. The volun-teer guards had built reputations as thugs, torturers and extortionists during the rule of former Governor Xicotencatl

Leyva, a PRI dinosaur par excellence. The larcenous excesses of his administration had prompted President Salinas to
force "Xico's" removal, paving the way for the PAN victory
in 1989. So the ruling party in Baja had a semblance of a
motive: revenge against the Salinistas for surrendering their
state. As the press published new photos and asked pointed
questions, fear and loathing filled the drafty, cavernous
headquarters of the PRI across the border highway from the
Tijuana River levee. Every move in Lomas Taurinas became
sinister, every contact with the suspects conspiratorial.
Reputations were stained; careers were trashed. Once-cocky
bosses fended off accusations. "What, now me?" stammered
Roberto Ventura, the organizational secretary of the party's
municipal council, when two reporters confronted him with
a front-page newspaper photo showing him near Aburto and
Tranquilino at the rally. The rather adventurous caption suggested that he was talking to them. Ventura bolted from the
room and closeted himself in an office with a campaign
worker named Mario Alberto Carrillo, the little sandy-haired
man who had apparently stumbled in front of Colosio just
before the shooting. Ventura was never accused of anything;
Carrillo was not so lucky. In another dramatic announcement after Easter, special prosecutor Montes rebaptized
Carrillo forever as El Clavadista (roughly, the Diver) and
accused him of having been in league with the assassin. The
Diver had hit the dirt on purpose to block Colosio, Montes
charged.

Armed with a pointer and an enhanced video, the moon-
faced Montes told a spellbound television audience that
Colosio had been the victim of a "concerted action" by at
least seven conspirators. Five were in custody: Aburto,
Tranquilino, the Mayorals and Rodolfo Rivapalacio, the
security team boss. At large were the Diver and an unnamed
guard in sunglasses who had ducked at Colosio's left.

left. Colosio's military guards testified that the suspects had obstructed and distracted them. Rivapalacio had organized the local team and penned Tranquilino's name on a typewritten personnel list at the last minute. He had also, according to Tranquilino's wife, shown unusual interest in Tranquilino's attendance by going personally to his house to recruit him. Rivapalacio's background was questionable. During his thirty-year career, he led the state police homicide and burglary squads. A veteran detective described him as the "unofficial chief" of the force at a time when bribe-taking was especially blatant. Rivapalacio had thrived financially and politically, acquiring a mansion with a pool and an apartment building. He was a leader of the municipal PRI. His fortunes had not suffered from the fact that the San Diego Police considered him their prime suspect in a vicious attempted murder north of the border in 1987: an assailant stabbed Rivapalacio's ex-wife seventeen times and shot her male companion. Rivapalacio denied involvement, but he also declined to cross the border to be questioned by San Diego detectives. "He's sharp and he's slick," said the fellow Baja detective. "Of all the suspects, he's the only one I could see being involved in something as big as the assassination."

Rivapalacio was free within two weeks. Despite the nation's lynch-mob mood, the judge presiding over the case ruled that the evidence associating him with a plot wasn't there. The other suspects were ordered held for trial. The image of conspirators enclosing Colosio in a deadly circle was compelling, a scene reminiscent of a Mexican historical mural. Like a mural, however, it was one-dimensional. Beyond fuzzy images, nothing confirmed a conspiracy. The suspects were not superspies. Innocent or guilty, they were pawns. Except for Rivapalacio, they fit the term coined for them by mystery writer Paco Ignacio Taibo II: "lumpenpolice." Their single conceivable motive was economic gain.

Having crossed swords with Mayoral and Rivapalacio in cases of alleged police abuse, Víctor Clark Alfaro said such a conspiracy had to have orginated with plotters above the Grupo Tucán or the state party. "These men did not have political reasons to commit an assassination," Clark said. "They would have to have been paid by someone. Their profile, their intellectual level, is not made for this."

The investigation produced no convincing proof of previous contact with Aburto or a mastermind, no clandestine meetings, no swollen bank accounts. The one nagging question that Rodolfo Mayoral and Sánchez never completely answered was whether they had spoken to Aburto at the rally, as the photos seemed to indicate; they said they did not know him. The Mayorals and Sánchez spent a year in Almoloya de Juárez, Mexico's most feared prison, a high-tech fortress populated by a gangster aristocracy of drug lords, fallen politicians and professional killers. The trio withstood physical abuse—the battered Sánchez appeared in court in a wheelchair and a neck brace—and psychological abuse. Rodolfo Mayoral later said: "A supposed psychologist came to see me and asked how I was doing after six months of being in Almoloya. I knew that I had only been there a month and that they were trying to make me doubt my mental health. At one point we were . . . put in a cell next to Aburto. I heard the guards telling him to implicate us because it would be easier on him if four people shared the blame. . . . One day I heard Tranquilino screaming. He was yelling for us to look out our cell windows to the yard because the guards were beating up his wife and brother. When I told him there was nothing there, he accused me of also being against him."

No one broke down and confessed because, they insisted, there was nothing to confess. Aburto denied any link to the three suspects. A Tijuana lawyers' association took up their

defense. The Mayoral family, living shabbily in a condemned housing project on the outskirts of town, spent a
small fortune on lawyers and collect phone calls to the
prison. After a judge acquitted and released the trio in 1995,
the crusty, gray-mustached Vicente Mayoral looked as if he
had spent ten years behind bars, not one. He had lost weight.
His skin had a cadaverous tinge. "The false accusations were
criminal acts against my family," Mayoral told reporters
after returning home, speaking in a slow, hoarse voice, the
web of wrinkles around his eyes deepening as he dragged on
a cigarette. "These were abuses that resulted from a hypothesis that was invented maliciously. . . . My son and I have
absolutely nothing to hide. The action we took was honest
and honorable. We risked our lives to arrest a person whom
I saw with a gun in his hand." For the Mayorals and others,
the limbo of the Colosio case was inescapable and
Kafkaesque. Carlos Monsiváis called it "a carnival of perpe-
trators who multiply in the same cell and suspects . . . who
are neither innocent nor guilty, but rather members of that
new species, the inhabitants of the 'lines of investigation' of
Lomas Taurinas."

The accused conspirators spent a year behind bars, but the
special prosecutor cleared them much sooner. Realizing
within weeks that his theory was crumbling, Montes brought
in a team of police forensic experts from Spain to assess the
videos and photos. Their stern verdict: the so-called concerted action looked like a bunch of people pushing and
shoving at a crowded public event. In June, Montes
announced his new conclusion: Aburto was a lone assassin
after all. This outcome had been predicted by a high-ranking
U.S. federal agent who assisted Mexican police on leads
north of the border. President Salinas picked the wrong
sleuth, the U.S. agent said. "It was like bringing in a dentist
to investigate."

But Baja Senator Fernando Gómez, the liaison between Montes and the state government, applauded Montes for his painful public reversal. "He couldn't live with the idea that he was convicting innocent persons," Gómez said. "He was very courageous."

The former special prosecutor later implied that he lacked support from President Salinas, reportedly describing him as more concerned with his own image than with the progress of the case. Although Salinas had appointed Montes, the president's maneuvers were typically inscrutable. The filing of the conspiracy charges reduced the immediate heat on Salinas, who appeared to distance himself from the special prosecutor and his multiple-suspect theory.

The hastily chosen replacement candidate, former Colosio campaign manager and electoral neophyte Ernesto Zedillo, faced a hotly contested election in August. Salinas wanted the case resolved and behind him. Unfortunately, Montes had opened the door to the idea of a massive conspiracy within Colosio's own party. It would not shut. Amid popluar outcry, Salinas appointed a new special prosecutor. The spate of "breakthroughs" died down, but the muddled denouement only stoked speculation. The passage of time made everything seem the work of a malevolent master puppeteer: The selection of such a physically treacherous site for the rally. The chaos and the breakdown of security. The nefarious background of the campaign security chiefs. The loud music that drowned out the shots. The investigation that lurched from one suspect to multiple suspects and back again. Even the fact that Lomas Taurinas was inundated with federal public works funds became fodder for distrust. A benevolent invasion of bulldozers and workmen built a towering statue of Colosio, a recreation center and a cement esplanade that wiped away the ungainly dirt plaza—and, Tijuanans muttered, the scene of the crime.

After Ernesto Zedillo of the PRI won the presidential election in 1994, the Colosio case was among his most urgent challenges. Not only did it symbolize lawlessness and impunity to many Mexicans, solving the case represented a personal obligation for Zedillo as the fallen candidate's campaign manager. The third special prosecutor, Pablo Chapa, returned to the videos. He reopened the question of the opposite bullet trajectories and the much-criticized explanation that Colosio had spun around between the shots. In February 1995, Chapa unleashed his bombshell. He said the crime scene had been altered and that the bullet that allegedly hit Colosio in the abdomen had been planted in the dirt where he fell. Rather than Aburto's gun, Chapa claimed, a second gun fired the second shot. Federal police in Tijuana arrested Othón Cortez, a chauffeur and aide for ruling-party bosses, and charged him with being the second gunman. Investigators pulled over Cortez, twenty-eight, as he drove with his wife and two small children. They hustled him away to a safe house where, Cortez later charged, they beat him, sprayed carbonated liquid up his nose and otherwise tried to extract a confession. The arrest revived all the paranoia and anticipation that had gripped Tijuana a year earlier. Cortez was as much an operative of the political machine, albeit at a low rank, as Aburto was solitary. Cortez knew many of the politicians, police and journalists in town. He had done errands for General Domiro García, Colosio's chief bodyguard, in the past. After the assassination, he drove General García to the airport.

The video of the crime showed Cortez visible from the shoulders up, standing just to the left and slightly behind Colosio as Aburto's pistol appeared from the right. The alleged second gunman appeared to nod abruptly before the first shot. But Cortez was right-handed and there was no gun in his right hand; when the images came back into focus, both his hands were visible and empty. If he really had fired, he got rid of the gun with amazing speed. Three witnesses now said they had seen him with a gun. But their accounts were less than compelling. Only one said he had seen him fire, and he happened to be an eccentric sculptor whose accounts were meandering and less than credible. In the continuing Kafkaesque logic of the investigation, Chapa also charged two more security men who had testified to seeing Aburto fire two shots. Since the new theory was based on the existence of a second gunman, the two guards were accused of perjury.

Now the public had a conspiracy. But the case against Cortez unraveled, proving as weak as the previous theory. A two-gun conspiracy and cover-up entailed many aspects that never surfaced: the second gun, contact with conspirators. During the year after the assassination, Cortez had gone about his business as before, an eager, glad-handing flunky of police and politicians. Far from dodging the press, his family rose to his defense. The fallout from the arrest brought two main results: General García, who for a fateful moment had been separated by the crowd from his assigned spot at Colosio's back, came under suspicion because of his reputed friendship with Cortez. The general denied guilt. The second result was predictable: frustration and confusion mounted. Chapa's doubt about the angle of the second shot was more understandable than his explanation. Theorists wondered whether Othón Cortez or someone else had been assigned to kill Aburto, Jack Ruby–style, and botched the job. Or whether one of the various men who pulled guns after the first discharge had shot Colosio accidentally and then remained silent forever, convinced no one would believe him.

Months passed without progress. The premise appeared increasingly far-fetched. A mastermind who found an

Aburto willing to pose as a mad gunman would be too clever
to muddle things with a second shooter. The story repeated
itself: another humble, working-class, ground-level suspect
was behind bars. Investigators were no closer to catching
anyone with power and money. Cortez was ultimately
acquitted and the case went back to square one.

"If they keep looking at the videos, they are going to
arrest everyone in the videos," said José Luis Pérez
Canchola. "The investigation has not deviated from the
videos and the direct actors. It has to go higher, to a motive,
to a mastermind. The tragedy is that in order to calm public
opinion, these arrests have to be made."

While Mexicans called for the masterminds to be brought
to justice, political and economic crises immolated the public image of Carlos Salinas. Soon the president and José
Cordoba, his chief of staff, became the nation's designated
villains. They were routinely and loudly accused of being
what Mexicans called "the intellectual authors" of the assassination. Cordoba was an aloof figure whose Spanish-
French ancestry made him the object of popular derision. As
the second-ranking man in the administration, he functioned
as the president's Cardinal Richelieu, attending particularly
to matters of national security—a role that made him the
focus of allegations about links to the drug cartels. The president, intentionally or not, cast a cloud over Cordoba days
after the assassination by sending him abruptly into the gild-
ed exile of an international banking post in Washington. And
Colosio's aged father, Luis Colosio Fernández declared that
Cordoba "had a lot to do" with his son's killing and called
for the former presidential chief of staff to be investigated.

Colosio's father did not offer proof. But the accusations
stemmed from allegations of top-level corruption in the
Salinas regime, the feud that dogged the Colosio campaign
and the perception that Salinas wanted to remain the power

behind Colosio's throne. The shadow candidacy of Camacho, the former mayor of Mexico City, greatly damaged Colosio. Colosio reportedly felt that Camacho's flirtation with a maverick bid had presidential approval: a Machiavellian thrust by Salinas against his own candidate. Colosio's allies and family asserted that the president and his chief of staff had felt threatened by Colosio's increasing independence and had even pressured him to step down. The Colosio camp cited an intriguing exhibit: a private letter written to Colosio four days before the assassination by campaign manager Zedillo, the protégé of Cordoba who replaced the candidate and catapulted from bureaucratic obscurity to the presidency. Zedillo's March 19 letter alluded to an apparent rift with Salinas, recommending that Colosio establish a "political alliance with the President. You must offer him all your loyalty and support so that he can conclude his mandate with great dignity." Zedillo urged the candidate not to criticize the government without prior approval. And he warned that Camacho was cultivating the "new priorities" of President Salinas in the hope of "substitution of the candidate." This rare inside revelation was a bombshell. "The letter is of utmost importance," wrote commentator Heberto Castillo, "because it establishes with clarity that there were serious differences between Salinas and his candidate."

Salinas and Cordoba had the means and resources to create an Aburto and sabotage the investigation. Motive was another question, however. Colosio acquired the inevitable posthumous halo of the noble savior, but no matter how sincere his rhetoric, he was a product of the system. His apparent dispute with Salinas was a legitimate line of inquiry that was not properly explored. But nothing known about Colosio—so far—offers a resounding reason why Salinas would have wanted to wipe out his own political offspring.

Sipping coffee in the book-lined study of his pleasant home in Mexico City, a former cabinet official in the Salinas administration shook his head. He found the accusations against Salinas illogical. Even the March 6 speech by Colosio, portrayed in some quarters as a landmark broadside against the system, was "part of the ritual. All the candidates do it." The former minister offered another theory. He blamed the drug mafias, suggesting that the assassination was a Colombian-style act of terrorism that fulfilled its objective of diverting the police from the fight against the underworld. "Who benefited? The security apparatus has been occupied with the assassination. Drug mafias have grown. Instead of chasing the ten biggest narcos, they are focused on this. The distractive action has been enormous."

As for the speculation that Salinas wanted to replace Colosio, the minister asserted that violence was not necessary. "In Mexico, if a president wants to get rid of a candidate, sixty seconds is more than enough time. He calls the candidate and tells him."

Reforma columnist Raymundo Riva Palacio, a noted commentator, also went against the grain by agreeing that common sense absolves Salinas. He wrote: "During a decade he prepared Colosio to make him great; he trained him, prepared him, took care of him; he built him a team and later a candidacy. With him the Salinas project would not only continue, it would create the best environment for the ex-president." Riva was less charitable to the former presidential chief of staff, however, suggesting that Colosio would have shut Cordoba out of the new government. "Cordoba did not have a prolonged future with Colosio. But he did with his old friend Ernesto Zedillo. . . . So Cordoba had a motive to want the elimination of Colosio: to move up Zedillo."

In testimony and in public statements, Salinas and

Cordoba denied wrongdoing. Salinas declared that, immediately after the assassination, hard-line PRI leaders tried to
pressure him to choose a replacement candidate from their
ranks. He said he did not know if there was a plot to kill
Colosio, but he suspected a plot to impose an Old Guard
candidate.

In fact, another school of thought painted Salinas and
Cordoba as the secondary victims of Old Guard ruling-party
chieftains intent on gaining control of the presidency. The
methods of the dinosaurs were legend: vote fraud, repression, alliances with drug mafias, murders of critics and foes.
The dinosaurs were automatic suspects in the Colosio case
and in the eyes of those who believed that Mexico's multiple woes in 1994 were part of a concerted destabilizing campaign. Salinas's depiction of himself as the martyr of
democracy fighting off the dark forces of the past, however,
ran up against contradictions. Some old-school politicians,
drug traffickers and other undesirables prospered during his
watch. Moreover, if anyone knew who stood to benefit from
Colosio's death and why, if anyone had the capacity to
amass information and decipher the machinations of the
elite, it was the president and his chief of staff. Salinas may
have lacked a motive to kill Colosio, but the idea that he
knew more than he disclosed was easier to accept, critics
said.

"Surely he has a great deal of privileged information,"
said Senator Alfredo Ling Altamirano of the PAN, who
served on a legislative commission monitoring the case. "It
is obvious that he has information about the internal struggle. If we are talking about a political motive, this is a line
of investigation. . . . There are power groups, and Carlos
Salinas knows who they are and who leads them."

Despite the almost unanimous, almost religious belief in
a conspiracy, no one conclusively linked the crime to the

political backdrop, the triggerman to a mastermind. Facts,
let alone proof, were lacking. A hard-nosed debater could
mount a rebuttal along the lines of *Case Closed,* the book
that concludes that Lee Harvey Oswald acted alone. And the
JFK assassination has aroused more inherent suspicion than
the Colosio case because of the murder of Oswald and
because of the physical difficulty of the single-sniper scenario in Dallas. In the Colosio case, the theory that defies
popular sentiment and common sense remains the strongest
by default: the deranged lone gunman.

"JFK was a conspiracy," said Jesús Blancornelas, the editor of *Zeta,* who clung with contrarian tenacity to the lone
assassin thesis. "But it is the assassination of Robert
Kennedy that bears a great deal of resemblance to the case
of Aburto. Or the assassination of Yitzhak Rabin in Israel."

"There are only two truths," Blancornelas concluded. "A
man died. And Aburto fired."

The absence of a conspiracy would be the ultimate irony
in a society riven by intrigue and well-founded paranoia
about official skullduggery. It would mean that the assassination was a coincidence without connection to the surrounding web of conflict. The portrait of the assassination is
unfinished and ambiguous, allowing more than one inter-
pretation. The Colosio case was not just about the crime
itself. It was about the context, which made the conspiracy
theories ever harder to resist. The shooting in the border
shantytown brought to light the secrets of the Mexican
power structure, showing that at times it functioned much
like the Tijuana underworld. The context came down to two
words: drugs and corruption.

CHAPTER SIX

Narco-politics:
Benítez and Beyond

In February 1994, a month before the Colosio assassination, the Mexican underworld was at war. The mafia headed by Héctor (Guero) Palma and the imprisoned Chapo Guzmán was fighting the Arellano brothers for control of the smuggling corridor in Baja California. The dominions of Guzmán and Palma extended across northwest Mexico and overlapped with the turf of the discreet, increasingly formidable Amado Carrillo Fuentes of the Ciudad Juárez mafia. The Palma/Guzmán alliance had good relations with Carrillo, who had pioneered the use of big jets to transport ten-ton shipments of cocaine; his nickname was "Lord of the Skies." Carrillo was simultaneously marching west toward Baja and east to challenge Juan García Abrego, the lord of the Gulf cartel, whose clout reputedly reached into the inner circle of the president of Mexico. García had been the dominant kingpin of the Salinas years, but as the administration came to a close, the drug mafias were fighting for position—like the political mafias with which they allegedly maintained alliances for mutual profit and protection.

On the evening of February 27, three weeks before the Colosio assassination, a killer on a motorcycle accelerated alongside a black Cadillac traveling seventy-five miles per

hour on Interstate-5 north of Los Angeles. His marksman-
ship was spectacular: all five shots from a 9-millimeter pistol hit the driver of the Cadillac and the passenger in the
front seat. Los Angeles County sheriff's detectives identified
the dead men as Manuel Salvador González, thirty-seven,
and Marco Antonio Trejo, thirty-five, who was Salvador's
driver and aide. The two reputed drug traffickers were
Mexicans who divided their time between homes in the Los
Angeles area and the state of Jalisco. Their pockets yielded
a treasure trove of clues.

Salvador's address book was a who's who of drug traffickers. He carried the business card of Liborio Nuñez
Aguirre, a jailed money launderer for the Guzmán organization. Weeks earlier, U.S. drug agents reportedly conducted
surveillance on the two victims as they drove around the
state meeting with suspected gangsters. The two were
ambushed while returning from such a rendezvous in
Bakersfield, according to investigators. Salvador, whose
brother was prominent in the methamphetamine trade, had
associated with a variety of traffickers of cocaine and
methamphetamine, including mobs that did not get along,
detectives said.

Complicating matters further, the victims' families and
other witnesses told surprised detectives that the dead men
were officials of the Mexican government and worked for
the Colosio campaign as security guards and collectors of
campaign funds. Salvador had worked in security for past
PRI campaigns in his native Guadalajara, the relatives said.
Shortly before the freeway murder, Salvador excitedly told
his family that he would soon assume a more prominent
security post with the Colosio campaign. The DEA looked
into the case as well, and investigators grew convinced that
the dead men were collecting contributions for the Colosio
campaign from drug traffickers. The documents on

Salvador's body suggested either that he had influential contacts or that he went to extraordinary lengths to gather inside political information. Salvador carried business cards and handwritten notes listing names and telephone numbers of top officials in the Colosio campaign, the PRI and the Mexican government. Prominent among the handwritten entries were the name and a phone number of Colosio's security chief, General Domiro García of the presidential guard (Estado Mayor), and several other officials of the presidential guard. Salvador's notes also included the names and numbers of Fernando Ortiz Arana, then the president of the PRI; an aide in the presidential press office; and police officials, customs agents and prosecutors in the states of Baja, Jalisco and Sonora. A scribbled note included a reference to Colosio's private secretary, but no phone number. Salvador carried a badge issued by the Mexican Congress and both a business card and a letter of introduction, the latter purportedly written by presidential chief of staff José Cordoba, identifying Salvador as "chief of northwest regional investigations" for the office of the presidency.

Mexican officials tried to quash the political angle. The PRI denied that the victims had any party affiliation. Mexican law enforcement officials also questioned the authenticity of the letter purportedly signed by Cordoba. They pointed out that the letter looked amateurish. It is not unusual in Mexico for gangsters—or public officials, or journalists—to flash credentials that are phony or have been issued indiscriminately. On the other hand, Salvador's parliamentary badge seemed genuine. It was canceled for unspecified reasons ten days before his death, according to a February 18 letter from the chief administrator of Mexico's chamber of deputies to the chief of parliamentary services. (The names of both those officials were also found in the victim's papers.)

In another peculiar twist, the freeway murders intersected with the 1993 narco-tunnel case in Tijuana in which gangsters had been overheard boasting about financial and social ties between the Reynoso brothers of Los Angeles, the Guzmán mafia and the Colosio campaign. The slain Salvador had been carrying the business card of a former employee and confidant of René Reynoso, the son of one of the executives. René was serving twenty-five years in prison for ordering a murder in Los Angeles—a crime that was also committed by a gunman on a motorcycle.

The investigation of the double murder on Interstate-5 bogged down in tensions between U.S. and Mexican law enforcement. The U.S. investigators remained convinced that Salvador and Trejo were simultaneously drug traffickers and Colosio campaign workers who collected drug money as contributions for the campaign. The likely motive of the murders was a methamphetamine rip-off; the likely killers had fled to Mexico. But investigators did not rule out the potential political aspects, especially after the subsequent flurry of murders in Baja involving both politics and drugs.

The freeway murders and the narco-tunnel case linked drug mafias to presidential politics. The cases suggested that drug mafias had tried to infiltrate the security and financing of the Colosio campaign before the assassination. It was a tangle of vague clues and unanswered questions: Was the presidential campaign receiving money and other forms of assistance from the Reynosos and other reputed drug lords? Would a Colosio presidency help some mafias and hurt others? Were gangsters fighting one another for access to the campaign? Why did a drug trafficker have phone numbers for the candidate's chief military bodyguard and top ruling-party officials? And did the I-5 murders have something to do with the Colosio assassination?

There were few answers. Some felt Colosio had been killed precisely because he had rejected the traffickers. And there was no smoking gun, such as a direct connection to Mario Aburto, Colosio's convicted assassin. Still, the freeway murders showed how the drug lords loomed over the treacherous landscape in which Colosio had run for president and been killed. The context of the Colosio assassination was a two-month surge of bloodshed in Baja during which the lines between drugs and politics dissolved. The narco-political violence in Tijuana offered a frightening vision of the anarchy that threatened Mexico. The tragedy played out in three acts. First came the March 3 shoot-out between federal and state police. Then Colosio. And finally the case of Federico Benítez, the director of public safety of Tijuana.

His friends called him Federico. The muckraking columnists of the Tijuana police pages ridiculed his rigid ways: they called him "Robocop." It was an ironic nickname. Upon becoming police chief in 1992, he had never worn a uniform, questioned a suspect or responded to a crime scene. He grew up in Tecate, a placid mountain town about an hour east of Tijuana known for a brewery, a health spa and the steep cliffside roads that separate the ninety thousand inhabitants from the rest of the world. A schoolmate remembers Federico Benítez as a serious, unathletic kid who got chosen for sports teams because of his height. "I could imagine him becoming a priest, maybe," the schoolmate said. "The last thing I would have imagined was that he would become a police chief." Benítez studied law. He worked for eighteen years as the manager of a *maquiladora* in Tijuana that assembled toys. His background and politics were solidly PANista: a career in the private sector, a devout Catholic, father of three. The administration of Governor Ernesto Ruffo Appel hired him in 1991 as a legal advisor, troubleshooting on matters such as juvenile justice. A year later, a sharp thirty-five-year-old architect named Héctor Osuna was elected mayor of Tijuana. Osuna had a lot of ideas for reinvigorating City Hall. He wanted an outsider to command the police, a "citizen chief" who would clean house. The mayor chose Benítez.

At forty, the new director of public safety was practically a father figure among the mayor's cadre of PANista whiz kids. And in the paint-peeling hallways of Tijuana law enforcement, Benítez stood out among the warhorse commanders in their leather jackets, boots and cowboy hats, pistols jammed in their waistbands. Benítez looked very much the technocrat in his big glasses and dark business suits. He was tall, gangling, severe. His face was narrow, acquiring a stern, bushy mustache that he grew and shaved off periodically. He walked with determined strides, angular elbows propelling him along. He was a valiant amateur: in that sense he resembled Javier Valenzuela, the founder of Grupo Beta. But Benítez did not share Valenzuela's political instincts or talent for inspiring loyalty. And he did not have the advantage of working with a small, carefully selected group of officers like Grupo Beta. Benítez embarked on a lonely crusade that left him surrounded by enemies and traitors.

In the course of fifteen months, Benítez fired four hundred officers, nearly a third of the municipal police force, more than the previous administration had dismissed in three years. He introduced human rights training. He raised salaries 20 percent and obtained new vehicles, guns, body armor, computers and communications equipment for the antiquated department. He modernized and professionalized the force, restructuring it into eighteen patrol areas designed to improve response times and break down barriers of fear and mistrust in the neighborhoods. He established bonds with the San Diego Police, the FBI and other U.S. agencies, whose investigators were always looking for a reliable ally south of the line. They realized he was not driven by the typical twin objectives: get rich and stay alive.

"We have never seen a chief like that in Tijuana who has gone out of his way to make a difference," said Assistant Chief George Saldamando of the San Diego Police. "He had vision."

When he met Benítez, Sergeant Vicente Villalvazo had dealt with countless *comandantes* in Tijuana. As the cross-border liaison of the San Diego Police intelligence squad, Villalvazo was one of those specialists who have developed out of necessity in U.S. agencies at the international line: A policeman who can go back and forth, speaks both languages, understands both systems and can maneuver in gray areas. Villalvazo had previously worked gangs, homicide, internal affairs. He was steeped in the complexities of Mexican culture and law enforcement. He rejected stereotypes and hoped for the best, but he had no illusions about his counterparts south of the border. He was cagey about trusting people. Chief Benítez succeeded in impressing this Chicano Diogenes; the incident with the polygraph did it.

Benítez asked Villalvazo for help because he wanted to administer a lie-detector test to some of his officers for an internal investigation. The polygraph machine owned by the Tijuana police was gathering dust because no one knew how to operate it. Villalvazo enlisted the help of a San Diego Police technician, who said the machine looked fine, but he needed to test it on someone. Startling his visitors from San Diego, Benítez volunteered immediately.

"I'll do it," Benítez said. "Right now. Go ahead, ask me anything you want." And he called his top aides into his office so they could watch him take the test.

Recalling the moment, Villalvazo, a husky man who speaks in a deep and gentle rumble, said: "I tell you what: I said I had another appointment and I left. I was afraid to get in an embarrassing situation, that he might get compromised by something he said in front of me."

Later, the technician reported that the test had turned into a full-fledged interrogation. Benítez answered a battery of questions about his integrity and passed with impeccable results. Unless Benítez was a psychopath, he was telling the truth. The technician told Villalvazo: "The guy's clean."

When you sat down and talked to Benítez, the stern visage faded. He could be engaging and playful. During an interview on Ash Wednesday, 1994, his eyes widened with adolescent enthusiasm as he described the heavy-duty motorcycles that he wanted to use for antigang patrols in rough terrain. Then he interrupted the interview and rose respectfully as Emilio Berlie, the city bishop, bustled into the chief's office. "You have to excuse me for a moment," Benítez said, grinning. "There is something I have to do. This is an important day." Benítez accompanied the bishop from his sparse office into the decrepit lobby of the one-story municipal headquarters on Eighth Street. The chief lined up with his uniformed officers to receive the traditional Ash Wednesday blessing from Bishop Berlie, who was assisted by a nun. When Benítez returned to his desk, the cross of ashes was still marked on his forehead, like a portent. Or a target.

Perhaps religious convictions forged Benítez's attitude toward his job, which was simple and personal. Lawbreaking was not to be tolerated. The job of every police officer, including the chief, was to prevent crime. When Benítez came across a truck disposing of old tires in one of the city's ubiquitous clandestine dumps, he personally escorted the driver to the federal environmental office to make sure he paid the fine. When his officers arrested agents of other police forces, his response broke the unwritten code: File charges. I don't care who they are. He enraged the racketeers who controlled immigrant smuggling, prostitution and gambling in the Zona Norte by shutting down a protection deal that had spread $100,000 a month among municipal commanders and down through the ranks.

Honest, inexperienced, PANista, Benítez was in every sense an outsider. The newspapers, still largely favorable to the PRI, pounded him. A City Hall aide and ally saw this as "a symptom that he was doing things well. He was affecting interests in very deeply rooted areas." But the chief could be abrasive and imperious; he alienated colleagues and subordinates. A veteran officer called him "a good organizer, but a bad policeman." The chief of another police agency in Tijuana remembers a telephone conversation in which Benítez demanded that he attend to a problem, shouted at him and hung up. Minutes later, Benítez called back and apologized for losing his temper. The fellow chief saw Benítez as a well-intentioned and courageous man whose methods were his downfall. "Not only was he inexpert in police work, he overcompensated for his insecurity by being impulsive and authoritarian. He made important changes without calculating the risks. He did not cultivate much support among his people."

The risks were the greatest in the arena where the chief charged the hardest: drugs. Technically, the mission of the city police was to patrol the streets and prevent crime; the federal police enforced drug laws. But with fifteen hundred officers, the municipal force was larger than the state or federal agencies and had the most direct contact with the citizens. At community meetings, people slipped the chief notes about the brazen street-level workings of the drug trade. Telephone tipsters reported houses where gangsters stored and shipped north stashes of cocaine and marijuana. The callers did not trust the state and federal police because the armed men guarding the shipments were sometimes state and federal agents.

"The citizens called him and they told him in this place they are unloading drugs, selling drugs," said María de los Angeles Villarino, the chief's secretary. "He advised his superiors at the city, state and federal levels. The citizens called and said, 'No one came.' He would go personally to the location and verify what was going on. He would radio state and federal police from the scene. That was how he worked with the citizens. Why did they call him? Because he would take their names and then he would call them personally. They would tell me, 'He won't call back.' And I would say, 'Yes, he will.' Gradually, this spread by word of mouth among the citizenry. That was how the major drug busts happened."

Benítez knew the municipal police were not supposed to meddle. But the underworld had bought off or scared off just about everybody else. This bothered him; he refused to stop his officers from searching suspicious vehicles or hitting obvious drug houses. Governor Ruffo liked the chief and began to rely on him for sensitive tasks as the governor grew wary of his own state police. On several occasions, Ruffo took Benítez aside and cautioned him about crossing the traffickers.

"Be careful," Ruffo urged him. "Don't get involved."

"What am I supposed to do if I run into them?" Benítez answered.

Later, Governor Ruffo recalled: "That was the way he was. He responded à la Federico Benítez."

The chief unleashed the Special Tactical Group and its indomitable chief, David Rubí. Acting on tips about convoys and stash houses, the Tactical Group racked up seizures of cocaine, marijuana, weapons. The municipal police confiscated more drugs in early 1994 than the Tijuana contingent of the federal police—the official antidrug agency. The threats against Benítez increased.

"He got bomb threats, death threats, calls to the chief's office," said Villarino, the secretary. "He never paid any attention."

Benítez ventured into a minefield of complex and shifting allegiances. The Arellano mafia retained its hold over the state police and agents in the federal ranks as well. But since the death of the cardinal of Guadalajara, lightning incursions by federal units from Mexico City kept the Arellanos off balance. The federal commanders who had engineered the arrest of Francisco Arellano in December 1993 were rewarded with top federal posts in Tijuana. They and other newly arrived federal commanders were rumored to be in league with the drug lords invading from Sonora in the east, the Guzmán-Palma alliance. The gangsters were fighting by proxy through the police forces. At least once a month in early 1994, the state police in Tijuana and Mexicali responded to reports of ominous armed groups of about thirty men riding in black Suburbans with tinted windows, who swaggered into restaurants and other public places. When challenged, the armed groups identified themselves as federal agents; the state police even recognized some of them. Yet the chief federal prosecutor in Tijuana said he knew nothing about it. The word on the street was that they were the personal retinue of Guero Palma, who was in town and flexing his muscles.

The tension burst into view with the machine-gun battle of the Third of March between federal antidrug agents and state police guarding one of the Arellanos. Federal prosecutors rather indiscriminately charged a dozen officials—state prosecutors, detectives, municipal police—in connection with the gunfight and the escape of the drug lord. Enraged by the death of the commander of the Arellano search team, the federal authorities flooded Tijuana with special brigades hunting the drug lords and accelerated a secret probe of corruption in Baja law enforcement. Their ultimate quarry was Juan Francisco Franco, the state attorney general, with whom Benítez did not particularly get along. Franco clung to his job as allegations hounded him; federal agents had already gone as far as searching his house. The federal investigation of him grew largely out of the persistence of Víctor Clark Alfaro, the human rights activist. Disgruntled state police officers helped Clark amass detailed allegations about the Arellanos' control of state law enforcement. The federal probe was a time bomb. If the Mexico City government brought down the state attorney general, it would be a shattering but risky attack on an opposition governor during an election year.

Federal police versus state police, Sonora gangsters versus Tijuana gangsters, PRI versus PAN—it was a grim panorama. The federal and state police stations, which are only about three blocks apart, resembled the camps of hostile armies waiting for the next clash. /

This was the climate in which presidential candidate Luis Donaldo Colosio came to Tijuana on March 23. Days earlier, the organizers of the local volunteer security team for the campaign met with Benítez about the preparations for the rally in Lomas Taurinas. The chief told the PRI security chiefs that he had heard rumblings about threats against Colosio's life, according to his secretary. "Members of the party were worried that there were threats about an assassination of Mr. Colosio," said the chief's secretary. "He tried to explain to them that there were threats, that the location was extremely dangerous. . . . I remember very clearly that they only asked for four patrol cars."

Nonetheless, the meticulous Benítez decided to set up the Tactical Group outside Lomas Taurinas. They intervened after Aburto shot Colosio; Benítez hurried to the hospital to take charge, clad in his usual suit and tie, pacing in the commotion with his radio at his ear. The next day, the chief supervised the inventory of the trunk that was turned in by a neighbor containing the assassin's possessions and papers, including Aburto's handwritten manifesto. Benítez played a visible, if ultimately secondary, role as the Colosio investigation evolved. At Governor Ruffo's direction, the chief responded to requests from the special prosecutor assigned to the Colosio case. Benítez dug into the shady histories of the Grupo Tucán security team. He requisitioned Aburto's factory personnel records and compared the signature with that on the assassin's handwritten manuscript. He compiled reports about the intervention of the municipal police after the assassination: they arrested the bloodstained agent of the National Security bureau running from the scene and recovered a spent bullet, apparently the one that hit Colosio in the abdomen. The chief was curious and clearly dubious about the official version, questioning the authenticity of Aburto's manifesto and the veracity of the testimony of his supposed girlfriend. Contrary to subsequent wishful thinking and melodramatic exaggeration, however, there is no evidence that Benítez conducted a parallel investigation or stumbled onto an earthshaking break in the assassination case.

"He never gave any motivation to think that he was personally interested in the case," said Governor Ruffo. "He was basically providing information that was requested of him. But it was not like he was involved in some kind of personal investigation."

What Benítez did was slightly less risky. In contrast to the secretive federal investigators, he was open and vocal. He expressed misgivings about the portrayal of Aburto as a lone assassin and noted contradictions in the official version, raising the possibility of a conspiracy and a second gunman.

Instead of the usual local reporters sniping at him, correspondents from Mexico City and the United States sought out the chief because he was a rare forthright voice. Benítez received them with good cheer, relishing the chance to swap theories and delve into the subculture of ruling-party intrigue which the assassination had exposed. He appeared to be enjoying himself.

The public was obsessed with the Colosio case. Meanwhile, Benítez was confronting a drug underworld that had dropped any pretense of discretion. On several occasions, the municipal police had encountered interference from other agencies during drug arrests. In April, Benítez responded to the scene of a standoff between the Tactical Group and turncoat federal and state police officers who were guarding two tons of northbound cocaine at a warehouse. The rival cops told the chief that the next move was up to him. He backed down and withdrew his officers. Afterward, he told his secretary that he had narrowly averted a bloodbath. "I am risking my life, my family's lives and the lives of the Tactical Group," the chief said.

The drug lords decided that enough was enough. The chief posed no dire threat, but he was obstinate. He made them look bad. "He was a pain in the ass, more than anything else," explained a DEA agent who knew Tijuana well. "The position of municipal chief can be pretty powerful, if you want it to be. They wanted to make an example of him."

Sometime around April 18, the gangsters reached out to the chief through the standard intermediaries—his fellow cops. The details remain hazy, but investigators believe Benítez attended two sit-downs. They alleged that the first took place in a restaurant or coffee shop, probably in the twin-towered Gran Hotel (formerly the Fiesta Americana), a plush skyscraper hotel on Agua Caliente Boulevard. Benítez met with Rodolfo García Gaxiola, a federal commander who had just arrived in Tijuana leading a special brigade from Sonora, according to charges filed by state prosecutors. García Gaxiola was only about twenty-eight, poised, a hotshot. He owned ranches and houses in Sonora. He had survived a nasty public spat with an army general who accused him of protecting Sonoran traffickers. His two brothers were also federal commanders. The García Gaxiolas rose rapidly thanks to sponsors in Mexico City, the Sonora government and, allegedly, the drug mafias.

At least one other federal official acompanied García Gaxiola to the meeting, according to the investigation by the Baja state police. Benítez brought along a municipal commander. The message from the mafia was simple: Benítez was interfering with business. Important people were prepared to compensate him generously if he agreed to call off the dogs. They offered him $100,000 a month.

Benítez refused. "I am not going after anyone intentionally," he said. "But I am going to do my job. I am going to do what I have to do."

"Very well," came the response. "Then we will also do what we have to do."

Benítez meticulously noted the meeting in his agenda, according to investigators. Shortly afterward, according to some versions, Benítez attended another meeting. This time, Benítez reportedly found himself sitting across the table from a kingpin who was wanted by the federal police: Ismael Higuera, aka El Mayel, the acting field operations boss of the Arellano clan. The fugitive gangster's nonchalant presence in public set the tone: the Arellanos still owned Tijuana. Once again, Mayel offered money. Once again, Benítez declined.

Benítez knew he had crossed a line. He told Mayor Osuna and other officials what had happened. He was not very expansive, and the mayor and his aides did not ask a lot of questions. During the final week of April, in fact, the chief's secretary alleges that the mayor, the attorney general and the governor avoided phone calls from Benítez. The chief kept putting in long hours. He wrote a report for the upcoming visit of a congressional committee looking into the Colosio assassination. He prepared for an offensive by opponents on the city council who wanted to evaluate his performance as a prelude to firing him. On April 27, he was talking to a friend from City Hall when a secretary brought in a sheaf of documents sent over by the federal police. Benítez grimaced. "Look at this," he told his visitor. "We caught these five guys this morning with money and crystal methamphetamine and now they let them go. We catch five in the morning, they let five go in the afternoon. This is what I deal with every day."

On April 28, Benítez attended the inaugural meeting of a community forum on public safety. He looked tired and distracted. In the afternoon, he had a long talk with his wife about insurance policies, bank accounts, family papers, what to do if anything happened to him. Back at the office, he sat down and talked to María de los Angeles Villarino. They discussed the standoff over the two tons of cocaine, and the $100,000 offer. He said he was disgusted with his own aides, who had urged him to accept the bribe. "He felt completely betrayed," Villarino said.

Shortly after 8 p.m., a call came in: a bomb scare at the Tijuana airport. The threat arrived by a strangely circuitous route. An anonymous caller phoned the Mexico City offices of Miguel Montes, the special prosecutor in the Colosio assassination case. The perplexed Montes relayed the information to Governor Ruffo in Mexicali, who informed the authorities in Tijuana. Benítez stayed in his office and monitored the police response by radio. When he was satisfied it was a false alarm, he left the station. He needed a haircut and the barber had agreed to wait for him. The chief and his bodyguard, Ramón Alarid, climbed into a blue-and-white city-issued pickup truck. As was his custom, Benítez drove. He maneuvered through the traffic in the Revolución district and merged onto the Vía Rápida, the anemically lighted crosstown expressway, speeding under bridges, curling southeast away from downtown.

The federal police carried out the ambush with textbook precision, according to investigators. It recalled the double murder on the freeway in Los Angeles. It was the antithesis of the Colosio assassination: fast, clean, a lonely place, an excellent getaway route. Professional. The killers used at least two vehicles, a white Jeep Cherokee and a red Ford Bronco. A federal commander probably coordinated the operation by radio. The Cherokee pulled in front of the pickup truck and slowed, forcing Benítez to reduce speed as well. The Bronco swung alongside the chief on the driver's side of the pickup truck. The shooter aimed an AK-47 at Benítez out the window. Despite the adrenaline, the darkness, the moving vehicles, the flesh-and-blood target, the shooter was steady as a surgeon.

"Every bullet he fired hit that man," a DEA agent said afterward. "The bodyguard was killed by rounds that passed through Benítez."

The chief's truck careened onto the shoulder of the expressway and crashed, partially overturning. The Cherokee and Bronco roared away. Minutes later, according to one account, two of the federal commanders who took part in the murder stood on the front steps of federal police headquarters, smoking cigarettes. Around them, sirens wailed and lights flashed as a citywide dragnet of officers set up meaningless roadblocks.

During a memorial on the plaza in front of City Hall two days later, Mayor Héctor Osuna looked haggard behind the

glasses that gave him the air of a graduate student.
Delivering his eulogy in front of an honor guard and the two
coffins, Mayor Osuna declared: "The society is tired of this
horror story." The scene at City Hall suggested a state of
siege. The Tactical Group manned battle stations around the
building and at the mayor's office. Bulletproof vests were
requisitioned after a caller phoned in a curt warning: "The
mayor is next."

Mayor Osuna was effective and visionary in many ways.
He could take credit for dramatic improvements in the city's
neglected infrastructure: streets, sewers, flood control. His
proposal to create a master plan for urban development was
unique in Latin America. But the Benítez case overwhelmed
him. Although he had lived in Tijuana most of his life, Osuna
apparently did not realize, or did not want to realize, how
tough the city could be, especially if you tried to change it.
He came out of a technocratic, upper-middle-class world of
upstart politics that did not prepare him or his inner circle for
the narco-realities of the border. An official who attended a
long late-night meeting in the mayor's office after the murder
said, not unsympathetically, that the mayor and his youthful
aides were visibly distraught. The mayor speedily appointed
a new police chief, an old-timer who wasted no time raising
the white flag. He made it clear that the city police would no
longer search suspected drug vehicles or otherwise mess
around with drug cases. Seizures plummeted.

Almost immediately, the Baja state authorities had a very
good idea of who had killed Benítez, as did the FBI and the
DEA. All the clues and suspicions pointed to the federal
police. But nobody was about to make public accusations,
much less arrests, after the federal forces unloaded another
broadside five days later. On a sunny afternoon, Sergio
Ortiz, the deputy state attorney general, arrived at his offices
in the state courthouse. A man with a revolver accosted him

on the front sidewalk, which bustled with court officials, lawyers and citizens. The man identified himself as a federal agent and told Deputy Attorney General Ortiz he was under arrest. The bearded, low-key prosecutor protested that he was not armed and that he would respond to the arrest warrant voluntarily.

"Either you come with me," the federal agent snapped, "or we are going to kill each other right here." Grabbing hold of the state's second-ranking law enforcement official by the back of his belt, he stuck the pistol in Ortiz's ribs and hustled him down the street to a waiting pickup truck. Thinking at first that Ortiz had been kidnapped, the municipal Tactical Group and state police led by a young prosecutor named Hodín Gutiérrez chased the pickup to federal police headquarters. Rushing to the front steps, the pursuers met a row of "goat horns": assault rifles wielded by federal agents in black raid uniforms, who shouted, "That's as far as you get, bastards!" Ammunition clips clattered as both sides racked automatic weapons to the firing mode. At that moment, the Republic of Mexico and the state of Baja California reached the brink of war. Then Raúl Loza, the bespectacled, black-mustached chief of the federal police in Tijuana, spotted a glowering David Rubí, chief of the Tactical Group of the municipal police, at the forefront of the opposing forces; the two were on amiable terms despite the tensions. "*Compadre*," Loza called out soothingly, "one moment!"

The moment passed; cool heads prevailed. The would-be rescuers fell back. A hundred heavily armed federal agents deployed onto the streets and rooftops around the headquarters, the calculated show of force turning the Río Zone into occupied territory. After interrogating Ortiz, federal authorities charged him with obstruction of justice in the shoot-out between federal and state police two months earlier, when he had been the highest-ranking state official to respond to the scene. They accused him of aiding the escape of the Arellano drug lord and locked him up in the La Mesa state penitentiary. The deputy attorney general was held in the prison director's office because the director, Jorge Alberto Duarte, was a colleague of Ortiz's on the law faculty of the Autonomous University of Baja California and feared he would be eaten alive by the inmates.

The federal agents made the arrest on the orders of Rodolfo García Gaxiola, the same commander who allegedly offered the bribe to Chief Benítez—and became the top suspect in the chief's murder. The federal forces transported Ortiz to the prison in an ostentatious armed convoy of Chevrolet Suburbans and Jeep Cherokees which stopped traffic and provided stirring footage for evening news programs on both sides of the border. Most of the Suburbans and Cherokees bore California license plates; police in San Diego were not surprised to discover that records checks showed many of the vehicles had been stolen in the United States. San Diego politicians were outraged. County supervisor Brian Bilbray said: "I think all of us who wanted to encourage free trade across the border did not mean this kind of free trade."

Two months of turmoil had boiled over. The state police, in league with drug lords, were accused of killing a federal commander in a shoot-out. An assassin had killed the presidential candidate, whose own campaign guards were suspects in the assassination. The federal police, in league with drug lords, were suspected of killing the city police chief. The federal police had arrested the deputy state attorney general and charged him with corruption. The scandalous parade of stolen vehicles taking Ortiz to jail crystallized the sense that the institutions of social order had broken down. It seemed that anything could happen next.

The aftermath brought another twist. Not only was Ortiz charged with protecting gangsters, federal agents said they were investigating him in connection with the murder of Benítez as well. Press officials in the office of the president of Mexico passed on a supposed tip that the federal police had the goods on Ortiz. The Baja deputy attorney general had bugged Benítez's phones, the tipsters said, and learned that the chief was gathering incriminating evidence against him for the governor. On its face, this allegation was odd. The police chief and the deputy attorney general were both close to the governor. In fact, the "tip" evaporated. Ortiz was never charged or implicated in the murder of the chief; he was acquitted of the charges that were filed. The campaign aimed at the national and foreign press by the federal authorities added to the impression that the government of Baja was under concerted attack.

On May 5, a national holiday, Governor Ernesto Ruffo took stock of his predicament. He was holed up in the air-conditioned sanctuary of the gubernatorial residence on a quiet, tree-lined street in Mexicali. In the front hall of the mansion, plainclothes detectives lounged by a rack of shotguns and a bank of security video monitors. The governor had never been fond of entourages and ostentation. His trademark was his unobtrusive style. Now he had tripled the size of his security detail and hurried in and out of public appearances surrounded by a phalanx of guards.

"This is a dangerous game," Ruffo said. "And I don't even want to call it a game, because I never wanted to be a player in such things. But well, these are things that fall into my area, and what can I do? Hopefully after this I can live a peaceful life."

The diminutive Ruffo wore a tan safari-type outfit with short sleeves and an open collar. Despite all that had happened during the past two months, he retained his jovial air.

But he seemed more deliberate, as if weighed down by what he had experienced. After years devoted to more civilized struggles—election reform, decentralization of federal power—violence and scandal had engulfed him and his government. The damage to Baja's image had been devastating. If there was a dark hand behind the Colosio murder and the rest of the strife, Ruffo was not alone in suspecting that Baja, because it was an opposition state, had been chosen on purpose to create the maximum political turmoil.

"I want the truth to be known, I want everything to be cleared up," Ruffo said. "I want it known that Baja California had nothing to do with this. Otherwise, Tijuana will never get rid of this image."

As far as Ruffo was concerned, his woes were exacerbated by a campaign, directed from Mexico City, to drive him out of office. This fate befell numerous ruling-party governors during the Salinas administration; all it took to oust a governor was a presidential decree. The prospect, however, of the president dumping the first-ever opposition governor during an election year carried explosive potential consequences. Salinas had "allowed" the PAN victory in Baja in the first place, had attended Ruffo's inauguration and projected a magnanimous attitude toward the border state—a convenient showcase for democratization. So Ruffo suspected that people in high places were proceeding indirectly, softening him up for removal by fomenting chaos in his state. The leaks about the Benítez case from Mexico City fueled his worries.

"That's when I said, Oh, boy," Ruffo said, raising his eyebrows. "This is very delicate. . . . Of course there is a natural political competition, it has never surprised me that there is a competitive attitude toward the record of this government. But this is extraordinary. This had never been seen before."

Ruffo had fallen to the nadir of his six-year term. He lost

trusted allies in the police chief and the deputy attorney general. He also lost his state attorney general, Juan Francisco Franco, who finally resigned in April. The federal police subjected Franco to marathon overnight interrogations but never charged him with a crime. Although few accused Ruffo himself of having ties to the drug lords, critics faulted him for staying loyal to the attorney general amid scandals and unsolved murders that left two possibilities: Franco was either compromised or paralyzed. The attorney general apparently survived by relying on the governor's sense of us-against-them. Ruffo felt that the federal investigation was more about bashing Baja than about solving the jigsaw puzzle of corruption.

Even if Ruffo deflected too much blame onto external forces, there was little doubt that Baja was experiencing a concentrated blast of the conflict spreading across the nation. The last year of a presidential administration in Mexico is always turbulent. Alliances and understandings disintegrate. New power groups push forward, trampling old ones if necessary. The institutionalized, larcenous free-for-all among public servants has a nickname, "the Year of Hidalgo," which plays off a profane rhyme about what should happen to the mothers of those who do not steal everything they can. In 1994, the system had never been as fractured politically, never as corroded by the money and savagery of the drug mafias. "If they talk about sixth years as difficult, perhaps this is the most difficult," Ruffo said.

The death of Benítez left Ruffo staring at the possibility of his own death. He was convinced that the killings of the chief and Colosio, whether related or not, had both resulted from an alliance between drug lords and politicians. Less than a decade after entering public life, the governor had learned a graphic lesson about a seemingly invincible form of power—narco-politics.

"It is a war," Ruffo said, looking uncharacteristically somber. "A chief of police dies. An honest man, dedicated, and to my judgment free of any corruption. It seems that the bad guys are beating the good guys."

At that moment, Ruffo had something in common with Benítez, and the other border cops, and even Cougar, the born-again gang member from Thirtieth Street. The governor was in over his head.

Nonetheless, Ruffo made a genuine effort to solve the Benítez murder. He created a special prosecution unit, a secret team of half a dozen detectives and prosecutors who reported directly to Ruffo. He picked people he could trust: the lead investigator was a distant cousin of the governor named Eduardo Sandoval, a tall, bearded, dashing detective who wore sport jackets and suspenders with his jeans and looked vaguely Arabic. Sandoval was a fixture at Bob's Big Boy, puffing on an ever-present big cigar. The special prosecutor Ruffo placed in command of the unit was an attorney in his late twenties with the sonorous name of Hodín Gutiérrez Rico. He was the kind of bright, serious and driven young man likely to catch the eye of a politician. His voice and manner were boyish, but his crisp, lawyerly speaking style lent him some gravity. He could still have passed for a recent law school graduate except for his weary look—receding hairline, dark circles under his eyes—characteristic of an ambitious prosecutor who has spent a few grueling years in the Tijuana trenches.

The "Hodines," as the governor called the special unit, worked out of secret offices and shared as little information as possible with fellow police. They were guarded and closemouthed to the point of paranoia, and with good reason: there were traitors everywhere. And they were hunting dangerous prey. The chief suspect in the Benítez murder, Commander García Gaxiola, wielded power beyond his rank. At one point, García Gaxiola and his two brothers, also federal commanders, held simultaneous commands in Baja California, Baja California Sur and Sonora, creating what Gutiérrez called "a triangle of control" in the northwest corner of Mexico. Gutiérrez had done a lot of reading on organized crime. He described his adversaries as the classic mercenaries employed by a Colombian-style alliance between drug mafias and the political system. "As the mafias jockey for territory, they can move their allies in the police around the map to fight for dominance," Gutiérrez explained one afternoon over coffee in a Denny's restaurant in Tijuana. The movement on that chessboard had gotten more agitated during the turf struggle touched off by the murder of Cardinal Posadas and the announced police anti-mafia crusade that, in reality, had "done very little," he said. "After Posadas, the very complex relationship between the cartels and the government became evident. The intermediaries in that relationship are the police. There is a supposed persecution after the cardinal's murder . . . but in reality not that much is done."

Although the unit kept its distance from other Tijuana cops, Hodín Gutiérrez and his men worked closely with U.S. agencies. The murder of the chief had alarmed the cross-border investigators of the FBI, the DEA and the San Diego Police a lot more than the average drug rubout because they had admired and worked with Benítez. FBI agents and other U.S. officers worked their well-entrenched network of informants and passed along leads to the Baja investigators which keyed them in on the Jeep Cherokee used in the ambush and two civilian enforcers, or *aspirinas,* who had helped shadow Benítez and organize the murder. Finally, Gutiérrez charged García Gaxiola and a midlevel commander named Marco Jácome with killing Benítez in revenge for his refusal to take the bribe money. But in a confusing move,

Gutiérrez also charged El Mayel, the lieutenant of the Arellanos, theorizing that he had ordered the hit. This puzzled some Tijuana journalists, who asserted that the mastermind had to be a rival Sonoran drug lord because the federal commanders were suspected of having connections to the Sonoran mafia. Gutiérrez responded that he had filed his charges based on the evidence available to him; this led some to believe that the decision to involve both mafias in the case was a strategic ploy, perhaps designed to play one side off against the other.

The federal commanders suspected in the Benítez case were transferred to other states after the murder. Going after them required the help of the federal police and meant a confrontation with the suspects' supposed political protectors in the state government of Sonora and the federal government in Mexico City. Ruffo and his investigators concluded that the accused killers were untouchable. The fugitive Commander García Gaxiola, for his part, sent a handwritten letter to a newspaper asserting his innocence and accusing the Ruffo administration of persecuting him for political reasons. The motive in the Benítez murder had more to do with police than politics. Despite speculation, the investigators did not believe that Benítez had been eliminated because he knew too much about the Colosio assassination. Nonetheless, the nexus to the Colosio case could not be ruled out altogether. The timing raised obvious questions. The one-two punch of the chief's murder and the arrest of the deputy attorney general came at a time when Benítez, the governor and others in Baja were expressing doubts about the investigation and speculated about a conspiracy. Why did the combined forces of the mafia and the federal police choose that precise moment to strike at Benítez? Why was the airport bomb threat, an apparent attempt to lure Benítez into the ambush, phoned in to the Mexico City office of the prosecutor in the Colosio case? The mafias used violence to send messages. The forces behind the Colosio assassination, assuming a conspiracy existed, could have ordered the hit on Benítez as a warning to others to back off.

"Theoretically, there could have been a convergence of interests between organized crime and politicians," Gutiérrez said. "It could be that one thing goes with the other. In Mexico, this phenomenon of symbiosis is occurring."

The special Baja unit worked closely during the year after the Benítez murder with the special federal prosecutor in the Colosio case. "We are two islands trying to establish an alliance," Gutiérrez said. The Benítez and Colosio assassinations certainly intersected at a lower level. Investigators traced the white Jeep Cherokee used in the murder to the commander named Marco Jácome, who, police said, had a lucrative sideline running an office where he conducted telephonic-eavesdropping-for-hire. Witnesses testified that Jácome had taken part in the ambush of the chief, then hid the Jeep at the house of one of his enforcers. Before he was charged in the chief's murder, Jácome had a previous claim to fame: he was one of the two federal agents on the rooftop in Lomas Taurinas who shot the videotape of the Colosio assassination which was broadcast in court and around the world. Jácome also participated in the initial stages of the Colosio investigation under Raúl Loza, the federal chief in Tijuana. Testimony of informants linked Loza to the Benítez murder as well, but he was not charged. In yet another strange subplot involving Sonora and the federal police, a nervous woman at a public phone called the office of the governor of that state in August 1994. She said she had learned of a plot against Colosio several months before the assassination. She offered to give names and details, but never showed up. The call was tape-recorded and experts in voice analysis later identified the woman as a former secretary in the federal attorney general's office in Tijuana, and the reputed girlfriend of a federal commander who was close to García Gaxiola.

The Benítez mystery, therefore, contributed to the Colosio mystery. The two main suspects in the Benítez case—García Gaxiola and Jácome—had alleged ties to drug lords; and Jacome and another suspect, Loza, had played roles in a Colosio investigation that was rife with gaps and errors. Although they were not tycoons or elected officials, the accused commanders eluded capture easily. This may have been a product of generalized impunity. Or it may have meant that somebody important wanted them to stay free.

The storm in Baja California abated, but the word "narco-politics" entered the vocabulary of the international discussion of the Colosio assassination, and of Mexico's future, thanks to one of the bravest, loudest, best-informed voices to denounce corruption: Eduardo Valle. They called him the Owl. He wore thick glasses and talked in a manic rasp. He was a scrappy, forty-seven-year-old investigative journalist. During a career of defending human rights and attacking corruption, he had been a congressman for a small leftist party, a political prisoner and a student leader. In 1993, Attorney General Jorge Carpizo invited Valle to work as his special advisor, a choice that demonstrated Carpizo's willingness to go to unorthodox lengths to shake up the system. Valle traded his typewriter for a pistol, yet another outsider joining the fray. He ended up leading a team of federal agents in pursuit of Juan García Abrego, the kingpin of the Gulf cartel, across northeast Mexico. Valle arrested important cartel lieutenants and scored other successes before concluding that the enemy was too big. In an open letter of resignation on May 1, 1994, he said Mexico had become "a narco-democracy" and that Colosio was killed because he resisted the rule of the criminals.

"Nobody can outline a political project in which the heads of drug trafficking and their financiers are not included, because if you do it, you die," Valle wrote.

Valle departed for Washington, D.C., on a self-imposed exile. He brought along suitcases full of top secret investigative files from the attorney general's office. He scared up gigs writing for various publications back in Mexico. And he rearmed himself with the weapons he knew best—words. He fired off articles and letters. He gave marathon interviews. He deluged his friends and colleagues in the Mexican and U.S. press with trenchant quotes, connect-the-dots theories and nuggets of official paperwork. He published a book entitled *The Second Shot,* a ringing indictment of corruption. The book presented a dense, sometimes dizzying thicket of information. It was written much the way Valle talked, in sardonic, passionate, complicated riffs. But the author provided prodigious documentation and spoke with rare authority. For all his criticism, he remained a patriotic Mexican. He served in a frontline assignment with direct access to the nation's chief law enforcement officer. And he was honest about his own personal frailties, such as a long-time drinking problem.

The common wisdom was that the unchecked rise of warlike drug lords in Mexico created a danger of "Colombianization." Valle saw a more insidious phenomenon. "There is a difference," Valle thundered during one of many telephone interviews he gave in 1994, his voice resonating in his lonely apartment in a modest Virginia suburb. "In Colombia, the drug lords have negotiated directly with the state, like one state dealing with another state. In Mexico, it has not reached this. It is concealed. The form has not reached the Colombian level, but the power has. In Mexico, the cartels are a state within the state."

Citing piles of phone records, wiretap transcripts, property deeds, investigative dossiers and documents seized from traffickers, the Owl depicted entire states, police forces, business empires and federal agencies as fiefdoms of the drug lords. He asserted that the ruling-party leadership and the presidential palace had been infiltrated by the mafias. A prime exhibit in the Owl's case was a character out of a spy novel: Marcela Bodenstedt. She was a twenty-eight-year-old blonde who had pursued ephemeral careers as a Mexican federal police agent and television news reporter. Law enforcement intelligence reports identified her as a trusted operative of the Gulf cartel, a kind of narco–Mata Hari. Valle traced her steps to several well-known drug traffickers and to a meeting in November 1993 with the minister of transportation. The Bodenstedt connection, Valle alleged, was just one sign that the Gulf cartel had won access to a strategic cabinet department that controlled airports, harbors, highways, telephones and other networks crucial to the smuggling industry.

"The meeting with Marcela is not the only proof of complicity," Valle exclaimed in his habitual high-volume roar. "It is pilots and owners of airplanes with unserved arrest warrants. It is landing strips that have not been investigated. It is structural protection."

The transport minister denied any drug ties and said the woman had merely come to see him about selling him a painting. Later, it was revealed that Bodenstedt had had an apparent romantic relationship with José Cordoba, the presidential chief of staff. Newspapers published wiretap transcripts of flirtatious telephone conversations between the alleged cartel operative and the nation's second most powerful official. But neither Bodenstedt nor the president's chief of staff was ever charged with a crime.

Valle admitted he had more evidence about the narco-political context than about the Colosio assassination itself.

But in his book, and in sworn testimony in the Mexican consulate in Washington, D.C., he tossed more embers on the fire. As a candidate, Colosio had rejected overtures from the boss of the Gulf cartel, Valle alleged. Valle testified that he had learned that the brother of kingpin Juan García Abrego planned to attend a campaign banquet in Colosio's honor. Valle said he notified Colosio and the invitation was blocked Valle also alleged that several campaign officials were operatives of drug lords. One of them was a former federal police commander and ex-convict who led a traveling civilian security force, which was funded by Old Guard politicos and assisted Colosio's military guards. The former commander was another example of the kind of cops entrusted with Colosio's life. Valle theorized that Colosio was killed by an alliance of drug lords and narco-politicians because he resisted their influence.

"I liked Colosio a lot," Valle said. "I am not going to permit that they say he was killed by a crazy solo assassin and leave it at that."

Like Chief Benítez, Valle was another newcomer to police work doing his best to fight the good fight. Although federal prosecutors shelved his accusations unceremoniously, they were variations on a familiar theme. Political scientists, human rights activists and opposition politicians all said the dominance of the drug mafias was a central fact of life in Mexican society and could have played a role in the Colosio assassination. Talking about how the Benítez investigation ran into the wall of narco-politics, Ruffo told reporters: "There is a lot of truth in what the Owl says."

What the Owl said about the Gulf cartel and the Colosio case complemented other evidence of drug lords meddling in politics, such as the narco-tunnel and freeway-murder cases in California which suggested that northwest border mafias were infiltrating the financing and security of the presidential campaign. The tentacles of organized crime appeared to reach from various directions into the PRI, the Colosio campaign and the investigation of the assassination. As in the case of the cardinal of Guadalajara, this created a swamp of scenarios. It could be that Colosio had bravely refused overtures from drug traffickers and paid the price. He could have been in cahoots with one faction of drug lords and fallen victim to a double cross or a preemptive strike by rivals. Narco-politicians could have bumped him off in the hope of forcing the Salinistas to select a more acceptable candidate. The president could have ordered the assassination as a result of a power struggle in which drug mafias were just one of several factors, then used corrupt cops to hide the truth. As suspicious as the bloodshed and mysterious subplots surrounding Colosio's death got, the problem, again, remained the scarcity of facts. And the use of a lone kamikaze assassin like Aburto was not typical of the gangsters; they tended to kill efficiently, firing car-to-car if possible, and disappear, like the murderers of Chief Benítez. Aburto did not match the mold of the hit man and he had no criminal record. If he was the instrument of conspirators, they did a remarkable job of erasing any fingerprints.

The context, however, got more suspicious. On September 28, 1994, a gunman murdered Francisco Ruiz Massieu, the secretary-general of the PRI and former brother-in-law of President Salinas. The killer struck in broad daylight outside a hotel in Mexico City. The killer resembled Aburto: a young ranch hand with a fourth-grade education, no police record and few credentials as a hired gun other than a willingness to get up close and do the job. The Tek-9 machine pistol he fired at point-blank range jammed after shooting a single, fatal bullet. The assassination of one of the brightest behind-the-scenes leaders of the ruling party, a likely future presidential aspirant himself, heightened the national crisis—worsening capital flight, investor anxiety, public indignation. Unlike in the Colosio case, the aftermath exposed a web of conspiracy and cover-up at the top.

Breaking a taboo that protects former presidents, in February 1995 newly elected President Ernesto Zedillo gave his blessing for the arrest of Raúl Salinas, the brother of former President Salinas, as the suspected mastermind of the Ruiz Massieu assassination. The motive allegedly mixed personal, political and business feuds. Investigators also arrested Mario Ruiz Massieu, the victim's brother. As deputy attorney general in charge of antinarcotics operations, Mario Ruiz Massieu had taken the helm of the investigation of his brother's murder and had rounded up suspects at a breakneck pace. Mario was at the center of a remarkable drama in which he excoriated PRI bosses for protecting the alleged masterminds and resigned, declaring: "The demons are on the loose." Nonetheless, investigators accused Mario Ruiz Massieu of hubris: even as he struck avenging poses, he was allegedly concocting a facade designed to conceal the guilt of Raúl Salinas. Described in chilling detail by Mexico City journalist Ignacio Rodriguez Reyna in the book *Ruiz Massieu: The Crimes of Power,* the investigation of Mario Ruiz Massieu's investigation concluded that his police had raped and tortured witnesses and had altered and fabricated evidence to protect the president's brother.

The tableau recalled the treacherous goings-on in Tijuana at a loftier level. If you believed the charges, the president's brother had ordered the murder of a top leader of the ruling party, his former brother-in-law. Then the second-ranking law enforcement officer in Mexico, the victim's own brother, had engineered the cover-up.

And there was more. Ruiz Massieu had become the federal antidrug chief in the spring of 1994 as the battles of narco-politics raged in Baja and elsewhere. During his tenure, cocaine seizures dropped. Prosecutors and commanders who had been fired returned to choice posts in smuggling centers such as Tamaulipas and Baja. Ruiz Massieu was accused of setting up a "franchising system," as one investigator called it: the prosectors and commanders paid up to a million dollars under the table for the assignments, collected bribes from local drug lords and sent weekly suitcases full of cash to Mario Ruiz Massieu in Mexico City, according to U.S. and Mexican investigators. From May to November, his assistant and accused bagman deposited $9.4 million in suspected drug money in Texas bank accounts.

Ruiz Massieu fled to the United States and protested his innocence. Repeated efforts to extradite him to Mexico were rejected by U.S. federal judges. They ruled that the evidence presented by the Mexican government was insufficient and contradictory. They appeared confused and suspicious about the case against him and the Mexican legal system in general. But a federal jury in Texas concluded in 1997 that Ruiz Massieu had been involved in drug corruption. After a trial on civil charges brought against the former top prosecutor by the IRS and antidrug agencies, the jury ruled that $7.9 million of the money in Ruiz Massieu's Houston bank accounts consisted of payoffs from drug mafias for official protection. The verdict authorized the seizure of the assets and gave the U.S. and Mexican governments a crucial victory.

Meanwhile, the investigation of Raúl Salinas furthered the belief on both sides of the border that the Gulf cartel of Juan García Abrego had enjoyed special clout during the Salinas years. García Abrego's base of operations encompassed the states of Tamaulipas and Nuevo León, the home of the Salinas family. The Tamaulipas congressman who allegedly organized the assassination for Raúl Salinas had suspected ties to the Gulf cartel, as did other players in the plot. (The congressman disappeared after the murder and is presumed dead.) Raúl Salinas was an agronomist who fancied himself a poet, a high roller whose brother assigned him to run the government's food-distribution program for the poor, a businessman with clout in the financial and ruling party elite. In 1994, a fugitive federal police commander told U.S. and Mexican investigators that Raúl Salinas was a friend and business partner of the head of the Gulf cartel. The commander, Guillermo González Calderoni, had carried out sensitive tasks for the Salinas family and was publicly accused of protecting the Gulf cartel. After the commander was arrested in Texas, he "said that he had personally delivered to Raúl recordings of telephone wiretaps of opposition politicians in the north," a Mexican investigator said. "He said he was personally aware of the relationship between [the drug lord] and Raúl. He said Raúl had meetings with García Abrego and that Raúl served as a front for García Abrego through his companies." Raúl Salinas was spotted in the company of the drug lord at restaurants, an airport and a private party, according to investigators and published reports. Like Ruiz Massieu, Salinas left a money trail. Mexican, U.S. and Swiss police found more than a hundred million dollars in European and Mexican bank accounts which the president's brother allegedly deposited under false names. They suspected that some of the money was drug-related, but tracing its origins was difficult. The money could also have come from politics, clean and shady business deals, government coffers. Prosecutors accused Raúl Salinas of other crimes, including enriching himself with public funds.

The Zedillo administration gained credibility by daring to arrest the former president's brother and by declaring drug trafficking Mexico's top national security concern. Understandably, many Mexicans were sensitive about such descriptions when they were made by U.S. politicians putting pressure on Mexico. Mexicans pointed out, accurately, that corruption has no borders. The pipelines that moved the drugs north and the profits south required the involvement of law enforcement officials, businesspeople and drug lords in the United States. And the fuel for the massive international machinery of the narcotics trade was the cash of insatiable consumers in the United States.

But narco-politics posed a pressing danger to Mexico's national security. When President Ernesto Zedillo took office in late 1994, an internal federal report outlined an ominous tableau. The report, entitled *National Program for the Control of Drugs 1995*, warned that the mafias threatened to overwhelm the apparatus of the state. The "consolidation" of half a dozen nationwide drug-trafficking organizations— including the Arellanos, the Gulf cartel and the Ciudad Juárez mafia—and ninety regional outfits has "revealed their great capacity to co-opt elements of the justice and political systems at the state and federal levels," the report said. And it came to this conclusion: "As a result of the financial capacity of the drug trafficking organizations, there will be a continuing tendency toward the infiltration of the financial and governmental structures. It should be noted that the power of the drug trafficking organizations could lead to situations of ungovernability, using whatever political or economic space in which the institutions show weakness or inattention; the advance of drug trafficking foments impunity and uncertainty in institutions . . . and increases the intimidation of the authorities and the forms of government."

The new president said repeatedly that impunity would not be tolerated. President Zedillo was described by those who talked to him as determined to pursue the Colosio case no matter where the trail led. This raised expectations. The mere fact that a second political leader was assassinated months later cast doubt on the idea that Colosio had been the victim of a coincidental, isolated crime. The newly revealed sins of the elite provided a kind of road map for conspiracy theorists. If the president's brother was using murder to resolve his feuds, anything was possible and no one was above suspicion.

In a historic gesture, Zedillo had turned the hot seat of the federal attorney general's office over to the opposition, appointing a PANista lawyer named Antonio Lozano. He was handed a daunting narco-political triumvirate of cases: Colosio, Ruiz Massieu and the cardinal of Guadalajara. The federal investigators worked closely with Hodín Gutiérrez's secret team of state investigators in Baja, requesting the case files on Colosio, Benítez and even the 1988 murder of Héctor (Gato) Félix. The Zedillo administration was investigating Old Guard political figures such as the Hank clan, which had been linked to the journalist's murder in Tijuana. U.S. investigators were working more closely with them as increasing resources and political pressure came to bear on the drug issue in both nations.

The killing of the Tijuana police chief seemed a perfect opportunity for the new federal sleuths to produce results. After all, Governor Ruffo had invested considerable personal effort in the case and he was a PANista, like the new attorney general. The federal investigators told Ruffo in March 1995 that they concurred with the findings of state investigators in the murder of Chief Benítez; they promised to round up the accused federal commanders. But years came and went with no arrests other than that of a single lowly accomplice. The chief suspect, García Gaxiola, obtained a judicial order in the state of Sinaloa blocking his arrest. The PAN learned in the federal attorney general's office what it learned in Baja: rebuilding the justice system would require more than well-intentioned newcomers.

"We asked [the attorney general] if he could assign us one federal police commander whom he could trust, just one, to resolve the Benítez case," Ruffo said later. "And he could not. . . . There are few officers whom they can depend on. In there they give an order and the bad guys know about it before the officers. . . . It turns out that the one who receives the order is the traitor."

More than a year after Benítez died, special prosecutor Hodín Gutiérrez sat in the Denny's diner in Tijuana. His head hung low over a cup of coffee and he kept his voice down. His boyish features looked frayed. The omnipotence of the mafias had reached the point where the murder of a municipal police chief, let alone a presidential candidate, could go unpunished. Instead of cherishing the chief's memory and demanding justice in his name, people forgot. Time passed. Scandals and bodies piled up. The drug underworld functioned unscathed and, ironically, generated prosperity and economic well-being.

"It's sad to say, but while the drug lords are here the economy is strong," Gutiérrez said. "This money activates the economy, injects new energy."

Although the city named a boulevard after the chief and paid him other tributes, Benítez's combination of honesty and impatience, bravery and abrasiveness, made him a solitary, flawed hero. When Benítez died, the reaction in his milieu—among police, politicians, reporters—was disconcertingly cynical. They had seen it coming. They had little sympathy for a rookie who seemed to fancy himself Gary Cooper in *High Noon*. During the frantic early days of the investigation, when Gutiérrez, the cigar-smoking detective Sandoval and their handful of investigators were literally sprinting after leads from City Hall to the governor's office to the streets, there was a lot of talk on the radio, and in the cantinas and the coffee shops, about how the municipal police were not supposed to muck around with drugs in the first place. Perhaps that reaction had less to do with how good or bad a policeman Benítez was than with generalized feelings of hopelessness and defeat. Benítez, at least, tried to make a difference.

Gutiérrez cared deeply about the case. But he was tired. Tired of working out of secret offices, worrying about his family, watching over his shoulder. The past year had shown him that his battle was ludicrously quixotic: Hodín with his pen and Sandoval with his cigar, dueling giants. "We are fighting a monster," he said. Mexico needed to design a national strategy against the mafias, to establish a commission of academics and politicians and police that would make the war the nation's top priority. "Otherwise," he said, echoing the warning of the journalist known as the Owl, "we will reach a point when Mexico has become a narcocracy."

The investigation had shown Gutiérrez the world through the eyes of Benítez. He had realized that the strength of the monster that he and the slain chief had been fighting transcended the borders of their jobs, their city, their nation.

"Every day, it becomes harder to do this job," Gutiérrez said. "There are powerful obstacles within the state police forces, people allied with the narcos. The federal police are another obstacle. And the third enemy is the bad guys themselves. So you are fighting on three fronts. It goes beyond the police. Organized crime has the support and participation of politicians. It happened in Colombia. And it is happening in Mexico."

Despite his fears and misgivings, Gutiérrez stuck with the job. Though he lacked the kind of experience and instincts that come with years on the street, he was smart and ambitious and had a formidable patron in Governor Ruffo. Two years later, Gutiérrez had risen to the third-highest post in the state attorney general's office and had investigated a series of high-profile and sensitive cases. He started getting death threats. He told a relative that he knew the contract on his life had already been signed, but he felt he was more protected if he stayed in his job than if he quit. After going out on a Friday night in January 1997, he returned with his family to his house in an upscale neighborhood in the hills near the racetrack. His wife took his infant daughter inside while Gutiérrez parked the car in the garage. And the gunmen struck.

If the killers of Benítez were surgeons, the killers of Gutiérrez were butchers. There were four of them; apparently they were ordered to physically destroy their victim, not just to murder him. They fired more than 120 rounds with automatic rifles. Then they climbed into a van and ran over the corpse, mangling it in the street beneath the wheels. The crime generated the usual flurry of indignation, speculation and gossip; once again, "corrupt police and drug traffickers were suspects," but the murder joined the Benítez case on the list of crimes likely to go unsolved. The message of the mafia was typically and brutally eloquent: what Hodín Gutiérrez had said about Mexico was coming true.

CHAPTER SEVEN

The Little Village of Jorge Alberto Duarte

Between the warden's office and the grounds of the Baja California state penitentiary in Tijuana, there is an antechamber: a giant open-air cage about the size of a two-story house. The cage contains a perennial hubbub of lawyers and relatives waiting to get into the prison interior and inmate messengers shouting out the arrival of visitors and packages for other inmates.

A commotion ripples through the cage. The fierce-looking sentries who guard the entrance swing open the chain-link gate; the mob of inmates on the other side of the fence parts in half. Two guards, holstered pistols on their belts and truncheons in their hands, stride forward, looking wary and purposeful. They are followed by a man who walks with his narrow shoulders hunched in a sweater, hands jammed in the pockets of corduroy trousers. The man is forty-one. He has a thick beard and unruly, reddish-brown hair; he looks like a former hippie who has matured into a serene and rumpled university professor. In fact, Jorge Alberto Duarte is a legal scholar by training and still teaches law courses at the university. But he is also the warden of a prison about which the National Human Rights Commission of Mexico once said: "The circumstances prevailing inside the state penitentiary create a tableau that is unique in the world."

Duarte makes his way through the crowd. It is like entering a hallucination, a Tijuana dreamscape, a penal institution
invented jointly by Dickens, Kafka and García Márquez.
Duarte passes taco stands in the open-air central plaza of the
prison, an inmate-owned general store with a hand-painted
imitation of a 7-Eleven sign in front, clusters of tattooed
men crouched around a basketball court at the heart of the
plaza. Duarte greets an inmate merchant who works and
sleeps in a little wooden hut where he makes and sells belt
buckles carved with funky border-culture icons: AK-47
assault rifles, Virgin Marys, Harley-Davidsons, the Mexican
and U.S. eagles. Duarte fends off a rasping inmate, an emissary of an imprisoned gangster who would like a word with
the warden. Duarte pats a little boy on the head. The boy is
four years old; he wears a blue sweatshirt, baggy jeans and
a look of solitary awe. His world is filled with wonders: huddled heroin addicts shooting up in a corner, point-blank gun-
fights. The boy mimics what he sees. In the prison chapel
where the Virgin Mary is framed by flashing colored bulbs,
he clasps his hands in prayer. In the cramped cellblock
where he lives with his family, he snarls profanities at the
other kids and scurries away when his parents try to give
him a beating. And when you ask him his name, the boy
responds with one soft word: "Máscara" (Mask). His melan-
choly visage inspired that moniker. He has been rechristened
by the inmates of a penitentiary that seethes with the surre-
alism of the U.S.-Mexico border.

Of the more than twenty-five hundred inhabitants
crammed into the four-acre prison in Tijuana's La Mesa
neighborhood, about three hundred are wives and children
of inmates. Because many inmates are migrants from southern and central Mexico, prison officials allowed their
impoverished kin to move in en masse long ago. For

decades, sympathy and payoffs have induced authorities to tolerate the construction and sales among inmates of unofficial dwellings, known as *carracas*. This customized housing has consumed space in the prison compound, created a multilayered economy—construction, property sales, illicit "taxes" on the entry of furniture and materials—and replicated the helter-skelter sprawl of the city outside the walls.

"They started building in an irregular manner," Duarte explains, "a dormitory here, a little house there, an athletic court here, so there was no planning for infrastructure. And this caused the inmates to ask the administration to let them build an area where they could sleep, because some people had nowhere to live, nowhere to sleep. . . . With the problem now, after thirty years, that we have two types of housing: the official housing, which is a cell for six people, and the individual dwellings with more comforts."

There are about two hundred *carracas* and sixty inmate-owned stores and restaurants constructed in two-story blocks that form the internal "streets" of the prison. The place bears little resemblance to the stark, high-tech confines of U.S. prisons. With its strolling families in street clothes, its shacktown skyline dotted by homemade television antennas, this penal village has earned its nickname: El Pueblito de La Mesa (the Little Village of La Mesa). It has developed its own architecture, economy and laws, a strange form of order that governs seeming anarchy.

Some of La Mesa's most disconcerting problems are blessings in disguise, the warden says. The presence of women and children helps keep the peace.

"The family occupies a fundamental place in Mexican society," Duarte says. "This helps us in the sense that if someone commits a crime and he retains the support of his family, there is a good chance he can be reformed. Through the family, it has been possible to maintain calm."

Duarte is leading a tour of the prison for a visiting federal bureaucrat, a woman lawyer who turns heads with her stiletto heels, emerald-colored sheath skirt and abundant chestnut curls. The lawyer represents the Interior Ministry in Mexico City, which controls prison budgets. She is here on a fact-finding visit, one of the ministry's periodic responses to the pleas by the administration of Governor Ernesto Ruffo Appel of Baja California: La Mesa needs money, before it explodes, before it's too late. Duarte narrates in a dry, patient monotone, making his case for more resources. On the sentry catwalk on the outer wall, baby-faced guards snap to attention as he passes; they wear rifles and uniforms adorned with jaunty personal touches—a scarf, a silver-and-black Oakland Raiders jacket. Duarte shows the bureaucrat an ancient, bedraggled cellblock known as the pigeon coop because of the wall of wire revealing a warren of cells connected by precarious splintered staircases. Men sit on benches smoking cigarettes in the gloom. In the women's cellblock, or "tank," Duarte introduces a gray-haired, bent-over, sixty-four-year-old woman from El Salvador. A Mexican court convicted her of smuggling immigrants bound for the United States. Her parole has been delayed by a federal paperwork foul-up. "We need the space," Duarte says. "Certainly there must be people who deserve to be in here more than her." Duarte ambles into a dank corner dormitory where men are warehoused in rows of wooden sleeping cubicles—if they can afford to buy one from the previous inmate-owners. Duarte asks an inmate to unlock his cubicle, which is slightly larger than a coffin. "Show the *licenciada* your little house, my friend. How much did you pay for that? $100? Thank you."

The societal structure of the prison resembles a funhouse mirror of Mexico. The rich inmates amass luxuries—televisions, Rolexes, designer sweat suits, cellular phones.

Protected by corrupt guards, they run lucrative rackets inside the prison—drugs, alcohol, prostitution, extortion, real estate involving *carracas* and businesses. The rich surround themselves with servants and gunmen hired from the ranks of the poor inmates, who scrabble to survive. A first-time visitor might be lulled by the bright colors, the almost festive bustle of fathers hoisting toddlers, mothers hanging up laundry. But the underlying reality is murderous. In other prisons, convicts fight with crude knives fashioned from toothbrushes. The warriors of La Mesa keep smuggled automatic firearms under their pillows and sleep in bulletproof vests when times get tense. A dozen people have died violently in the past year.

"It doesn't look like it's dangerous," says Mario, a tall, rugged and gregarious Chicano from San Diego, who is serving ten years for marijuana possession. "But there are criminals in here that will kill you for a *quina* [about 20 cents]. You can't forget you're in a penitentiary. You gotta remember, they got guns in here."

Duarte acknowledges the dangers with a shrug. Every so often, the guards join forces with SWAT teams from the Tijuana police and sweep through the prison at dawn, looking for guns. But the Uzis and the sawed-off shotguns evaporate before they arrive. Generally, the raiders just find a few knives. There are too many leaks, too many hiding places. Sometimes inmates or reporters who cover the police beat will saunter up to Duarte and ask, "So, *licenciado*, what time is the sweep tomorrow?"

Duarte's critics in Tijuana politics and the press call him naive and overwhelmed, an academic who improvises as he goes along. They accuse him of ceding power to criminal kingpins. "The warden is an instrument of the mafia," mutters the incarcerated boss of a Tijuana squatters movement, his massive hands cradling a mug of coffee in his *carraca*.

But it is hard to find anyone who does not describe Duarte as honest and well intentioned. He is gentle, austere, deeply religious, a man of books and ideas sent into a lion's den. He works closely with human rights advocates and has largely won them over. They say the problem is too huge to blame on one man. The prison is a metaphor for Mexico's ills—violence, gangsterism, governmental neglect, opulence amid squalor.

"He's a very good person," says José Luis Pérez Canchola, whose human rights office has done in-depth investigations of conditions in La Mesa. "But there is nothing that can be done. He takes a very pragmatic attitude: without resources, there is only so much he can do. The situation in there is desperate and it creates hatred and rancor. It is a human rights disaster." Compounding the injustice, and violating the Mexican Constitution, the facility mixes together men and women, suspects awaiting trial and hardened convicts. Professional killers live next to first-time drug mules next to wrongly accused victims of a ponderous legal system based on the Napoleonic code. Or, as Mario calls it, "the Napoleon law: guilty until proven innocent."

It is depressingly easy to go to jail in Tijuana if you don't have power or money, says a former chief of the prison guard corps. "Mexican law is very special. Say you run somebody over. You are waiting for trial because you can't make bail. You end up in a cell with me, and I'm some young guy who enjoys killing. For three months I'm on your case, harassing you, making your life miserable. Finally, you lose control and stab me to death. And then you end up doing time for both of us."

Having done time on both sides of the border, though, Mario from San Diego has come to an interesting conclusion: "They should take this and apply it in the U.S. You got the stores, the wives and the kids. Morale-wise, a guy doesn't feel locked up. In the U.S., it's all steel and concrete. There's homosexuality, frustration. He comes out angry and violent. He goes from a black-and-white world to color. And he can't handle it."

After the lawyer from the Interior Ministry makes promises, shakes hands and leaves, Duarte returns to his office. It is unheated and threadbare, dominated by a mournful but brightly colored portrait of Jesus Christ. A demented cacophony drifts in from the prison compound as Duarte works at his desk: voices, whistling, *ranchera* music, the crow of a rooster, a hacking tubercular cough, the pounding of carpenters' hammers. Duarte leans forward, his narrow, almost Asiatic eyes intent over his beard. He says he is doing the best he can under the circumstances; he has nothing to hide.

"They talk about guns in here; we wish they weren't in here, but we know they are," he says. "So we are open about it. I think you are making a big step forward when you speak the truth. We cannot lose the human aspect. If all we do is toughen the system, it will not work. This is the reality with which I have to live. Gradually, working within the limits of the economic conditions, we can go about changing the situation."

If Tijuana is a microcosm of change and conflict in Mexico, the La Mesa prison is a microcosm of the microcosm. True to its nickname, the prison is a tough little border town: the ultimate product of the surreal, noble, brutal extremes that make the border unlike anyplace else in the world. All the cross-border currents come together within the walls: immigration, smuggling, drugs, mafias of every description, political and police corruption, hybrid cultures. In the prison, the pretenses of the outside world disappear. The legal and illegal economies intertwine and the state openly shares power with organized crime. Other Latin American prisons have overcrowding, violence, liberal visiting policies and inmate kingpins who are the real power behind the walls. But there is no other prison with all the elements that give La Mesa its roiling energy: the luxury and poverty, the architecture, the shops and restaurants, the hundreds of resident wives and children, the booming internal economies, the heavily armed combat. The prison juxtaposes savagery and dignity, despair and humanity.

In July 1992, the administration of Governor Ruffo sent Jorge Duarte into the madhouse to make it more civilized, hoping Duarte would succeed where many had failed. Duarte had previously served as deputy warden of La Mesa and director of the Tijuana Juvenile Hall. The mission fulfilled his sense of social commitment: "I always asked myself, What can I do to help my people? Socially, this work has many repercussions." He took the top post at a time when drug wars and political intrigue in Baja were making the world of La Mesa even harsher. Like the other recently appointed reformers in town—Javier Valenzuela of Grupo Beta, Federico Benítez of the municipal police— Duarte was unorthodox in background and approach. He was not the classic head-bashing warden; he shunned paramilitary airs and round-the-clock bodyguards. He had a deadpan sense of humor. On the day he was named warden, he told reporters in his distinctive drawl: "I had always dreamed about this job. Believe it or not."

The prison is in a middle-class, centrally located neighborhood of narrow streets a few blocks from Boulevard Díaz Ordaz. It was built in 1956, intended as a municipal jail for six hundred inmates. Then Tijuana surged from a honky-tonk town to a metropolis of more than a million and a half people, the growth fed by migration, tourism and the transborder manufacturing industry. Notorious for vice since the

silent-movie days when stars from Hollywood caroused in
its casinos and beach hotels, Tijuana evolved into a base for
multimillion-dollar, multinational criminal enterprises.
When he talks about the roots of the prison's crisis, Duarte
laments the short memories among California politicians
who think the border's problems can be wiped away by hurrying Border Patrol reinforcements and fortifications to the
line. "If we look back historically, this state has always been
one of the routes which many people travel to the U.S. Not
for twenty or thirty years, for more than 100 years, this has
gone on. The United States has labor that its citizens won't
do. Who's going to do it? The Mexicans. It is a natural crossing. Although there's a border, a wall, the statements of a
governor, it's not going to stop that easily. And it brings us
serious problems."

Population growth overwhelmed Tijuana's physical and
governmental infrastructure, including law enforcement.
Migrants filled the shantytowns and squatter camps spreading from the city. Often hoping to cross to California, sometimes the migrants ended up behind bars instead.
Border-related federal offenses, principally drug and immigrant smuggling, now account for almost half the prison
population. But Baja does not have a federal prison.
Construction of a new penitentiary east of Tijuana ground to
a halt in a murk of ineptitude and pilfering, leaving a ghost-
ly shell in the mountains. "Schubert's Unfinished
Symphony," Duarte sighs. And officials of the Baja
California government accuse the bureaucrats in Mexico
City of worsening the plight of La Mesa by failing to provide enough prison funds to the state; they see this as a typically cynical political assault by the ruling party on Baja, a
bastion of the opposition. The prison offers an easy target
when the ruling party or its allies in the press want to take
shots at Governor Ruffo for failing to get tough on crime.

The fiscal neglect and political conflict intertwined with the rise of the drug cartels, which attracted legions of aimless, hungry young Mexicans—and U.S. citizens like the Thirtieth Street homeboys—eager to take a fistful of cash to pull a trigger or smuggle a suitcase north. They filled prisons on both sides of the border. In addition to trafficking bosses, hit men, smuggling mules and wayward cops, fully 30 percent of the inmates of La Mesa are addicts, hustling and marauding for the next fix. The result: a penal time bomb.

It explodes periodically. In 1978, the warden, his assistant and two guards were gunned down, one of numerous multiple shootings. There were violent escapes in which inmates used tunnels and bribes; the most notable to flee was a suspect in the 1985 murder of Enrique Camarena of the DEA. Wardens fell regularly in the wake of scandals, including a former military officer who was appointed in 1989 to clean house. Governor Ruffo's administration has put considerable effort into superimposing a modern institution on the existing one. The state has spent more than $5 million on new construction, fired scores of guards and improved pay and training for new ones. But the pattern has become familiar. The press thunders about the latest crisis. The government promises changes. The attention subsides.

Given all the ingredients for disaster, it is intriguing that the prison manages to avoid the kind of massive riots and losses of life that have occurred in penitentiaries in Brazil, Venezuela and elsewhere. Duarte credits continuous dialogue with inmates and one of the few comforts he can offer: visits, conjugal and otherwise. Visitors are crucial to psychological and economic survival. On Tuesdays and Thursdays, spouses of inmates line up outside the main gate waiting to spend the night. Many of the adults among the three hundred relatives who live inside full-time support their families by commuting to jobs outside the prison. On Sundays, the crush of visitors doubles the population.

Duarte approaches his job as a scholar; he has toured prisons in the United States, Cuba and Russia. The trips reaffirmed his quiet patriotism. Mexico may lack big budgets and technofortresses, he says, but the liberal Mexican policy governing visits is the most humane. "You ask how it is possible that the fourteen hundred inmates who are not locked up remain under control? Because we give them their general visits, their conjugal visits. This is fundamental. We don't understand another philosophy; prohibiting conjugal visits is nothing more than punishment. It is not readapting or rehabilitation, just punishment. This shocks us philosophically."

Where some see a particularly bizarre version of the stereotypical Mexican jail, others are impressed by the pragmatic arrangement governing this self-contained universe. "The government accommodates the people and the people accommodate the government," says Carlos Chacón, a San Diego Police sergeant. Chacón got to know the border as a member of the San Diego Police undercover squad—immortalized by Joseph Wambaugh in *Lines and Shadows*—that went out into the canyons on the U.S. side in the 1970s to protect immigrants. Chacón got to know the La Mesa prison because he is an expert on Latino prison gangs. "The government doesn't have a lot of money, so they are forced to work together," he says. "The government knows it can't provide everything for the inmates, so it allows the families and the inmates to provide for themselves."

In some ways, Chacón says, La Mesa is more humane than the barren landscapes of U.S. prisons dominated by racial warfare and sexual violence. While the presence of guns in La Mesa is obviously outrageous, the experience of U.S. prisons shows that jailhouse mafias do not need firepower in order to shed blood. "A guy in Pelican Bay [California's top-security prison] can still order a murder in another prison," Chacón says. "What's the difference? The power to kill is still there."

Duarte maintains that La Mesa is like nowhere else; only slow and careful reform will bring change without blood-shed. He says: "This government has made a very big effort. We built new cellblocks, vocational workshops, a kitchen, a Catholic church, remodeling the exterior of the entrance, the cafeterias. It is not fair to say that nothing has changed. We are not going to solve a problem that began thirty years ago in an administration of six years. . . . I don't make decisions by shooting from the hip: one day I'm going to do this or that, I'm going to prohibit this. Especially not in a place like this. It is very delicate. The safety and security of many people depend on the decisions you make. You need a lot of tact, a lot of care."

Jesús (Flaco) Araiza descends a circular outdoor stairway. His cowboy boots thunk on the metal.

His nickname means Skinny, but it refers to his height, about six three. Flaco looks solid. In his late twenties, his light skin and dark hair typical of the Mexican north, he is decked out in white jeans, a sharp embroidered shirt and a cowboy hat. As official "coordinator" of the inmates' governing council, Flaco oversees everything from work assignments to arbitration of property disputes—he is Duarte's counterpart on the inside. When Flaco leads a tour of the prison, though, he does not need an armed escort. He does not totally deny the newspaper stories identifying him as a *capo*, one of the half dozen inmate chieftains who are La Mesa's shadow government. He scoffs at some of the melodramatic details.

"They said I wear two guns in my belt," he growls, his

voice gravelly and deep in his throat. "They said I walk around with twenty bodyguards. Do you see any bodyguards?" Nonetheless, Flaco can field a personal security force in a hurry if hostilities break out. "Oh yes. You have to. You're not going to make it on your own."

And he is not bashful about his influence. "The authorities don't interfere. We run the businesses, the sales of *carracas*. Among ourselves. And if somebody acts up, if they go around robbing the visitors and causing trouble, I give them an ass-kicking."

If you are rich, upon arrival in La Mesa you fork over $40 to skip the three months of maintenance work required of newcomers, who trundle garbage cans and slop cafeteria food into pails that poor inmates have to come up with themselves in lieu of plates. You tip the guards to avoid getting up at 6 a.m. for roll call. You tip the industrious messengers who race each other to bring news of a visitor in the cage. You hire cooks, servants and bodyguards, who are plentiful and affordable. One enforcer, a strapping Chicano convict, earned meals, a couple of marijuana cigarettes, a place to sleep and about $5 a day as a sentry at the steel door of a drug dealer's *carraca*. Sometimes he had to push people out. Sometimes he had to pull them inside. "Let's say a guy owes money," the enforcer explains. "The *capo* says, 'Bring me George.' So we go get 'im, we get a stick or a steel bar. We beat the shit out of him, cut his hair off, shave his eyebrows. And he's still gotta pay. That way, everybody gets the message."

Few rules govern goods entering La Mesa, except that you have to pay. Guards charge $20 for admitting radios, hair dryers and other appliances. A dour, insomniac engineer accused of accidental homicide brought in a personal computer, which he uses to design a subsidized housing project for a low-income neighborhood outside the prison in Tijuana, commissioned by a development firm that appar-

ently does not discriminate against accused felons; he
hunches among full-color blueprints, the printer whirring
day and night. It costs more to sneak in Scotch, marijuana
and other prohibited items. The price for a smuggled pistol
goes as high as $5,000.

The real estate market flourishes. The top of the line, a
two-story town house complete with Jacuzzi, costs $50,000.
But lack of space has finally put to a stop the construction of
more *carracas*. Home buyers use inmate brokers and property deeds to avoid rip-offs and pay a tax for services levied
by Flaco's "governing council," comprised of influential
inmates who govern, theoretically, in tandem with the
administration. Strolling the open-air corridor known as the
Boulevard of the Eagles, Flaco summons his *chalán,* or
valet, and tells him to run ahead and unlock Flaco's *carraca.* Lined with shops, food stands, second-story *carracas*
and small cellblocks, the "boulevard" throbs with foot traffic, noise and menace. The walls are maroon, green and
blue. It looks like an old and rough street in the Zona Norte,
Tijuana's fabled red-light district; it feels like being inside a
pinball machine.

Like the other home owners, only Flaco—not the
guards—has the key to the barred security cage enclosing
his wooden front door, which is reached by a circular staircase. "It's my own little jail," he says. "And I'm the jailer."
The interior suggests the studio hideaway of a slumming
wealthy bachelor, or the presidential suite in a hotel that has
seen better days. Flaco paid $3,000 and did $7,000 worth of
remodeling; inmate workmen raised the ceiling to accommodate his height. He has a cellular phone on a countertop
holder, a television/VCR with pirated cable channels from
San Diego, a wet bar with stools, an air conditioner, a heater,
a kitchenette with stove and microwave, a bathroom. The
closet overflows with rodeo-style shirts wrapped in plastic

covers. A big box on a couch contains a radio-controlled toy car that his son plays with during visits. Flaco is serving seven years for possession of 350 kilos of cocaine, but he does not really feel the time. He makes money—he owns a soda fountain and Señor Frogs, a prison restaurant named after a well-known Tijuana eatery near the international border crossing. He gets what he needs.

"The *capos* don't escape because they don't want to," Flaco says. "They are comfortable. They run their businesses from in here, over the phone."

Flaco roams the grounds like a sleepy young prince. He calls orders to a cleanup crew, jokes about his hangover with a deferential guard, hands a coin to a beggar. He leads the way up to the roof of a new six-story cellblock, gesturing panoramically at the expanse of *carracas* with their rooftop blue drums, which are used—both in the prison and in the neighborhoods around it—for storing water. An inmate once tried to escape by jumping off this cellblock roof into a dumpster. Unfortunately, the dumpster never made it past the no-man's-land between the inner and outer walls. "Stupid bastard. He thought he was home-free." Flaco has no sympathy for freelance troublemakers. He says the *capos* mete out swift justice to child molestors, or *violines* (a punned diminutive of the word for rapist). "Nobody messes with the kids in here. Because if they do, we kill them."

In the central plaza, Flaco points out a chunky, shambling inmate of about forty-five who, though not particularly imposing to look at, is one of La Mesa's hired gunslingers. "A couple of months ago, he killed a guy in a shoot-out. He put nine bullets in him and didn't get a scratch. So he must be pretty good." The inmate gunslinger limps toward the infirmary accompanied by his eldest son, a loping rawboned teenager with hard-rock curls down his neck. The father is recovering from a beating a few weeks earlier

which nearly caused a riot. The commander of the prison
guards got a tip that the gunslinger had been hired to kill him
in revenge for a crackdown on drugs being smuggled into La
Mesa. So guards hauled the suspected hit man into the commander's office and tried to pummel the truth out of him
with nightsticks. The inmates mutinied, firing shots into the
air. Although the commander was college-educated and
known for rejecting bribes, the warden decided that he had
gone too far. Reluctantly, Duarte gave in to the protests and
dismissed the commander and two deputies.

Flaco nods with satisfaction. "The warden is a good man.
We work with him. But if they try to bring back the *comandantes*, we'll show them a riot like they wouldn't believe."

For all his swagger, Flaco has plenty of competition. The
self-proclaimed king of the jailhouse gunslingers is Tomás
González Zamacona, aka Commander Sapphire, a renegade
federal police officer. A sinewy thirty-six-year-old with a
black beard and a legendarily demonic disposition, Sapphire
led a parapolice band of killers and kidnappers who did contract work for drug lords. The Baja state police finally managed to arrest him; a nervous squadron of detectives
deposited him in La Mesa in 1992, glad to be rid of him. He
quickly muscled in on the prison real estate and protection
rackets. When Flaco protested, Sapphire slapped him
around. When a federal judge came to take Sapphire's depo-
sition in a murder case, he sent word from his *carraca:* "I'm
not coming out." So the judge left. On a Saturday night two
months ago, rival gunmen confronted Sapphire and a side-
kick next to a row of burned-out shops. The combatants
emptied an Uzi and heavy-caliber pistols at each other, spent
bullet casings dancing on the cement, bystanders dropping
on their bellies. One man died. Sapphire suffered a leg
wound (self-inflicted, rumor had it; perhaps he hoped to be
taken to a hospital and escape).

Describing Commander Sapphire, the Chicano inmate named Mario sounds like the manic Dennis Hopper character who sang the praises of Colonel Kurtz in the movie *Apocalypse Now*. "I know him personally," Mario says. "A man in his position, he's not gonna come in here and be at the bottom. He's gonna want to be on top. If somebody disrespects a woman in here, Sapphire sends his guys over. He wants order. Don't disrespect his code."

Sapphire's code seems based largely on fear. The former chief of the prison guards thinks that, sooner or later, someone is going to get up the nerve to put a bullet in his back. The former chief says: "Sapphire is crazy. He has half of his neighbors in there terrorized. I know people who end up in the prison from time to time, and they already told me: His days are numbered."

Commander Sapphire's war on the official and unofficial power structures of La Mesa troubles Duarte, who is working on a secret plan to transfer him to a maximum-security federal prison elsewhere. But Sapphire's upcoming trial in Tijuana poses an obstacle. And no one relishes the mission of extracting him from La Mesa. "Sapphire is a danger," Duarte says. "Why should I deny it? Hopefully, the transfer will be possible at some point." Still, Duarte downplays the presence of the gangs and says that he keeps the peace by maintaining constant communication with the inmates. "In any prison, you are going to have inmates who are more powerful, or richer, than others. You will have inmates who are more dangerous."

Duarte says he has a good relationship with one of the most powerful men, inmates or otherwise, inside the walls: Antonio Vera Palestina, the assassin convicted in the ambush murder of Héctor (Gato) Félix, the *Zeta* columnist. Vera's business empire inside La Mesa includes the *maquiladora*, the prison's own little outpost of the low-wage, transnational manufacturing industry that dominates the economy along the U.S.-Mexico border. When Duarte pays a call on Vera's sweatshop, a husky youth at the door of the mini-*maquiladora* scrutinizes the visitors before ushering them in. The youth wears a cowboy hat and a jeans jacket and has a short thick whip under his arm—a close-quarters weapon of choice among La Mesa's hired thugs. Inmate employees sit at rows of sewing machines, making sportswear and children's clothes to be sold in California. Vera subcontracts for Tijuana assembly plants. He turns a profit and provides about one hundred sorely needed jobs for inmates, paying between $5 and $13 a day, which is not much worse than on the outside.

Arms folded, Vera confers with Duarte, surveying a wall that the warden has agreed to have knocked down. Vera plans to expand production and keep the workshop operating twenty-four hours a day, just like a real *maquiladora*. Vera is forty, a veteran of the elite "Jaguar Squad" of the Mexico City Police. Compact and brisk, he sports a blue designer warm-up suit and a graying, martial mustache. Stenciled on his cap are the English words "Commander in Chief." He has the flat wet eyes and jutting lower jaw of a pit bull. And in 1988, that was what the enraged journalists of Tijuana called him: an attack dog who killed on the orders of his master. Vera was convicted of killing Félix, who was cut off in his car and gunned down as he drove to work. In previous weeks, the victim had written columns ridiculing Jorge Hank Rhon, the owner of the Agua Caliente racetrack and heir of one of Mexico's richest, most powerful and most criticized political clans. There was talk of a bitter personal rift between Félix and Hank; Vera worked as chief of security for Hank's racetrack; he received periodic sums of money from the racetrack after the murder, while he was a fugitive in Southern California. Hank denied any role in the crime and was never charged. During his campaign in 1989, Ruffo promised to capture the killers. The police tracked down Vera and the other two gunmen within the first years of the governor's term. The Mexican human rights commission and journalists' groups called for the police to keep going and follow the evidence pointing to Jorge Hank as the possible mastermind. But Governor Ruffo either would not or could not pick that kind of fight with the ruling party. So the case remains in limbo. The magazine *Zeta* still prints a page every week under Félix's byline which updates the status of the case and demands justice.

Behind bars, the convicted triggerman Vera has not shied away from turf battles with other gangsters, especially Commander Sapphire. But Vera makes a point of getting along with the warden. His conversation with Duarte about expanding the garment workshop appears polite, even amicable. Duarte says later: "Vera is not a problem for me."

Nonetheless, the word in La Mesa is that Vera has not reconciled himself to the idea of spending the next quarter century in prison. As Flaco would say, for the time being Vera chooses to remain. His adult son visits to help run the business. They seem to enjoy a steady flow of capital—the wages of silence, according to those who claim Vera took the rap for a mastermind. Vera lives in style and comfort. He and his gang inhabit their own fenced complex of *carracas* with a central patio, where the henchmen lift weights and Vera's Rottweiler frolics. When Vera strolls the plaza on his Sunday constitutional, the stolid bodyguards trail close behind him, cowboy hats bobbing. In La Mesa, the attack dog has been transformed into a master.

During her first days as an inmate, Norma Yvette Araujo became one of the homeless.

Norma was pregnant, recently divorced and the mother of

two small children. Originally from Mexico City, she moved to Tijuana to be closer to her parents and eight brothers and sisters, who were legal immigrants living in Los Angeles. She worked five years as an accounting clerk at a *maquiladora;* and she occasionally smoked marijuana with her friends. One day, the police caught them with five grams and Norma found out why legislators and prosecutors want to reform Mexico's drug laws. The system castigates small-timers harshly, while shielding drug barons. The problem goes beyond corruption; because of weak racketeering and conspiracy statutes, the police have to catch kingpins practically with their hands on the goods. As Duarte explains, "The majority of people here for drug crimes are not drug traffickers. They are mules, as we call them, who carry small doses. To help themselves economically, they agree to make the trips. Normally, the trafficker isn't going to end up here."

Five grams of marijuana resulted in a seven-year sentence for Norma, the same as Flaco Araiza got for 350 kilos of cocaine. When Norma arrived, the guards assigned her to the women's tank, but there was no room. Somebody gave her a blanket and told her to go away. After dark, when the villagers of La Mesa need no encouragement to lock themselves in, Norma joined the approximately five hundred inmates who had no recourse but to sleep outdoors, in stairwells or in the hallways known caustically as "los freeways." Norma curled up in improvised shelters and shivered through the baleful sights and sounds of the night: robberies, drug deals, enforcers barging into *carracas* and torturing debtors. She did not sleep for twelve days.

"I had never been in prison and they had told me many things about this place," Norma says. "I was terrified. The tension was incredible."

Finally, a resident of the woman's tank left and Norma borrowed $300 to buy her vacant cell. Many of the former homeless have moved into two newly built high-rise cell-blocks, which have a capacity of 1,350. But the working poor still live as they live on the outside: they get by. They truck and barter. They make money by their wits, with their hands and, in some cases, with their bodies. They baby-sit, push brooms, shine shoes, serve food, do errands, sift through the garbage like the unionized scavengers of Mexico's urban dumps. Artisans make and sell pottery, jewelry, model sailing ships, heart-shaped wood lockets with intricate miniature carvings of lovers' names and kissing birds. Everything has a price, from a space on a clothesline to the shelves of a discarded filing cabinet converted into a bunk for two inmates. Only drugs and death come cheap.

"Everything is more expensive than on the outside," Norma says. "Every diaper costs fifty cents. A bottle of milk that costs two dollars outside costs four dollars."

Norma's family in Los Angeles are her cross-border lifeline. They are helping her raise the baby daughter who was born four months after Norma was locked up. "It was very tough and very sad for me that she was born here. I had her with me for the first three months, then my brothers took her to Los Angeles. They bring her for ten days, a week, fifteen days. So she gets used to me. So she doesn't forget me."

During a Sunday visit, Norma watches her eldest daughter, nine-year-old Esmeralda, scamper back and forth across the sunny plaza to the makeshift video arcade, a tent housing a row of Nintendo games swarming with children. Esmeralda hugs her mother's legs, asks for change, introduces her playmates. She does not wander far. Esmeralda and her ten-year-old brother live a few blocks from the prison in a charity-run shelter for inmates' children. When she was little, Esmeralda delighted in the nonstop carnival of activity in which her mother lived, but now she is old enough to understand. Most inmates shower children with affection, but as the kids get older the prison becomes a factory that produces adolescent criminals. They steal, they get in fights. When they get in trouble, they taunt the guards: What are you going to do? Send me to prison? Esmeralda is old enough to be afraid.

"She says, '*Mami,* I don't like this place,' " Norma says. "She has seen two or three fights. Then there are people who talk to her and scare her. . . . The environment is very intense for a child. The children see many things, they hear many things. They realize many things. And if you watch them, after a while when they play they talk like the inmates, the same words, the same profanities. As they grow up, they reach a moment when it's not good for them to be here."

Norma sends Esmeralda back to the arcade and navigates through the mob, nodding, saying hello—neighborly encounters in the town square. Norma, thirty-two, has a demure, determined walk. Her smile reveals several gold teeth in a pleasant, weary face. Her gleaming black hair cascades halfway down her back. Her wardrobe is well kept: crisp jeans, a brown corduroy sport jacket over a sweater. She has structured her days so as to keep busy and win early release for good behavior. She studies literature and English. She acts in the inmate theater ensemble that occasionally is escorted out by guards to perform at hospitals and university festivals; in a work entitled *Caresses,* she plays a wife who listens to her husband rant at her, then calmly gets up and kicks the hell out of him. She also works at the prison garment shop owned by Vera, earning as much as $80 a week and free meals. Duarte considers her a star convict.

"The warden told me I might get out early because I participate in many activities," Norma says. "It occupies my time. It clears my head, because I have moments when I am fed up with all this. I have seen and learned things I could never have imagined. I have seen babies who had to be detoxed because they were born addicted. When they killed Chichiloca—he was an inmate—I was in the front door of the women's tank. I saw the way they killed him with a bullet in the head. Right in front of me. You get used to it. Well, I don't get used to it, because I'm sensitive and I get scared, but it doesn't have the same impact anymore. You see it as something normal."

When she is released, Norma wants to join her family in Los Angeles. She is one of many inmates who have relatives, memories or aspirations in California. The border figures centrally in their odysseys, narratives invariably driven by migration or smuggling: the illegal immigrant gardener who killed his estranged wife in suburban San Diego, fled south and discovered that Mexican courts convict Mexicans of crimes committed anywhere in the world. The northbound drug mules whose frightened gait tipped off the federal cops at the Tijuana airport. The handful of foreigners—a Jamaican, a Peruvian, two Filipinos—who washed up in Tijuana on the tide of vague doomed adventures.

On the Boulevard of the Eagles, panhandling addicts circle and a couple embraces passionately against a wall. Norma sits down for a cup of tea at the newest, most exotic business in La Mesa: an Asian food stand. Decorated by a hand-painted image of a dragon, the little stand with the picnic table in front is operated by Chinese and Taiwanese sailors. Two dozen in all, they were the crews of the three smuggling ships full of illegal Chinese immigrants bound for California which the U.S. Coast Guard intercepted off the coast of Ensenada in July 1993. Many of them had drifted into smuggling after a 1991 ecological accord outlawed gill-net fishing and battered Taiwan's fishing fleet; organized crime converted the vessels to more profitable use. The sailors kept the dilapidated smuggling vessels functioning on the long voyage to Baja, tending the balky engines.

They lived in threadbare quarters that were decorated with Asian pinup girls and that were comfortable only in comparison to the squalor belowdecks. After the delirious and very public ten-day stalemate at sea, after Mexico deported the immigrants back to China, the sailors were left marooned in La Mesa awaiting trial on smuggling charges.

The sailors communicate in bits of English and Spanish, asking Norma—and anyone else who seems knowledgeable—when they might be able to leave.

"How many time can go?" asks Kai Li Wang, twenty-four, a ship's cook from Taiwan. On the smuggling ship, he fed the clandestine passengers from giant cooking pots, slopping rice into metallic pans. Now he earns his keep behind the counter of the prison "restaurant." A bullet hangs on a chain around his neck, the jailhouse symbol clashing with his boyish short hair and bewildered expression. Norma sips her tea with two hands, cocking her head sympathetically as Kai recounts how the Mexican navy took charge of the boats from the U.S. Coast Guard and arrested him: "Boat is go to San Diego. But I don't know why is come here. Coast Guard and Mexican navy change. Here too many time. No good."

Kai lives in one of the new cellblocks, enduring cold showers, cold food, insects and rodents scuttling in the night. He and his mates have absorbed a simple lesson: In La Mesa, you need someone to watch your back. Almost everyone belongs to some type of group or hierarchy. The occupants of six-man cells designate leaders; the American inmates stick together; the eighteen Mexican Jehovah's Witnesses run a monastic cooperative at the end of the boulevard, a bolted, dungeonlike sanctum that somehow functions as living quarters, woodworking shop and church. The Asians follow the orders of the captains of the three ships. The captains oversee the restaurant and represent their men in dealings with the authorities and their attorney. An exasperating sort, the lawyer has collected $250 for services that thus far consist of dropping by to report that the case has not progressed. His clients, subsisting on the income of the food stand and meager sums wired by relatives in Asia, hope for deliverance. Now that the furor over the smuggling ships has dissipated, they feel forgotten.

"It's like a closed book," one of the captains complains through an interpreter. "It was an international case, but it's like a closed book now. It's been five months and we haven't been to court yet."

Later in the afternoon, her children departed for the shelter and, the shadows lengthening, Norma goes home. She rounds a corner into a cul-de-sac between cellblocks, where a group of addicts duck behind a crate to inject themselves with heroin, oblivious to water sloshing and splashing from a row of laundry basins. The interior of the women's tank is fastidiously clean, softly lit. Cardboard and blankets cover the bars of the cells for privacy; mellow colors, candles and crepe paper decorate the central common area. The approximately 125 women chip in to pay a male inmate to sit and guard the entrance.

"As a woman, you have to be careful," Norma says. "And stay away from the people who can hurt you. I say hello to everybody. But there are certain *carracas* I will not visit, certain places I will not go."

One of the paradoxes of La Mesa is that there are relatively few violent sexual assaults of the kind you might expect in a penitentiary, coed or otherwise. That does not mean it is safe, however. Women fall into prostitution and sexual exploitation. If a young girl catches the eye of the big shots, according to the former chief of the guards, "by the time she's fifteen, three of those bastards will have had their way with her."

The administration makes noises every year about evict-
ing the wives and children. The families respect Duarte and
listen when the warden proposes a slow exodus: This place
is no good for your children, señora. Why do you want your
wife and children living like convicts, señor? We can help
you look for a home or a social service agency. But Duarte
already knows and sympathizes with the answer. Many of
the wives commute each day to outside jobs, supporting
families that came from faraway states. They cannot afford
rents or baby-sitters. If they were kicked out, they would
sleep in front of the prison gates. They react ferociously
against the idea of separation. Norma doubts they will ever
leave.

"It's the economic state of the people," Norma says. "It's
pure necessity that keeps them here."

The Feast of the Virgin of Guadalupe, the sacred day of
the patron of Mexico, brings a visit from the bishop of
Tijuana. Bishop Emilio Berlie has dignified tufts of gray in
his hair, a resonant tenor voice and a telegenic profile.
Dispensing laminated pictures of the Virgin with inspira-
tional messages on the back, the bishop glides past the
scruffy men lining the fence between the central "plaza" and
the prison chapel. Guards with shotguns clear the way for a
visiting choir from a neighborhood church: middle-aged,
middle-class citizens attired in festive ponchos, trying not to
stare at the tumult around them.

In the chapel, Jorge Alberto Duarte makes his way unob-
trusively to a pew. He stands next to Mother Antonia, a
beloved American nun who lives and does charitable works
in the prison, his head bowed. Inmate families in their
Sunday best pack the chapel, a simple structure with a
peaked frame. Fathers look sternly scrubbed in sunglasses
and long sideburns. Mothers sing in sweet harmony, their

upswept hair arranged with ribbons decorated with images of Minnie Mouse. The makeup streaked on their cheekbones resembles war paint. Their arms overflow with bundles of white baptismal regalia: thirty-two babies born in the prison will be christened on this twelfth of December, 1993.

In his sermon, the bishop celebrates the reverence for the Virgin of Guadalupe among Mexicans everywhere. "The Virgin is so popular in California," he jokes, "that they gave her a green card." The congregation hangs on his words, so rapt that you can hear the chatter from the basketball court. The bishop summons Duarte and Mother Antonia and blesses the keys of the newly built chapel. Then he baptizes the thirty-two babies. Finally, the congregation emerges onto the steps of the chapel to face the mob in the plaza: the forlorn migrants, the hyped-up addicts, the splayfooted gang members.

The chant begins: "*Bolo!*"

The word refers to the custom that calls for the godfathers to dispense alms to the poor after christenings. The chant builds. On cue, the godfathers toss a shower of coins through the chain-link fence into the plaza. Dozens of men lunge, wrestle, scrabble for the skittering coins. The frenzy seems sure to end in bloodshed. But when the coins have been recovered, it subsides. The men dust themselves off, unscathed, laughing.

In the southwest corner of the compound, a block of expensive *carracas* ends in a balcony overlooking a grocery stand that specializes in U.S. products. (The groceries are shipped in three times a week from Price Club, a discount center in the nearby San Diego suburb of Chula Vista.) The *capos* sun themselves and smoke joints on the balcony, dispatching their servants to buy snacks. The grocery has three parrots painted on its wall. Cages containing real parrots, which inspired the painting, hang from hooks next to the stand. Beyond the *carracas* and the parrots, a tall chain-link fence encloses a brand-new vocational school and administrative complex that was completed and opened to inmates just weeks ago.

The prison's past confronts its future, Duarte says. Propped on his elbows on the railing of the catwalk on the prison's outer wall, he points out the contrast between the new concrete complex, with its empty, guarded perimeter, and the raucous ramshackle "street" on the other side of the fence. "Little by little, no? It is changing into a modern prison, but it can't be done from one day to the next. Little by little. Nobody is going to come in here unless they are in the school, the workshop, one of the programs. It is not going to be like the other side, where they can move around freely."

To build the school, Duarte had to battle. The funds were available. The demand was enormous. But there was no space. He had to demolish thirty-three *carracas* renowned for their size and luxury. Duarte conducted tense negotiations with the big shots and their families, seventy residents in all, who occupied the only feasible site. In his polite, almost plodding tone, Duarte explained the benefits the project would bring. Job training, like a prison is supposed to have. Psychological treatment and evaluations to separate violent inmates from harmless ones, convicts from the accused. A decent infirmary to treat tuberculosis and other diseases. Drug rehabilitation for the army of addicts.

But the owners howled. I invested a lot here, *licenciado,* they said. I spent thousands of dollars. I put in this special lighting here, I fixed up the walls there. Duarte promised to find them new homes in the compound. He appealed to their sense of community: You have to make a sacrifice for the common good. The owners cursed, blustered, threatened.

The warden did not budge, so they appealed to the state and national human rights commissions, the governor, the interior minister and President Salinas himself. They fired off letters and held press conferences expressing the indignation bred by the upside-down world of the prison, where seemingly outrageous practices have become inalienable rights.

"It was not easy to convince them, above all so there were no eruptions of violence," Duarte says with a faint grin. "They exhausted all their recourses. . . . But when it's a collective benefit, not just the whim of the warden, there was nothing left to do except convince them. We relocated them a few at a time, until there was just a group of ten or fifteen left. Finally, we relocated them too, and then everything calmed down."

He savors these victories, little landmarks in the civilizing process. He shows off photographs of the featherweight boxer accused of murder who hooked up with a trainer in the prison, got acquitted and now fights professionally as El Recluso (the Inmate) Gómez, bounding into the ring in baggy warm-ups with cartoonish jail stripes. He talks about talented inmate musicians—the band that succeeded in recording an album under the name Ghosts of the North, the trio that strides into his office to sing him "Happy Birthday." He describes his campaign to have the city government prohibit employers from seeing the rap sheets of nonviolent ex-cons applying for jobs—"very important steps to prevent stigmatization."

Duarte's dedication grows from a deeply Catholic sense of duty. One of his closest allies is Mother Antonia, the American nun. Duarte's friends and admirers among Tijuana's government functionaries, cops, human rights watchdogs and journalists marvel at his dogged resilience. But they worry. He has not cultivated strong and loyal protectors. As his decision to fire his bright young commander indicated, his strategy tends to isolate him. Unless he relents and takes the bribe money that is offered, implicitly and explicitly, on a recurring basis, he will find himself in a showdown with the *capos* and corrupt guards. The stakes are high; the internal prison economy—like the other underground economies of the border—generates fortunes. The former chief of the prison guards says: "Commander Sapphire has ten or twelve pistols. After he uses them, he gets rid of them so they can't be traced. Each one costs him $5,000 to sneak in. Imagine how much he has spent just on pistols. Somebody is getting rich just on the pistols."

The ex-chief of the guards is as hard-nosed as they come. And thoughtful. Although he works in another law enforcement job in Tijuana now, he still gets agitated when he recalls his years in the jungle. If they keep ignoring the problems, he says, the prison will blow up in their faces. They should show some balls. He has a few suggestions: Tax the rich inmates. Use the money to post bail for the poor ones and buy them bus tickets so they can go back to their home states. Pull the files and see who has fines that could be taken care of. You cut crowding, calm things down, make everyone happier. If the *capos* insist on fighting, put two of them in a cell and solder it shut. See which one turns the other into a woman. Get tough, before they get tough with you. "I don't know what they are waiting for," the former chief says. "Guys like Sapphire, they could hit them with a revolution in there."

This is not Duarte's language. Whether naive, stubborn or both, he does not stray from his gradual course. There are simply too many people crammed into La Mesa. Until the government comes up with enough money to build a real prison, he says, no other approach is possible. And the danger only strengthens his dogma of negotiation and nonviolence, his fascination with innovative, progressive methods of rehabilitation. Wistfully, he recalls a trip he made to study Islas Marías, an experimental island prison near Mazatlán. It is a pastoral penal colony. The inmates are a controlled number of carefully selected, nonviolent offenders from rural areas. Their families come to live with them, though unlike at La Mesa the process is tightly regulated. The convicts spend their sentences cultivating the land and tending farm animals. The place sounds like Duarte's idea of a warden's paradise.

"It is a really beautiful island, very tropical," he says. He leans on the catwalk in the late afternoon breeze. His eyes scan the beehive of La Mesa as if he were seeing it for the first time; he smiles at the memory of his week in the island penal colony. "It was very interesting. I liked it very much. It has beautiful beaches. I would like to go back, spend another week. When the boat left, I felt like one of the inmates. There was no way to get back until the next boat."

March 8, 1995

At about 10 p.m. on a cool Wednesday night, Jorge Alberto Duarte headed for home.

After finishing the law class he taught at the Autonomous University of Baja California, he drove his yellow Volkswagen Beetle southeast. His route took him past the city bus station, past the plant that produces butane gas. The fast dark road rose and curved through a landscape of stark hills. After a last belt of housing tracts carved into canyons, this was where Tijuana's urban sprawl finally trickled to a stop.

Teaching the class made for a long workday, but Duarte cherished the intellectual respite. The past year had been grueling. The wars of narco-politics had reverberated inside the prison walls. After the Colosio assassination, relatives of the accused assassin, Mario Aburto, took refuge briefly in La Mesa with Mother Antonia. They held press conferences to protest Aburto's innocence and denounce persecution by the authorities; they ended up obtaining political asylum in the United States. After the murder of the Tijuana police chief and the hostilities between state and federal police, Duarte rose to the defense of his fellow law professor Deputy Attorney General Sergio Ortiz. When the federal police arrested Ortiz in May, Duarte refused to send his colleague into the prison compound; instead, he let him sleep in the warden's office until he made bail.

Those were minor upheavals compared to the power struggle among the prison mafias that started in September with a death foretold. A gunman killed Commander Sapphire, the *capo* once described by a police detective as "the devil himself." The killer crept up on Sapphire in a rare unarmed and unguarded moment and shot him in the back of the head. Sapphire collapsed onto the railing of the second-floor catwalk outside his $20,000 *carraca*. A long list of people wanted Sapphire dead; it was said that the killer's boss was allied with Antonio Vera. Whether or not Vera had anything to do with the murder, it effectively consolidated Vera's supremacy among the *capos*. In addition to the *maquiladora* and his other rackets, Vera maneuvered into the post of inmate coordinator after Flaco Araiza resigned in order to lower his profile and concentrate on winning early parole. To Duarte's dismay, Vera was a brutal taskmaster, allegedly using extortion and beatings to administer the job assignments and property sales. And Vera did not keep the peace. In November, snipers barricaded themselves in a cell-block and opened fire, wounding a guard. The resulting standoff looked like the catastrophe that authorities had always dreaded. A lockdown was ordered. Heavily armed guards and SWAT teams deployed, and the state director of prisons and the secretary of government, the number two official in Baja, rushed in from Mexicali. They decided to order a commando assault on the forty barricaded inmates.

But Duarte objected, refusing to risk a bloodbath. He threatened to resign if the police stormed the cellblock. Ultimately, he prevailed. Instead of attacking, they sent in Mother Antonia to negotiate. The nun strode through the field of fire into the cellblock, her full-length white-and-black habit billowing like an apparition. She went among the gunmen; she prayed and cried with them. A few hours later, they surrendered.

The tension got steadily worse, however. Duarte had been warden for almost three years, a long time inside La Mesa. His world was closing in on him. On this Wednesday night, as Duarte rounded a final bend toward home, he had a lot on his mind. He turned left and descended a long hill into Fraccionamiento del Lago, a subdivision popular with schoolteachers and government workers. On weekend afternoons, Duarte's neighbors were accustomed to seeing him make the long walk down the hill, unaccompanied and nonchalant, to the neighborhood taco stand.

The row of town houses on his left occupied narrow lots with small gated patios in front, an expanse of bumpy, undeveloped land in back. His house was about a block down: gray and white, partly renovated, decidedly not the home of a public servant making money on the sly.

Duarte's nine-year-old son appeared in the doorway to greet him. Duarte parked next to the gate of the front patio. As he got out of the Volkswagen, a Dodge Aries lurched up alongside. Two ex-convicts tumbled out of the sedan and rushed him.

Their names were Jorge Humberto (the Jackal) Rodríguez Peralta, twenty-two, and Ramiro (El Mike) Garibay Velázquez, twenty-one. Both were born in other states, grew up poor in Tijuana and did time for robbery in La Mesa. El Mike had a peach-fuzz mustache and had worked sporadically as a mechanic. The Jackal, a spindly illiterate with a tic that distorted his face into a perpetual grimace, had worked as a servant for Antonio Vera in the prison. The ex-convicts had spent several hours in the car, staked out a few yards from Duarte's house behind an old bus smeared with graffiti. They were soaring on heroin, fear and adrenaline.

El Mike put a 9-millimeter pistol to Duarte's head. The assailants tried to drag Duarte into their car. He clung to the Volkswagen, his grip leaving fingermarks on the metal. His terrified son ran back inside to his mother, who called the watch commander's office at the prison and screamed for help. The gunmen wrestled Duarte into their car. About one hundred yards up the long incline, the old Dodge sputtered and conked out. Duarte seized the opportunity, shouting and struggling. El Mike and the Jackal panicked. They hauled him out, throwing him down on the street. The Jackal picked up a piece of concrete and slammed it against Duarte's head. El Mike leaned over with the pistol and squeezed off five shots at close range.

The newspaper photos by veteran Tijuana journalist Miguel Cervantes Sahagún, who stumbled on the scene minutes later because he lived nearby, would show Duarte huddled facedown in his sweater and slacks, two rivulets of blood oozing downhill, his body looking frail and crumpled.

El Mike managed to start the Dodge. He floored the accelerator. Left behind, the Jackal stumbled in a drugged stupor down an embankment behind the houses, plopped down and fell asleep. Minutes later, he was rousted and handcuffed by several carloads of enraged prison guards with machine guns who had zoomed to the scene. Homicide detectives arrived. Some inspected the crime scene; others took charge of the Jackal and hurried to the prison. The next morning, crowds of weeping inmates converged on the chapel to attend a Mass for the warden. On Friday, the governor and state attorney general went to Duarte's funeral. They announced afterward that Antonio Vera had been charged with ordering the murder. The motive: Duarte had reportedly refused an offer of $40,000 to let Vera and five other inmates escape. The charges were based largely on the Jackal's confession and circumstantial evidence. On the morning of the murder, Vera had stomped up to the warden's office and demanded an audience, threatening and scuffling with a guard after he was turned away.

Governor Ruffo's press conference was interrupted by word of a riot, instigated by Vera because he feared the murder case would cause his transfer to another prison. Vera's henchmen incited the addicts to burn and loot, offering them free drugs. There was a fatal stabbing. After another SWAT deployment and hours of negotiations, the authorities convinced Vera that he would not be moved from La Mesa. In exchange for the cease-fire, they agreed to let him talk to the press. Guards ushered reporters and photographers to the catwalk overlooking Vera's compound. Vera appeared below in the chain-link cage, dressed as if for a fancy rodeo: cowboy hat, cowboy suit, snakeskin boots. Vera bellowed up at the assembled press corps, his canine features twisted, an executioner raging in his private dungeon. He proclaimed his innocence. He railed against the governor, the police and the magazine *Zeta*, which had let loose with both editorial barrels at the news that the assassin of its columnist had struck again.

"If anyone was Duarte's friend, it was me," Vera roared. "If I had really wanted to escape, I would have escaped long ago, because this is the most insecure prison in the world."

The denials did no good. Weeks later, lulled into a false sense of security, Vera allowed himself to be transported to court for a hearing. It was a carefully prepared ruse by the police. The caravan sped him to the airport. Assisted by agents of the federal Interior Ministry, the police flew Vera to the city of Guadalajara and locked him in a top-security federal prison, far from his *carraca,* his *maquiladora,* his allies big and small. An hour after his departure, inmates in La Mesa fell on his henchmen and beat them bloody.

Yet suspicions endured. As always, the story seemed more complicated than the official version. Doubtful reporters and former colleagues of Duarte thought his death did not fit the style of a revenge hit; the killers could have simply fired from the car. Leads surfaced about corrupt guards and an imprisoned gang of kidnappers from the state of Nayarit who may have been involved. Was the crime actually the result of a botched escape plan that called for the gunmen to use Duarte as a hostage to spring their bosses? Was a high-ranking guard promised a luxury car and a bag of cash for his help? The paranoia of the conspiracy theorists was fed by Vera's political connections and by the events of the past year; Duarte was killed soon after the arrests of Raúl Salinas in the Ruiz Massieu case and the alleged second gunman in the Colosio case.

The questions went unanswered. A court ultimately cleared Vera of the murder charge in the Duarte case. Once again, the identity of the mastermind would remain a mystery as far as the legal system was concerned. In the summer, Duarte's widow, María, attended a groundbreaking ceremony for a major expansion of the penitentiary. The governor and high-ranking officials offered condolences and kind words about her husband. Spurred by the murder and subsequent attention to the crisis at La Mesa, the state decided to expropriate adjacent land and double the size of the facility. This would enable a long list of reforms that Duarte had urged. The transformed penitentiary was to be renamed in

Duarte's honor. Candidates in the upcoming gubernatorial elections promised to build a new state prison, perhaps two prisons, by the year 2000.

Compared to the assassinations of Colosio and the cardinal, Duarte's death did not get a lot of attention outside Baja. He was just another casualty at the border. Duarte had done his work patiently, painstakingly and without fanfare. He knew the prison was an institution built on the fragile alliance of the official but tenuous power of the state with the secret but overwhelming power of the border underworlds. With little to gain, he ventured into the no-man's-land between those forces and tried to govern the miniature society in an honest and humane way. Perhaps he was naïve; perhaps he failed to grasp the enormity of the danger. But if there were any heroes at the border, he was one of them.

This is the reality with which I have to live, Duarte once said about the prison. And in the end, in front of a small house on the edge of the city, that reality reached out and claimed him. Duarte chose faith over money; he would have shrugged off the fact that his assassins valued his forty-two years in jailhouse terms. The killers were each paid 2,000 pesos—according to the exchange rate at the time, about $300.

The Prisoner in the Window

The U.S. port of entry at Tecate looks like the old black-and-white photographs of the border crossing in Tijuana in the early years of the century.

There are a couple of narrow vehicle lanes, a small aging building for customs and immigration offices, a clump of low-slung stores and warehouses. The port of entry occupies a narrow pass in the mountains. Scattered in the wilderness on the U.S. side are farms and semirural hamlets, far enough from San Diego to offer country living, close enough to be called suburbs. The Mexican side, in keeping with the border pattern, is more populous: the city of Tecate spreads gently down into the valley. In sleepy and remote Tecate, the town that Federico Benítez left to become a lawyer and then a police chief, the town that is synonymous with a Mexican beer, the border for many years was little more than a back alley. The houses on the Mexican side faced across an imaginary line at the brush and mountains to the north. Only the best-organized smugglers operated in Tecate, using the winding back roads and forest trails to move drugs and small numbers of Chinese and other lucrative non-Mexican immigrants. The region was known as La Ruta Verde: "the Green Route."

The final years of the century have changed Tecate, as they have changed the rest of the border. Miguel Barragán saw that for himself on a warm day in late 1995 when he went to Tecate to try to make some money. The grizzled smuggler of immigrants had been discouraged by the Border Patrol's walls of brown steel and green uniforms at the San Diego line. So he toiled east up the steep highway from Tijuana in an orange 1975 Datsun sedan that looked as if it had been chewed by giant teeth. After an hour-long trip, Barragán drove into downtown Tecate past gloomy hotels doing brisk business: migrants lining the balconies, migrants carrying infants down cinder-block hallways to rooms with barred windows. He drove past the Tecate bus station. It was not much bigger than the rest room of the Tijuana bus station, but the Tecate bus station was packed with groups of migrants getting out of buses, sticking close to Tijuana smugglers with big-city sneers who led the way through the hectic lobby. Barragán drove past the Zócalo, a quaint, tree-lined park with a gazebo in the center, where smuggling bosses sat at plastic patio tables in front of a small restaurant, calling the shots about a block from the police station. A duo of elderly guitarists, Gonzalo and Bernabé, sat on a bench serenading migrants who squatted beside duffel bags and stared at the dark mountains to the north.

Barragán rounded up five clients and negotiated a price to take them as far as San Diego. The Border Patrol had only recently begun to build steel fences at the Tecate line; Barragán maneuvered the Datsun across the border in open land near a cemetery. His clients ran crouching behind the Datsun as it bumped over a small ridge. Two men crammed themselves into the trunk, and two women and another man piled into the backseat. Doors slammed and Barragán headed off down a lonely dirt road trailing a sheet of dust.

The smuggler did not get far. The U.S. Border Patrol had been watching from a bluff the whole time. The agents intercepted the Datsun and extracted the huddled, sweat-drenched passengers. Barragán, who was forty-three, allowed himself a gap-toothed grin beneath his red baseball cap. His soggy eyes suggested he might have had a drink or two earlier in the day. After working as a driver of a delivery truck in Tijuana, he had returned only recently to smuggling—a result of the economic crisis, he said. It was not a pleasant job switch. He raised long, stringy arms, like a decrepit boxer warding off invisible blows.

"I did this a lot about ten years ago," the smuggler said. "But it was a lot easier in Tijuana then. Now you have Governor Wilson, Proposition 187, the Border Patrol. I have to come all the way up to Tecate to make a little money."

Tecate was the future. The headlong transformation of the city in 1995 displayed both the success and the limitations of border control. The campaign of hype and substance kept rolling along in San Diego. The border kept rising on the political agenda in Washington. Attorney General Janet Reno even designated a special representative on Southwest border issues: a border "czar." Her choice was Alan Bersin, the U.S. attorney in San Diego. He had a lot of energy, ideas and connections; he had attended Harvard with Vice President Gore and Yale with President Clinton. The appointment of Bersin effectively elevated border enforcement to the top echelons of the Justice Department. The federal government had recognized the weakness of the traditional approach of dividing the border into jurisdictional and geographical fiefdoms. The far-flung bureaucracies often bred inefficiency, corruption and infighting among agencies with overlapping tasks, such as the INS and Customs. Bersin's mission was to build borderwide on his innovations in San Diego: multiagency task forces, special courts to speed up deportations and an overhaul of inspections at the ports of entry in 1996, which finally reduced the long lines and chaos that had confronted legal crossers for

years. It seemed that every week brought a new initiative—
and press conference—focused on smugglers, immigrants
with criminal records, desert drug runners, corruption
among U.S. inspectors. No one was ignoring the border or
Mexico anymore.

But during the 1996 presidential elections, there was continuing debate about the results. Republicans said the border
buildup was not enough. The Justice Department was forced
to conduct an internal investigation when Border Patrol
agents complained that supervisors were cooking the arrest
numbers to make it look like they were catching fewer people than they were. More arrests, in this case, would mean
that the much-trumpeted deterrent of Operation Gatekeeper
was not working as well as advertised. If true, it was an ironic reversal of the complaints just a few years earlier that the
Patrol let immigrants cross in order to catch them, encouraged the freeway-runners and otherwise resorted to sneaky
tactics to drive up arrests and budgets.

The experience of Tecate made it hard to argue that nothing had changed, however. Tecate was suddenly awash in
migrants, smugglers, fast cash, Border Patrol reinforcements
and the other trappings of the culture of illegal immigration.
The citizens of Tecate were up in arms; they felt that Tijuana
had suddenly been superimposed on their town. That was
the constant refrain: We don't want to be another Tijuana. In
the semirural areas of San Diego County, small Border
Patrol outposts were recording as many arrests in a day as
they had previously racked up in a month, increases of 1,000
percent. The buildup in San Diego had partially achieved the
goal of pushing the crossing flow east, away from the urban
Tijuana–San Diego corridor. The crowds of immigrants
weren't going all the way to Tecate because it was fun.
Crossing through the mountains was a deadly proposition if
you did not know where you were going or what you were

doing. In the good old days in Tijuana, migrants could hur-
dle the fence at Stewart's Bridge or the river levee, board the
trolley and within minutes disappear into an urban sprawl
that did not stop until Los Angeles. They could do it on their
own, on foot, or hire a guide. But in Tecate, you could get
lost in the mountains, break your leg, die of hypothermia.
Robbers and rapists had hours to stalk you and finish you
off.

Consequently, the immigrants were pushed into the arms
of organized crime. Big-time smugglers thrived. The
recruiters at the Tijuana bus station turned clients over to
guides who transported them by car, bus and truck into the
mountains. The prices jumped accordingly: the standard
$300 fee for the trip to Los Angeles as much as doubled.
Along with the money came corruption. The police in
Tecate, especially the federal agents, muscled in on the
action. Mexican federal agents in Jeep Cherokees stood
guard for smugglers as they hurried loads across the line.
When the PANista mayor and the municipal police chief of
Tecate complained to the newspapers, they were treated to a
serenade: someone fired gunshots outside both their houses
in the night. They interpreted this as a reminder that the federal police were not beyond taking out local officials who
got in their way. The Mexican federal government hurriedly
put together an offshoot of Grupo Beta, known as Grupo
Alpha, to calm things down in Tecate.

"The peace of our community is at stake," said Pablo
Contreras, Tecate's thirty-three-year-old mayor, who said he
was pained by the backlash against migrants on both sides
of the international line. "We have identified the wrong
enemy. In times of crisis, we always identify the weakest,
the poorest, in this case the migrants. What has to be done is
create more work in the interior, improve the economy and
the policies to keep them in their states of origin."

But until the long-term solutions the mayor called for could be implemented, the immigrants were being driven increasingly into the margins: dangerous terrain, high-priced mafias, criminalization. The border had hardened. In the United States, the authorities were cracking down on illegal immigrants with criminal records—a good use of limited resources. But anti-immigrant zeal also produced ideas that seemed gratuitous and counterproductive, such as federal legislation that cut off public benefits to legal, law-abiding immigrants in 1996 and an initiative in California to deny prenatal care to illegal immigrants. A campaign against smugglers led to an alarming phenomenon in Southern California: frantic police chases of rattletrap, overloaded smuggling vehicles, often filmed by helicopter news crews. Crashes killed and injured dozens of immigrants. The smugglers were increasingly aggressive, occasionally demented. The authorities were not always in control either, judging from the internationally televised incident in April 1996 in which sheriff's deputies clubbed a Mexican man and woman after a freeway chase east of Los Angeles.

The chases and the transformation of Tecate represented a paradox of the border: increased control at the immediate line in San Diego caused conflict to bubble up elsewhere. Immigrants would save more money in order to pay higher smuggling fees. They would go to Tecate and Arizona. They would take to the deserts and mountains, to the air and water if necessary. Some might be discouraged and remain at home; others might stay put once they made it to California, disrupting the traditional network of periodic cross-border trips. But immigrants would keep coming.

There were no fast solutions, no easy answers. Immigration had been slowed, but the trade-off was that the smuggling mafias were becoming a bigger, tougher business. The lines between transporters of drugs and immigrants started to blur. They were still distinct worlds, but in Baja there was more talk about "narco-polleros": smugglers who moved both drugs and people. Border-crossing was losing whatever was left of its once-casual air. If the buildup at the international line endured, in the future illegal immigration from Mexico would come to more closely resemble the expensive odysseys of Africans bound for Europe or seagoing Chinese transported by global syndicates.

The narco-political mafias that held sway in Tijuana and elsewhere were also booming, despite a few victories by the administration of President Ernesto Zedillo. The Mexican military arrested Guero Palma, the archrival of the Arellanos, and the federal police caught Juan García Abrego, the boss of the Gulf cartel and the reigning drug lord of the Salinas years. Within hours of his capture in early 1996, the portly García was sent off to the United States to face trial on a massive indictment. The police had to wrestle him onto a jet, literally screaming and kicking. García had U.S. citizenship, like many residents of the border, and could therefore be deported. He was convicted on drug charges in Texas. By unloading him, the Zedillo administration set a precedent that would have been unthinkable a few years earlier, and countered ingrained nationalistic fears of allowing the United States to meddle in Mexican affairs. There seemed to be a new pragmatism on both sides, less stolid rhetoric, far more cooperation on everything from the Clinton administration's billion-dollar bailout of the economy to the pursuit of the kingpins.

But García's capture was not as impressive at it seemed, because he was already in decline. Palma, to the chagrin of prosecutors, was found innocent in several of the serious cases pending against him. The Mexican drug groups had only gotten stronger, partly as the result of an all-out offensive in Colombia which swept up the leadership of the Cali cartel and threatened political figures all the way up to the Colombian president. The woes of their Colombian colleagues allowed Mexican kingpins such as Amado Carrillo of the Ciudad Juarez cartel to consolidate their control of the international business they had entered as junior partners. Despite his billion-dollar fortune and an army of allies—who allegedly included Mexican generals—law enforcement pursued Carrillo vigorously. He did not enjoy his dominance for long. In July 1997 the drug lord turned up dead in a Mexico City hospital after undergoing plastic surgery to change his appearance. Although there was speculation that Carrillo was murdered, he had been in poor health because of drug and alcohol abuse. Authorities called it an accidental death caused by medication administered after the massive surgery. The unexpected demise of Mexico's most-wanted fugitive was a triumph for the police and for the Arellano brothers of Tijuana, who found themselves in an ideal position to muscle in on Carillo's empire. The Arellanos' wild ways made their survival all the more remarkable. They had become the top dogs. This meant even more riches and glory; it also meant that U.S. and Mexican investigators would press the hunt for the bosses of the Tijuana cartel like never before.

In Tijuana, the big cases—the cardinal, Colosio, Benítez—were not solved, or at least not to the satisfaction of those who still cared about them. There was a new spurt of half a dozen assassinations in 1996 as Tijuana traffickers conducted a purge of current and former prosecutors and police commanders. Those who compared the Colosio case to the assassination of John F. Kennedy pointed out that several of the victims in 1996 had participated in the interrogations of Aburto in the early days of the Colosio investigation. Again, the murders took the form of messages: a gunman in athletic gear ran up alongside Arturo Ochoa Palacios, who had been Baja's chief federal prosecutor at the time of the Colosio murder, during an early morning jog at a popular outdoor recreation center. In front of numerous witnesses, the gunman calmly opened fire with a handgun and ran away, leaving his victim crumpled on the track. A few months later, a federal police commander who had declared war on the Arellanos was machine-gunned in a taxi after arriving at the Mexico City airport from Tijuana. The gangsters chose the locations and the brazen methods for maximum terroristic impact: we can kill who we want, where we want, when we want.

Despite the links to the Colosio case, Ochoa and the other victims had worked in drug enforcement at a particularly violent and volatile time. A reasonable explanation for the murders was the continuing struggle within the interconnected web formed by the mafias and federal law enforcement. Attorney General Lozano ordered an unprecedented cleanup, firing seven hundred federal police agents, commanders and prosecutors around the nation. But Lozano, Mexico's first opposition-party cabinet minister, was fired in late 1996 partly because of the failure to solve the Colosio and Ruiz Massieu assassinations. Lozano had begun his tenure as a star, a potential contender for national elected office. His abrupt departure occurred amid a delirious episode of skulduggery involving Pablo Chapa, the special prosecutor assigned to the two 1994 assassinations and the murder of Cardinal Posadas. Chapa was accused of planting a skeleton on the estate of the imprisoned Raúl Salinas in an elaborate hoax concocted—with the help of a witch-turned-informant—to implicate Salinas in a second murder. As a result, the prosecution of Salinas as the mastermind in the Ruiz Massieu murder was damaged. And Chapa, who in 1995 had charged previous sleuths with cover-ups in the assassination cases, ended up a fugitive from justice himself.

The new team at the attorney general's office promptly ran into another scandal n February 1997 when an "incorruptible" army general named as Mexico's drug czar was arrested after only eleven weeks on the job. He was charged with protecting Amada Carrillo, the boss of the Ciudad Juárez mafia. The revelation merely appeared to repeat a perverse pattern that had existed for more than a decade in Tijuana and other border areas: the general was accused of taking bribes from one gangster while building a heroic image by locking up competing gangsters. Because the scandal erupted shortly before the yearly decision by the White House to "certify" Mexico as a partner in the war on drugs, it caused an uproar in the U.S. Congress. Declaring themselves exasperated with rampant corruption south of the border, prominent Republican and Democratic senators set out to block the certification and punish the Mexican government. The drug problem in Mexico had never occupied such a central spot in U.S. domestic politics or on the U.S. national security agenda. President Clinton went ahead and granted certification despite the criticism. The economic and political ties between the two nations were too deep; any other decision would have had a disastrous impact. Nothing comparable to the courageous judicial drive against narco-politics in Colombia had taken place in Mexico, but the Clinton administration asserted that President Zedillo and those around him were sincere in their determination to go after the drug lords and the political protectors with whom the mafias were suspected of having done business during the Salinas years. Mexico unveiled new tools such as tougher statutes against organized crime and money laundering, and an elite antidrug force whose agents would be rigorously screened, highly trained and well paid with good benefits. Clinton visited Mexico for the first time in May 1997, reaffirming the partnership between the two nations whose futures would be inextricably intertwined whether or not the latest rhetoric translated into action.

Despite the upheaval in Mexico City and the intermittent slaughter in Tijuana, the democratic process in the state of Baja continued to function smoothly. The east victory in the 1995 gubernatorial elections of Héctor Terán, a sixty-four-year old PAN stalwart and former senator, made Baja the first state to elect a second opposition governor. The PAN solidified its roots. The vote was seen as a referendum on the six-year tenure of Governor Ruffo. The governor's name dominated the campaigning by both parties; Ruffo had to remind everyone that he was not running. In the end, the voters' assessment of Mexico's first experiment with opposition rule was largely favorable. "It was an honest government," said Victor Valle, a political scientist at the College of the Northern Border. "These were virtues we lacked in the past."

During his last visit to Tijuana as governor, Ruffo held court in a tiny borrowed office in a government building. After more than a year on full alert, his bodyguards looked noticeably relieved by the idea that he would be stepping down in a few days. They lounged outside, watching journalists and political operatives jockeying for one last audience. Inside, Ruffo sat alone behind a sparse desk, sleeves rolled up, no necktie, no retinue of aides. Just a short, affable man at the end of a long and grueling journey. The final years had cost Ruffo friends, allies and his marriage. But at forty-three, he looked ahead as a leader of national standing and international renown. He was the dean of PANista elected officials, who now ran four states and several important cities. Although the PRI "dinosaurs" had watered down ambitious proposals by President Zedillo to reform federal campaign laws, the PAN looked forward to the presidential elections of the year 2000 as a full-fledged contender.

And in the summer elections of 1997, the center-left opposition achieved an historic breakthrough when Cuauhté-moc Cárdenas of the PRD won the governorship of Mexico City.

The high-profile job converted Cárdenas into a formi-dable condidate for the presidency and handed him the unenviable task of governing one of the globe's most chaotic capitals. The PRI's hegemony had suffered a grievious blow. But for President Zedillo, the clean and peaceful ascent of the opposition in the capital was a clear sign of his commitment to democratic transition and held out hope that he could lead a modernization of the ruling party. In practical terms, the Cárdenas victory was not a complete disaster for the ruling party because it further divided the nationwide opposition vote between the PAN and the PRD.

Democracy was progressing in Mexico. But change, as Governor Ruffo knew firsthand, meant danger. His harrowing experience had left him convinced that some of the politicians who ran Mexico had "acted like a gang. It is very sad that they functioned like that. I see the next few years as a time of unavoidable Mexican political transition. All moments of transition have risks."

In his relaxed manner, Ruffo did not discourage speculation that he might run for president one day, though he dutifully added a disclaimer: "Hopefully, there will be another candidate I can help. Better to live normally and be just another soldier." His strengths and weaknesses as a potential candidate seemed wrapped together in the fact that he was a local, instinctive, almost accidental politician. His followers in Baja and the PAN were enthusiastic about his prospects; others saw him as a long-shot candidate at best, especially after he lost an internal party competition for the presidency of the PAN. But as governor, Ruffo had showed agility, a knack for learning quickly, and resilience when all hell broke loose. Leaving aside electoral aspirations, he seemed a likely prospect for a leadership post within the national party and a cabinet post if the PAN ever won the presidency of Mexico. For the moment, he was simply happy to have survived.

Ruffo said he had been in the right place at the right time: the southwest corner of the continent at the end of the twentieth century. "Things happened naturally," he said. As he spoke, he doodled a map of Mexico on a piece of paper in front of him. He drew arrows in the border region, scribbling hard to highlight the intensity of movement at the San Diego–Tijuana line: drugs, immigrants, trade, political reform, foreign investment, transnational industry, cultural collision.

"Baja California is full of people who made a decision: to search for a better life," the governor said. "We are used to autonomy, to having to organize things on our own. The distance from the center of Mexico left us naturally isolated. Being at the border brings advantages and disadvantages. Here you have drugs and immigration, what Americans most resent. And the *maquiladoras*, which are what they most want. We have everything here. The best and the worst, all mixed together."

That mix of profound forces, the collision and blending of the legal and illegal, was what made the border a magical place: it transformed Ruffo into a historic figure, migrants into martyrs, intellectuals into cops, cops into social workers, teenage homeboys into jet-set hit men, gangsters into tycoons, politicians into gangsters, a prison into a village, Tecate into Tijuana. The border opened a window onto how the world really worked. It created heroes, assassins, survivors. So many people made the leap across the line, El Brinco, in so many different ways. And for some it never ended; it became a way of life, a continuous journey back and forth between hope and despair.

Shortly after the strange episode of the three Chinese smuggling ships of Ensenada, an immigrant named Jiang Xun Ping stood in a second-floor window in Tijuana, contemplating that journey.

Jiang was a prisoner of the border. He had been one of the hundreds of immigrants whom the U.S. Coast Guard intercepted and turned over to the Mexican navy to be deported to China. But he was not flown back to China with the rest of the passengers; he suffered an attack of appendicitis at sea. When the smuggling vessels docked in Ensenada, he was rushed to the hospital for surgery. A few days later, he was discharged from the hospital, and the police moved him to Tijuana. As Mexican officials went about making the arrangements to get him onto a plane to China, they put him in a new jail. It was positively luxurious in comparison to the smuggling boat: a clean, unlocked room on the second floor of the headquarters of the Grupo Beta police unit at the San Ysidro port of entry.

Jiang was twenty-nine, bespectacled, painfully thin. His Mexican police guards took a liking to him. The burly officers climbed the circular indoor staircase of the Beta headquarters to check on Jiang and keep him company, heavy footsteps thumping on metal. The officers ordered meals for their prisoner from a Chinese restaurant and tried to communicate with him through the employee who delivered the food. Jiang, a former factory worker, explained to them that he had sold everything he had in order to pay the smuggler. His slender hands moving precisely, Jiang drew pictures for his visitors on a notepad. He sketched a map, connecting China and California with a dotted line, and added the figure $20,000—the fee he had paid the gangsters for the voyage. He bummed a cigarette and tried to describe the filth and frenzy of the smuggling ship. From his wallet, he pulled a black-and-white photograph of his wife, who was already in New York. He had a piece of paper with a telephone number that he was supposed to call upon arrival. He yanked up his frayed button-down shirt to display the scars from the appendectomy. He studied his visitors, looking alternately accusatory and beseeching, as if each new face represented potential salvation.

"Poor little guy," muttered one of the Mexican officers, who preferred saving migrants from robbers to locking them up. "I almost hope he escapes."

The headquarters of the Beta unit sits next to the San Ysidro port of entry; Jiang's window was just a few feet south of the top of the rusty border fence. He watched the twilight waves of cars rolling south on the I-5 freeway into Tijuana, during the late afternoon rush hour. He listened to the melodic metallic clatter of the pedestrian turnstile advancing the flow from San Diego; it sounded like a calliope or steel drums. He saw blue-uniformed U.S. Customs agents with a drug-sniffing dog on a leash, laborers stooped beneath straw hats and backpacks, urchins with shopping carts helping with luggage. He saw idling Border Patrol vans and busy buses operated by the detention and deportation section of the INS.

The green-and-white buses emblazoned with the eagle insignia of the Justice Department collected prisoners from the Metropolitan Correctional Center, Border Patrol stations, Los Angeles and Northern California, and shuttled around the clock to the border crossings—a southbound countercurrent to the buses that rumble incessantly into the Tijuana bus station. The ritual at the San Ysidro port of entry was fast and efficient. The INS buses stopped at a fenced parking lot. A uniformed officer of the Mexican immigration service emerged from the Beta headquarters and unlocked a gate next to the pedestrian entrance for legal crossers. He nodded at the U.S. Border Patrol agent north of the gate. The buses unloaded prisoners: disheveled, nonchalant, sweaty, ready to try again. The Mexican guard scanned faces, looking profoundly disengaged. But once in a while his hand intercepted an incoming shoulder, bottling up the line for an interrogation. Are you Mexican? Where are you from? What neighborhood? What street? Non-Mexicans were sent back to the United States to be disposed of in some other way.

The released immigrants trooped back into Tijuana alongside revelers from San Diego bound for the bars of Avenida Revolución: shaven-headed U.S. Marines, tattooed homeboys in baggy pants, high school girls in shorts and halter tops, ambling tourists in serapes. The revelers and the released prisoners flowed together obliviously, their worlds intersecting without seeming to touch. They drifted into the crowd of taxi drivers hustling for fares, the vendors and beggars and smugglers, the smoke from the taco stands, the dance music and cantina neon.

The prisoner in the window could have tried to escape. Jiang could have climbed out the unbarred window and hurled himself across the steel fence, risking a sprained ankle for a shot at the promised land. But he did not move. He seemed awed at having reached the end of his journey at this spot so close to his destination. It was as if he were hovering, suspended in time and space. His police guards stood next to him and said nothing, watching along with him.

Finally, the prisoner in the window gestured at the view. He asked: "America?"

And when he was told that indeed it was America, the prisoner sighed.

Index

316

Made in the USA
Middletown, DE
17 November 2015